E.K.
C.C.

This book is one of a collection bequeathed by J. Hugh Campbell, History scholar and instructor at this College from 1975-1983.

OCEAN OF DESTINY

OCEAN OF DESTINY

A CONCISE HISTORY OF THE NORTH PACIFIC, 1500–1978

J. ARTHUR LOWER

University of British Columbia Press
Vancouver

OCEAN OF DESTINY

A Concise History of the North Pacific, 1500–1978

Canadian Cataloguing in Publication Data

Lower, J. Arthur, 1907–
  Ocean of destiny

  Bibliography: p.
  Includes index.
  ISBN 0-7748-0101-8

  1. North Pacific region—History.
2. Canada—Relations (general) with the North Pacific region.
I. Title.
D358.L69   909′.09′644   C78-002153-3

International Standard Book Number 0-7748-0101-8

Printed in Canada

Publication of this book has been made possible in part by a grant from Dr. Walter H. Gage

and

with the help of a gift to scholarly publishing made in honour of Dr. Harold S. Foley for his distinguished services to the University of British Columbia.

Contents

Tables

Maps and Illustrations

Photographic Credits

Plates 1, 2, 3, 4, 5, 6, 18, 19, 20, 23, 24, and 25 appear courtesy of the Provincial Archives of British Columbia. The Public Archives of Canada provided Plates 15 (C–20509), 16 (C–20473), 17 (C–59448), 22 (C–75740), 26 (C–30368), and 30 (2–2028). Plates 7 and 13 are from the Public Archives of Hawaii, Honolulu, and Plate 8 is from the Whaling Museum, New Bedford, Massachusetts. The British Museum supplied Plates 9, 10, and 11, and Plates 12 and 27 are from the Republic of China Information Services. Plate 21 comes from the photographic collection of the Canadian Pacific Railway. Plate 28 is from the Anglican Church of Canada Archives, and the Japanese Canadian Centennial Society supplied Plate 29. Plate 31 was provided by the Embassy of Canada, Tokyo, and Plate 32 is from the Pacific Biological Station, Nanaimo.

Preface

For four centuries immigrants from Europe extended their control westward across North America until they reached the Pacific coast. As Canadians and Americans, they retained their historical, economic, and cultural ties across the Atlantic bridge to Europe. The Pacific Ocean appeared not only to limit their territorial expansion but also presented a physical and psychological barrier separating North Americans from the alien civilizations of Asia. Only in recent times have Canadians and Americans come to realize that the Pacific also is a bridge, and that their history, especially in the west, has been influenced by events in Asia.

Regular trans-Pacific contacts have existed for over four hundred and fifty years. For the last two centuries traders have been transporting goods between the north-west coast and Asia. However, this traffic made little impression on the continental-minded eastern North Americans. Not until the end of the nineteenth century did Canada and the United States recognize that they were maritime nations as well as continental, and, as such, that they had maritime responsibilities. Canada continued to depend on the British navy for protection. The United States began to demand recognition as a naval power, and to strengthen its defences on both coasts built the Panama Canal. In the twentieth century the Pacific became of increasing importance in defence, trade, conservation of resources, and international diplomacy. The recognition of Pacific significance was accelerated after the 1930's. The United States fought three costly wars in the Pacific, while Canada actively participated in two of them. The centre of international politics moved from Europe to the four powerful nations of the North Pacific. Events on each side of the ocean became of vital concern on the other.

Thus it is now accepted that there is a trans-Pacific relationship which involves all of the North Pacific nations, but what is not recognized is that contacts have existed for two centuries. Many books, theses, and articles have been written on the North Pacific. Generally these are concerned with a north–south approach to the Asiatic coast or the north-west American coast and deal with regions, individual countries, or smaller units such as local communities in either Asia or North America. Few writers have been concerned with an east–west, or trans-Pacific, approach. Since the Second World War, this deficiency has been overcome by numerous books and articles concerning the relationship of the United States with Asia, particularly with China or Japan. However, very few have dealt with the relationship between Canadian history and events on the Asiatic coast.

Written from a Canadian viewpoint, this book outlines Canada's connections with the history of the North Pacific. The chronological approach correlates events on both sides of the ocean and, by so doing, adds depth to an understanding of Canadian history. Canada has a long history of Pacific involvement. Its historic ties clarify its position as a major North Pacific partner and confirm Canada's present responsibilities in that region.

This book owes much to numerous individuals in a variety of archives, libraries, government offices, and organizations. Special thanks are offered to the following: John D. Tennant, Chief, Pacific Division, Department of Industry, Trade and Commerce; John K. Burbridge and D. D. Vanbeselaere, Department of Industry, Trade and Commerce; A. Douglas Small, Pacific Affairs Division, Department of External Affairs; W. R. Hourston, Director, Pacific Region Fisheries Service, Environment Canada; L. Margoli, Pacific Biological Station, Nanaimo; Jim Durant and Joy Williams, Public Archives of Canada; Debby Sullivan, Bernice P. Bishop Museum, Honolulu; Agnes C. Conrad, Public Archives of Hawaii; Cymbre A. Ferguson, Whalers Village, Lahaina.

ASIA

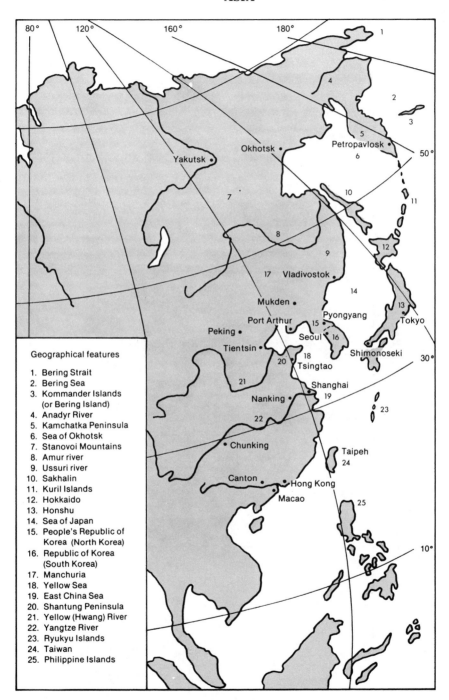

80° 120° 160° 180° 50° 30° 10°

1. Bering Strait
2. Bering Sea
3. Kommander Islands
   (or Bering Island)
4. Anadyr River
5. Kamchatka Peninsula
6. Sea of Okhotsk
7. Stanovoi Mountains
8. Amur river
9. Ussuri river
10. Sakhalin
11. Kuril Islands
12. Hokkaido
13. Honshu
14. Sea of Japan
15. People's Republic of
    Korea (North Korea)
16. Republic of Korea
    (South Korea)
17. Manchuria
18. Yellow Sea
19. East China Sea
20. Shantung Peninsula
21. Yellow (Hwang) River
22. Yangtze River
23. Ryukyu Islands
24. Taiwan
25. Philippine Islands

Geographical features

Yakutsk
Okhotsk
Petropavlosk
Vladivostok
Mukden
Port Arthur
Peking
Tientsin
Pyongyang
Seoul
Tokyo
Shimonoseki
Tsingtao
Shanghai
Nanking
Chunking
Taipeh
Canton
Hong Kong
Macao

NORTH PACIFIC

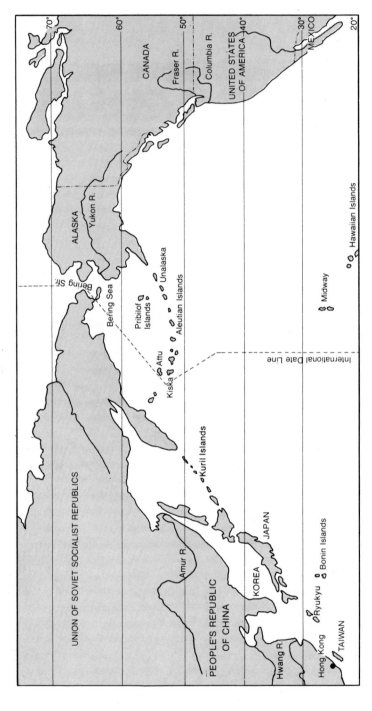

NORTH AMERICA

U.S.S.R.

International Date Line

2
3
60°

4 ALASKA
141°
Fairbanks
Anchorage
Valdez
Dawson
5
Whitehorse
Skagway
Sitka
14
BRITISH
6
COLUMBIA
50°
15
Prince Rupert
CANADA
7
8
9
10
16
Vancouver Barkerville
11 17
Esquimalt
New Westminster
Victoria 13
19 12 Seattle
Astoria
WASHINGTON
Portland Fort Vancouver
18
40°
OREGON 20
22
21
U.S.A.
San Francisco
Montérey
CALIFORNIA
Los Angeles 23
30°
San Diego

MEXICO

Coastal features
1. Bering Strait
2. Bering Sea
3. St. Lawrence Island
4. Yukon River
5. Kodiak Island
6. Prince of Wales Island
7. Portland Canal
8. Dixon Entrance
9. Queen Charlotte Islands
10. Vancouver Island
11. Nootka Sound
12. Puget Sound
13. Juan de Fuca Strait
14. Stikine River
15. Skeena River
16. Fraser River
17. Columbia River
18. Willamette River
19. San Juan Islands
20. Snake River
21. Sacramento River
22. Cape Mendocino
23. Colorado River

1

The Unknown Ocean

China is in compas 3,000 leagues and 1,800 leagues long. . . . Yet by the account of other bookes, they do finde it bigger and more leagues. . . . This mightie kingdome is devided into fifteene provinces that every one of them is bigger than the greatest kingdome that we doo understand to be in all Europe. (Gonalez de Mendoza, 1588)

To most North Americans phrases such as the "Atlantic Community," "North Atlantic Triangle," and "North Atlantic Treaty Organization" (NATO) are a way of life. They are familiar with the "Iron Curtain," the "European Economic Community," and the "European Common Market." How many have envisioned a "North Pacific Community"? A North Pacific Economic Community is not inconceivable; Japan, by force, had established the basis of its "Co-Prosperity Sphere" before, in its ambitious haste, it overextended its resources. Might not a similar economic, even defensive, organization be structured in the North Pacific by peaceful negotiations? Numerous bilateral economic, cultural, and defence agreements exist among the North Pacific nations as well as multinational agreements on investment and conservation. Much publicity has been given to the slaughter of seals off Newfoundland, but what has happened to the Pacific seals? North Americans are concerned with problems of the North Atlantic, whether they be trade, defence, offshore limits, or conservation of resources, but only in recent years have they recognized that similar critical problems exist in the North Pacific.

NORTH ATLANTIC TIES

The ties across the North Atlantic to Europe are natural outgrowths of history. Most North Americans have European ethnic backgrounds. For over 350 years colonizers and settlers landed on the Atlantic coast, but almost 200 of these years had passed before they had penetrated to the Mississippi–

Great Lakes region. Today, with very few exceptions, the eastern sections remain the most densely populated regions of North America.

The historical bonds with Europe are strong—the early explorers and settlements, economic ties, religious and political theories, memorials to wars which at first were extensions of those in Europe and, later, were struggles for independence in the United States and Latin America against European powers. Even the two great wars of the twentieth century in which Canada and the United States participated were basically European. Most Canadian and United States' histories see the history of the western half of the continent as the extension of the core eastern settlements followed by increasing expansion of economic and financial control strengthened by improved east–west ties through transportation and communication.

Although admitting that the world was round, Europeans found it difficult to conceive of it as a circle without ends. From the centre, Europe, the explorers and traders moved either towards the Far East or the Far West. The Pacific coasts of Asia and North America seemed to be the ultimate ends of long journeys. Even today the International Date Line is more than a place where a day is gained or lost; it indicates the mental limits of European expansion and the dividing line between two cultures.

For five centuries Europe has been expanding its domination throughout the world, but its control is obviously ending. With its retreat, new power blocs are rising to fill the resulting vacuums. The most realistic power centre of the near future is the North Pacific region.

THE NORTH PACIFIC

The North Pacific region consists of only six nations (seven if Korea is accepted as permanently divided): Canada, China, Soviet Russia, the United States, Japan, and Korea (see table 1). Although area does not imply international significance, it is worth noting that the first four are the largest in area. China has by far the largest population of any nation, but the Soviet Union, Japan, and the United States are also among the most populated. The United States, Canada, and Japan are among the world's leading traders, but the communist states are rapidly expanding. All of these nations are richly endowed with natural resources. Each year their international influence spreads into new regions of the world by trade, military and financial aid, or political greed.

Of the five permanent members of the U.N. Security Council, China, Soviet Russia, and the United States face the Pacific, while the other two, the United Kingdom and France, have a long history of Pacific involvement. Japan, the United States, and the Soviet Union are world leaders in technical advances, with China threatening to equal if not surpass them. In the select "atomic club," the Soviet Union and the United States are the undisputed leaders, again threatened by Chinese ambitions. During the earlier years of the twentieth century it was common to speak of the "Great Powers"; today they have been displaced by the "Super Powers," Soviet Russia and the United States, with China rapidly becoming a third. Finally, if we consider the "danger spots" of the world—those which threaten to kindle a devastating third world war—we recognize the dormant "Cold War" and the idealistic rivalries of China and the Soviet Union. The possibility of a military re-surgence in Japan is not inconceivable. Unrest and civil war in the African nations, the Middle East, south-east Asia, South America, and other places are affected by the indirect or sometimes open involvement of these powers. Even strategic Korea, unhappily divided, maintains the tensions among its three neighbours.

TABLE 1: POPULATION AND AREA, NORTH PACIFIC COUNTRIES

	Population		Area		
	Total (000's)	Annual rate of increase	Total (km.)	Density	
Canada	22,998	1.2	9,976,169 (3,851,809 sq. mi.)	2	
China (People's Republic)	800,000	1.7	9,597,000	85	
Japan	110,050	1.3	372,313	295	
Korea (People's Republic)	15,087	2.8	120,538	125	
Korea (Republic)	32,905	1.7	98,484	334	
Taiwan	15,902		13,592	85	
United States	204,879	.9	9,363,123	22	
U.S.S.R. (Asia)	62,474	1.6	16,831,000	4	
Total	249,747	1.0	22,402,200	11	

Source: U.N. Statistical Yearbook, 1974; Canadian Statistical Review, May 1976.

Thus the North Pacific Rim, although it may not be termed a "community," is nevertheless an area which must be considered as a single region, if not a unit, in the modern world. With increased air transportation and the rapid expansion of world trade, this concept is becoming obvious to those involved in travel, trade, and international affairs.

PREHISTORY

To archaeologists, the concept of the Asia–North America connection is more realistic than the European–North American union. Numerous times, especially towards the end of the last ice age, possibly 40,000 to 50,000 years ago, Asia and North America were joined by Beringia, where now there is Bering Sea.[1] This so-called land bridge was a great plain which periodically, depending on the expansion or recession of the glaciers, was an extension of the mainland of Asia or North America. As in the main bodies of the continents, flora and fauna spread eastward and westward across the plain, introducing North American animals and plants to Asia and vice versa.

More important was the movement of people. Driven by unknown forces from southern or central Asia, they moved northward, establishing themselves in Sibera, and pushed onward across Beringia to North America. It is generally accepted that in periodic waves, following established routes, they dispersed throughout both North and South America.[2] When Bering Sea separated the continents for the last time the Americas were populated.[3]

For centuries the Amerinds continued to migrate from place to place; there are indications that some movement was still in progress when the Europeans arrived. Eventually settling in definite areas, they developed economic, political, and social mores adapted to their environments. Linguistic groups, subdivided by dialects, occupied vast territories.[4] Tribal units introduced their own customs. In modern terminology the continents could be said to be divided among a multitude of nations—large and small, weak and strong, rich and poor.

Along the Pacific coast of North America were numerous groups extending from the Aztec civilization of Mexcio northward to the Eskimo cultures of Alaska, and similar groupings continued into Kamchatka and eastern Siberia. Even after Bering Sea separated the continents, contact and trade were maintained between the western Eskimos and their Asiatic kinfolk. With their seaworthy umiaks the Eskimos traded furs, seal oil, and possibly jade for the domesticated reindeer of the Tchukchus.[5] The north-west coast of America was one of the most densely populated areas of the continent. Living in a land rich with natural resources, often depending largely on the ocean, the various linguistic groups developed individual characteristics and are recognized as being among the most socially advanced native peoples, as well as having highly skilled characteristic art forms.

THE CHINESE EMPIRE

Although the coasts of the North Pacific were occupied by numerous basically primitive people, the major part of the Asiatic coast was controlled by a distinctly contrasting civilization. This was China. When European explorers finally reached the North Pacific, they moved freely with little serious opposition along the coast of North America or Siberia. Movement northward from the south Asiatic coast was delayed for three centuries by the formidable barrier of the Chinese Empire. Much of the history of the North Pacific is affected by European attempts to overcome the isolationist policies of the Chinese governments.

China began on the Hwang-Ho River several thousand years ago, and its history, which is the longest continuous one of any nation, has endured through numerous dynasties until they were replaced by republican governments in this century. Over the years the Chinese extended their empire far inland and controlled the coast from Burma and Siam to north of Korea. Its long history is marked by periods of greatness followed by decline as the numerous dynasties rose and fell.

In Greek and Roman times the Chinese Empire extended far west into Mongolia and Turkestan. By overland routes and via the Red Sea, luxury items such as silk and rhubarb as well as spices such as pepper were obtained by the Romans. In the seventh and eighth centuries the Nestorian Christians apparently had some success in China, but their sect, for some unknown reason, faded out. In the thirteenth century the Mongols for a short time extended their rule to the Tigris-Euphrates valley and across Russia to Poland. Marco Polo and other traders made the long overland journey to "Cathay," although they did not establish regular trade routes. About the same time European missionaries, following the same route, established missions and gained some converts in China, but their activities were abruptly ended at the end of the fourteenth century by the Mongol conqueror Timor.

China developed a high degree of civilization. In China originated the religions of Confucius and Lao-tse (Taoism), while from the first century it became the centre from which Buddhism spread to Korea and Japan. These religions became the bases of the rigid social customs of the people. The Chinese are credited with the idea of decimals, the compass, cast iron, gunpowder, porcelain, paper, printing by movable type, the mechanical clock, and the stern-post rudder. Tea-growing and sericulture were highly developed. Inoculation against smallpox was known in the sixteenth century. The arts of poetry, painting, and music still offer inspiration.[6]

Supervision of the huge Empire required a highly organized, centralized government. Manners, customs, rites, and institutions became formalized and static. The Chinese called themselves the "Central Kingdom" surrounded by barbarians. They had heard of other places—England, Venice, India, Russia, France—but these were small appendages occupied by the "outer barbarians" whose insidious influences must be checked. "Pride and vanity form the basis upon which the Chinese built their peculiar system of information regarding other lands and people. Around 'the Flower of the Centre,' as their sages teach, dwell rude uncivilized races, which are in reality animals, although they have externally human forms."[7] The barbarian threat was most serious from the north whence, periodically, invaders conquered China, established a new dynasty, and continued to dominate the Central Kingdom until they, in turn, were overthrown and the cycle repeated. Even until she was dethroned in 1911 the empress-dowager could not believe that China was not the greatest empire and could not understand the audacity of barbarians who expected to meet her face to face as equals.

Even with their efficient organization the limited methods of communication made it impossible for the Chinese to oversee the outer fringes of their empire. The peoples on the outskirts nominally accepted the suzerainty of the Chinese Empire and, as long as they paid tribute, no attempt was made to impose Chinese beliefs on them or to change their way of life. Tribute came from the island of Formosa, from Indo-China, and from the coastal tribes of Siberia, but each developed its own culture. Periodically these subject peoples sent their tributes through envoys who performed the traditional kow-tow, kneeling three times and knocking their heads on the floor nine times before the emperor or his representative. Although accepting tribute, the Chinese were unaware of the geography of the northern coastline.

After the downfall of the Roman Empire and through the Middle Ages, Europeans lost direct contact with the Chinese. By the ninth century Arab traders had reached the coasts of China and were later to extend their trade to the Philippines. The Arabs took control of the sea routes through the Indian Ocean, and by the fifteenth century trade between Europe and the Far East was under their control.

Except for coastal trading by Chinese junks which covered an area from Indochina to Korea, including the offshore islands, the Chinese, preoccupied with their vast empire, were a "land" rather than "maritime" people. They knew of Japan, where Chinese merchants visited on the islands. Japanese pirates were a continuous source of irritation. Two Chinese attempts to invade the islands in 1278 and 1281 were complete failures, largely because of storms, and their failures indicate China's inclination to land rather than sea expansion.

Periodically there were spurts of Chinese maritime activity. As early as 219 B.C. Hsu Fu may have sailed to Japan.[8] During the Tang Dynasty (518–907 A.D.) Chinese vessels travelled as far as the Euphrates River, but the greatest period of Chinese maritime activity was in the Ming Dynasty during the first half of the fifteenth century, when numerous expeditions penetrated the Indian Ocean. The most famous admiral, Cheng Ho, is reported to have visited the Philippines, Java, Ceylon, and the coast of Africa. On one voyage, to show the greatness of the Chinese Empire, he led an expedition of sixty-two large ships with 27,800 men into the Indian Ocean. For some unknown reason this great maritime period of Chinese history ended abruptly, and China returned to its "land" philosophy.

The isolated islands of Japan also had a long history, which claimed that the empire was formed in 660 B.C. Throughout the centuries contacts with China had influenced its development, but such influences were usually absorbed into the Japanese culture rather than changing it. Because of its location Japan was one of the last coastal regions to be pressured by Europeans from either the north or south.

Were the Chinese or Japanese aware of America? In Cassiar, British

Columbia, have been found relics of oriental origin such as Chinese coins minted in China 2000 B.C. and near Telegraph Creek were brass bowls 1,500 years old.[9] Records in the Chinese archives document the voyage of Hwui Shan who left China in 458 A.D. and returned in 499 A.D. He is reported to have passed the Aleutian Islands and sailed to Mexico, establishing settlements.[10] It would seem that the records were lost in the archives and knowledge of the expeditions was forgotten until 1752, while another century passed before the records were subjected to serious study.

Recorded examples leave no doubt that disabled Japanese junks reached North America, but whether any returned is doubtful. C. W. Brooks states that every junk found adrift or stranded on the coast of North America, or on the Hawaiian or adjacent islands, has on examination proved to be Japanese, and no single instance of any Chinese vessel has been reported.

This may be explained by the existence of the Kuro Shiwo, literally, 'black stream', a gulf stream of warm water, which sweeps north-easterly past Japan toward the Kurile and Aleutian Islands, thence curving around and passing south along the coast of Alaska, Oregon, and California. This stream, it is found, has swept these junks towards America at an average rate of fully ten miles per day. The absence of Chinese junks in the Pacific is accounted for by the existence of an ocean stream of cold water emerging from the Arctic Ocean, which sets south close in along the eastern coast of Asia.[11] T. A. Rickard, supporting this statement, says: "Out of the sixty recorded wrecks of Japanese junks up to 1875 twenty-seven were stranded on the Aleutian Islands, six on the coast of Kamchatka, two on the shores of Alaska, and two on both the Hawaiian and Brooks Islands, beside one on Nootka Sound, one on the Queen Charlotte Islands, while the others were scattered elsewhere on the northwestern coast of America."[12]

Rickard also mentions three junks, in 1805, 1815, and 1833, which had living Japanese aboard and states that one, with no living survivors, was found as late as 1927. He supports the theory that the iron which is mentioned by many of the first explorers who met the natives came from the wrecks of these junks and other wrecked vessels.

Brooks claims that many words used by coastal tribes are similar to those of Japanese and supports this by stating that in 33 cases there were 222 persons saved; from this one can estimate the probable extent of Japanese blood infused into the Indian tribes around the shores of the Pacific.[13] Beachcombers on the west coast today find credible proof of these theories as they continue to collect Japanese glass fishing floats.[14]

THE WORLD IN 1500

The world in 1500 was still insular. Throughout most of it the peoples were living in primitive tribal units at varying stages of development, knowing little of the world beyond their own immediate territories. In the land mass of Eurasia four large blocs of advanced civilizations existed. Catholic Europe was still fragmented into small units, but there were signs of incipient nationalism, while aggressive attitudes towards change, unification, and expansion were evident. The belief in a global world was gaining acceptance. The Moslem world had passed its western peak and was retreating in Europe, but it still controlled North Africa and the trade routes between Europe and the Far East. The subcontinent of India was torn by internal feuds. The Ming Dynasty in China was on the decline, but it still controlled a vast empire extending south, west, and north until it faded out into the lands of the far distant barbarians.

Each of these civilizations was aware of the others, but each lived within itself and knew little beyond its own boundaries. Traders, travellers, and missionaries had carried information and misinformation among them. Before its western extremities dissolved, the Mongol Empire had brought Asia to the borders of Europe for a short time. The Arabs carried trade goods between Europe, north and east Africa, and southern Asia as far as the coasts of China.

The islands discovered by Columbus and Cabot were still considered offshore islands of Asia. There was no idea that the Pacific Ocean existed separately from the Atlantic, nor was there recognition of the vast expanse of water to be covered from the newly discovered lands to Asia. Thus, knowledge of the geography and people of the North Pacific Ocean was non-existent.

This was the unknown world which was divided in 1493 by a papal bull and verified by the Treaty of Tordisellas, by which Spain and Portugal were entrusted with the task of implanting Christianity and commerce in the new lands. The first half of the sixteenth century was to revolutionize the geographical concepts of Europeans as they infiltrated into the Pacific Ocean and thus introduced five centuries of rivalry in that region. These centuries were to see colonizing empires rise and fall until only six nations were left in the North Pacific. Three of these (China, Korea, and Japan) have survived from pre-European days. The other three (Russia, the United States, and Canada) are outcomes of the European power struggle.

2

Europe Discovers the Pacific
(1500–1750)

Goods they had within bord, to wit, an hundredth and 22 thousand pezos of gold: and the rest of the riches that the ship was laden with, was in silkes, sattens, damasks, with muske and divers other merchandize, and great store of all maner of victuals with the choyse of many conserves of all sortes for to eate, and of sundry sortes of very good wines. (Thomas Cavendish, 1587)

By the fifteenth century luxury goods as well as the wanted spices from the Far East were in demand in Europe. However, the unreliability of the long overland trade routes and whims of Arab traders who monopolized the sea routes through the Indian Ocean and Red Sea made supplies uncertain. With the capture of Constantinople in 1453, followed by penetration into south-eastern Europe, the Turks strengthened their stranglehold on commerce. In Europe the distribution of eastern goods was controlled by the Italian states, especially Venice and Genoa. These factors made the costs prohibitive, especially to those states, farthest from Asia, along the Atlantic coast.[1] The necessity of breaking the uncertain monopolistic control of trade through middlemen forced the Atlantic states to find a direct route to the legendary wealth of Cathay (China) and to the Spice Islands.

The search for an unobstructed route to the Far East eventually led to the exploration of the North Pacific. Its coastline, with the exception of the unpopulated polar regions, was the last to be explored by Europeans. The overland routes were across the widest expanses of both North America and Asia and the crossing of these vast continental masses were major undertakings in themselves. The Arctic routes—the North-west Passage and the North-east Passage—were impenetrable ice-bound barriers to early navigators. The only feasible routes, and the longest, were by sea—either by the Cape of Good Hope or Cape Horn—journeys which demanded months of arduous, dangerous toil. Moreover, once these two capes had been rounded, the expansion into the North Pacific was handicapped, as we shall see, by political barriers.

THE PORTUGUESE

The Portuguese were the first Europeans to open a route to the Pacific, after half a century of probing along the coast of Africa by numerous expeditions supported by their government. Bartholomew Diaz rounded the Cape of Good Hope and within a few years Vasco de Gama reached India (1498). Using their superior weapons the Portuguese were able to destroy the Arab shipping monopoly and to force the native peoples to trade. By 1511 they had seized Malacca and five years later they reached the coast of China. Here, apparently, the officials of the powerful Chinese Empire turned them away. Forty years were to pass (1557) before they were granted permission, subject at all times to Chinese authority and on the understanding that they would help to suppress piracy, to set up a single trading post at Macao where they could obtain goods from Canton. This was a revival of Chinese policy, as similar trading posts had been established in the twelfth century by Arabs and Persians. The Portuguese occupied Macao for thirty years before they were granted sovereignty of the colony. Macao for many years was the centre of European trading into China and exists today as Portugal's only remaining colony.

With the Portuguese came Roman Catholic missionaries, led by the Italian Jesuit Ricci. The greatest of these was Francis Xavier. Born in the border country between Spain and France, Xavier was sent to Asia by the king of Portugal in 1542, the same year that the first Portuguese reached Japan. After seven years in the Portuguese settlements in India and Indonesia he reached Japan on a chartered Chinese junk. For two years he travelled throughout Japan baptising the people and spreading information on Christianity. In 1552 he died at Canton on his way to bringing Christianity to China. Xavier was the forerunner of many Jesuit priests who laid the foundation of the Catholic religion in Japan before they were expelled in 1613.[2]

THE DUTCH

Portuguese domination of the Far Eastern trade lasted for less than a century and received its death blow when Portugal was annexed by Spain in 1580. Portuguese control was displaced by the Dutch, whose East India Company (1602) during the seventeenth century, by establishing bases and by controlling the Cape of Good Hope route to the Far East, gained control of the former Portuguese possessions. By 1700 all that remained of Portugal's Far Eastern Empire were Timor, Goa, Diu, and Macao.[3] The Dutch pressed on to China and Japan but also were faced by the isolationist policies of these two countries which obstructed Dutch expansion northward. Nevertheless, when Japan, having experienced European traders and missionaries, expelled all foreigners, the Dutch were permitted to establish a trading post on an island off Nagasaki. This port became the funnel through which news of European events, European goods, and especially European weapons, entered Japan.

Although some Dutch ships entered the Pacific via Cape Horn, Portugal and Holland concentrated on developing the trade route eastward around Africa. By this route they reached India, the East Indies, and other islands of the South Pacific and advanced as far as southern China and Japan. The route around South America was opened by Spain, which became the first European nation to link both sides of the Pacific.

THE SPANISH

The belief that Columbus had discovered a direct route to Cathay was soon shattered as the American continents were revealed. Expansion into the new lands was comparatively rapid. When Balboa crossed the Isthmus of Panama (1513), he not only became the first European to see the Pacific Ocean (which he called the South Sea) from America but he also laid claim for Spain to the entire coastline "from the Pole Arctic to the Pole Antarctic." Within a few years Cortez had conquered Mexico and had established trading posts on the Pacific coast.

The spread of Spanish control and the exploitation of new lands were major enterprises. After the easily accessible treasures were removed, new mines were opened, missions and settlements were established, ports were planned, and trade between them and the mother country was organized. The aristocratic, highly centralized Spanish government which had encouraged the early speculative discoveries was gradually replaced by leaders who were more interested in exploiting what they had than in encouraging new discoveries of questionable value. Spain was deeply involved in the complexity of European alliances and wars, attempting to expand its influence throughout that continent. Internal rivalries, jealousies, and uncertain leadership throughout the bureaucracy were reflected in the colonial leaders. It has been said that Cortez was forbidden by the authorities to explore northward for fear that he might become too powerful.[4]

The lack of Spanish interest in the unpromising Pacific coast north of Mexico is understandable. Spain was heavily committed to more attractive prospects in other directions. The discovery of the wealth of the Incas in Peru drew the Spanish southward, and before 1550 settlements were established in Chile as far south as Santiago and Valparaiso. There were also the prospective riches of Asia to be tapped. While the gold of the Incas was available, that of California was unknown. Had this resource been developed by the natives, the Spanish might have been drawn north instead of south, leading to speculation that both Canada and the United States might never have reached the Pacific. Spain did move northward east of the Rockies, where it developed a vast inland empire.

SPAIN'S INLAND EMPIRE

Persistently searching for an "Eldorado," the Spanish were intrigued by the legendary "seven golden cities of Cibola." The search for these was led in 1540–42 by Governor Francisco Vasquez de Coronado. His famous expedition found no great cities, no gold, no silver, but it did travel far inland to the Rio Grande River, the Arkansas River, and into modern Kansas. It saw buffalo herds, met the fierce Hopi tribes of Arizona, and showed the difficulties of the northern route overland to the Pacific coast.

These expeditions from Mexico, combined with others into Florida and along the Gulf of Mexico, committed Spain to a vast new empire. Missions and settlements were established, and the boundaries of the inland empire were pushed northward. Eventually Spain was to control, along with the Gulf coast, the land as far north as the Missouri River. Modern histories of early Canada and the United States devote much space to the French–English or English–American rivalries, but little attention is given to the fact that Spanish expansion threatened to block the westward movement first of France, then of Britain, and eventually of the United States.

In its occupation of the east coast of North America and the Gulf of Mexico, Spain was faced with numerous rivals, some of which retained their island possessions until modern times. In the interior of North America the first strong opposition came from France, whose traders were pushing west and south. In 1677 Robert Cavalier de la Salle reached the mouth of the Mississippi, and in 1699 Jean-Baptiste Le Moyne de Bienville established a post which was to be the beginning of the French settlement of Louisiana, an immense territory controlling the Mississippi valley, extending French territory from Canada, enclosing the British colonies, splitting the Spanish colonies along the Gulf of Mexico, and intensifying the rivalry between Spain and France. Near the end of the Seven Years' War (1762), to prevent British possession, France ceded Louisiana to Spain, which thus solidified its coastline, and established a buffer between Mexico and the aggressive British–American colonists. Retroceded by Napoleon in 1800, it was purchased by the United States in 1803, but not until 1819 was the border with the United States established.

SPAIN CROSSES THE PACIFIC

Meanwhile Spain had found a route to Asia. The circumnavigation of the globe by Magellan's ship the *Victoria* (1519–22) had resulted in the discovery of the Philippine Islands. The significance of this voyage, which revealed for the first time the immense width of the Pacific Ocean, was the wealth (including twenty-six tons of cloves) that was carried back to Spain. Magellan's second ship, the *Trinidad*, unsuccessfully attempted to return across the Pacific, the first of many such failures. As early as 1527 Cortez attempted to exploit this new source of wealth by sending an expedition from the west coast of Mexico to the Moluccas, where it met strong oppositon from the Portuguese traders.

In the succeeding years four other expeditions using the north-east trade winds sailed westward from Mexico, but they could not make the return voyage against the prevailing currents and winds. Not until 1564 did the *San Lucas*, sailing north-east from the Philippines, make the discovery that by thus sailing north of the prevailing winds a return voyage was possible. The return of the *San Lucas* made possible a new trading pattern and in the following year the first of the Manila galleons crossed the Pacific.

The Philippines, which were annexed by Spain in 1565, were an extension of Spanish America and became a stepping-stone to the Asiatic market. From them Spanish traders and missionaries made contacts with the neighbouring peoples and became bitter rivals of the Portuguese.[5] A steady flow of Chinese junks connected Manila to the Canton trade, while from Manila numerous vessels plied the seas discovering the new lands of the South Pacific as far as Australia and establishing shipping routes among the islands. Flushed by their successes in America, the Spanish considered the conquest of China and the establishment of a new empire from Japan to Java centred in Manila. In 1592 Spanish missionaries entered the Japanese field in competition with the Portuguese. Nineteen years later Sebastian Vizcaino visited Japan and surveyed some of the coast. But Spanish resources were already overextended and by 1663 Spain had withdrawn from all of its settlements in the South Seas except for the Philippines.[6]

CALIFORNIA

Cortez planned to explore northwards along the coast of America, but a series of misfortunes plagued his efforts. Four ships were built at Zacatula, but they were burned before launching. Later attempts were delayed by dissension among the officials. Two ships left Acapulco in 1532 but were driven back by storms. The following year Mendoza's crew mutinied and killed him, but the mate, Fortún Jiménez, continued until he reached Lower California, which he believed to be an island. Jiménez and twenty of his crew were killed by the natives when they landed, and the survivors barely escaped to carry the news of their discovery back to Cortez. Two years later Cortez with one hundred men attempted unsuccessfully to establish a colony on the Bay of Santa Cruz, and it was at this time that he is believed to have named the new land, still believed to be an island, California.

Little exploration northward followed these beginnings. In 1542–43 two ships under Juan Rodriguez Cabrillo, a Portuguese in Spanish employ, made the first expedition. He is believed to have discovered San Diego harbour, thus becoming the first European to land on the west coast of what is now the United States. During the voyage Cabrillo died of blood poisoning, and it was under his pilot, Bartolomew Ferrelo, that the expedition continued northward. Ferrelo is believed to have reached about 42° N, possibly the south-west coast of Oregon. As he reported little of value no attempt was made to follow up his efforts. The voyages of the Manila galleons southward along the American coast resulted in a general knowledge of the coastline, but as they did not stop, few details were known. It is believed that on one of the galleons Francisco de Gali saw Cape Mendocino in 1584 and that ten years later Sebastian Rodriguez de Cermenon ran aground near San Francisco Bay.

THE MANILA GALLEONS

The annual voyages of the Manila galleons lasted for 250 years, from 1565 until 1815, and represented the first regular transportation services joining North America to Asia. Most of the exotic eastern products which they carried were sold to the wealthy Spaniards in Mexico or Peru, although some were transshipped to Spain.

At Manila were collected the riches from many countries of the Far East— India, Ceylon, the East Indies, China, and Japan. It became a centre to which were brought precious stones, spices, porcelain, carpets, exotic woods, ivory, silks, lacquered furniture, and cloths of varied textures and designs. In return, the Spanish sent the silver of Peru and New Spain.[7]

Numerous Dutch and English privateers attacked the Manila galleons, but only four of them were actually taken. The first of these, the *Santa Ana*, was captured by the Englishman, John Cavendish: "The whole company of the Spaniardes, both men and women to the number of 190 persons were set on shore. . . . about 3 of the clocke in the afternoone, our Generall caused the kings shippe to be set on fire."[8] Cavendish claims to have captured eight other smaller vessels. It is stated that on his return his sailors were clothed in silk, his sails were damask, and his topmast was covered with cloth of gold.[9]

Most of the galleons were built in Manila, with Chinese labour, and averaged about 700 tons, although in the eighteenth century some reached 2,000 tons and carried as many as 500 men. The two- or three-month voyage westward was difficult but the eight- or ten-month return could be disastrous. Without a landfall, food and water became scarce and stale, with resulting scurvy and death. In spite of the hardships the annual voyages continued. With their primitive methods of navigation the returning ships sailed eastward until they reached the coast of North America, and then continued southward without stopping, following the 800-mile coastline to Mexico.

It was possibly a desire to find a suitable way-port for the returning galleons that caused the Spanish authorities to send out Sebastian Vizcaino on a northward exploratory voyage in 1602-3. With three vessels and 200 men he charted the coast as far as northern California, possibly to Cape Mendocino. Accompanying him were three Carmelite friars, who left an account of the voyage, describing the appearance of the coast and the people. Vizcaino missed San Francisco Bay, but his glowing report of Monterey became significant in later plans for settlement. Cabrillo's and Vizcaino's were the only official attempts to explore the coast north of Lower California until 1769. For 150 years Spain was inactive on the north-west coast.

Spain was justified in calling the South Pacific the "Spanish Sea." After 1580 the annexation of Portugal removed opposition in the Indies for many years. The Manila galleons, although travelling on a comparatively narrow track, were the only vessels making trans-Pacific voyages. Spain had a strong post in Manila from where explorers, traders, and missionaries penetrated the Asiatic islands and mainland. Moreover, Spain controlled the eastern approaches to the Pacific around South America, and only Spanish ports existed on the American continents north of Cape Horn.

NEW RIVALS

Meanwhile, changes in the power structures of the European nations resulted in new rivalries. Events such as the Reformation, the growing interest in science, the rise of England under Elizabeth, developments in banking and finance, the decline of the Italian states, ambitious princes who desired more power and independence, and the threat of the Ottoman Empire all combined to disrupt the authority and prestige of the Roman Catholic church as well as to create new economic patterns and systems of alliances. Three nations challenged the Spanish–Portuguese power: Holland, England, and France. The resulting rivalries were to have drastic effects on colonial policies.

We have seen that, rounding Cape of Good Hope, the Dutch displaced the Portuguese in south-east Asia. Through the Straits of Magellan an Englishman, Francis Drake, was the first to threaten the Spanish monopoly in Pacific America. In 1579 he led a buccaneering expedition which raided the Spanish ships and ports along the west coast of South America and

Mexico. Fleeing from pursuit he sailed far north seeking a northern passage (Straits of Anian) home. "We coniecture: that either there is no passage at all through these Northerne coasts (which is most likely) or if there be, that yet it is unnauigable. . . . though we searched the coast diligently, even unto the 48 de. yet found we not the land to rend so much as one point in any place towards the East."[10] How far north he sailed is a matter of dispute, some authorities maintaining that he reached Vancouver Island "from whom high and snow-couered mountains, the North and Northwest winds send abroad their frozen nimphs." Failing to find a passage, he turned south and landed at a bay, again the source of dispute, near San Francisco, where he left a brass plaque after claiming "New Albion" for England. Thence he sailed westward to the Moluccas, the first Englishman in the Far East. Here he made a treaty of friendship and commerce with the Sultan of Ternate before completing his circumnavigation of the globe. Thomas Cavendish (1586–88) followed him within a decade.

Except for the fact that Drake had sailed farther north along the Pacific coast of North America than any previous European, his voyage added no significant discoveries. Drake brought much treasure back to England; his expedition did arouse interest in the unknown and fostered the growing nationalism in England. Two centuries later England was to use his landing at New Albion as a nebulous claim for territory on the Pacific coast. When Drake did not return to Mexico, there was some fear in that country that he had found a northern passage which would permit the entry of more English raiders and Vizcaino's expedition may have been an attempt to forestall further intruders. The English expeditions had crossed the Pacific on the approximate route used by the Spanish galleons, and thus contact with Asia remained in a narrow band while the North Pacific remained unknown.

THE STRAITS OF ANIAN

This lack of knowledge did not prevent considerable speculation and rumours about the northern ocean. Imaginative maps were drawn showing a hypothetical coastline, undiscovered islands such as the immense Gama-land, and numerous "Straits of Anian." Three reports concerning this strait illustrate some of these misconceptions.

A Greek, Apostolo Valerianos, commonly known as Juan de Fuca, claimed that while sailing for Spain in 1592 he discovered a strait opening into an inland sea between 47° and 48° North latitude. Following so soon after Drake, he may have been sent north by the viceroy of Mexico to check on the possibility of other expeditions coming from the north, but his claims of discovery have never been taken seriously. A report of 1788 claimed that two hundred years earlier Captain Lorenzo Ferrer Maldonado had followed a series of channels from the Pacific to the Atlantic. An earlier account published in 1708 asserted that in 1600 Admiral de Fonte had sailed from the Atlantic to the Pacific in the approximate latitute of 53° North. Although, except for de Fuca, these reports are obviously imaginative, they did much to influence the map-making and theorizing of the North Pacific region and to strengthen the belief until the end of the eighteenth century that the Straits of Anian existed.

HOLLAND, FRANCE, AND BRITAIN

By 1600 the Spanish monopoly in the Pacific was being challenged by the Dutch, English, and French. The Dutch entered the Pacific from both east and west, motivated by the rich trade of the Orient as well as the expectation of looting Spanish territories or galleons. Attempts to trade with Canton in 1604 and 1607 were refused because of Portuguese influence on local officials. An attempt to seize Macao failed. Having destroyed a Spanish fort, the Dutch occupied Formosa in 1642, but twenty years later they were expelled by the Chinese. These setbacks delayed but did not stop the Dutch. Their explorers ventured far north in the Pacific, past Korea and Sakhalin, adding to the knowledge of the coast. During the seventeenth and eighteenth centuries several Dutch representatives reached Peking where, in spite of their willingness to perform the kow-tow, they gained little.

England and France were also expanding their commerce. While the Spanish and Portuguese were reaching the Far East by the southern routes, Britain and France were attempting to find a northern route. John Cabot, followed by later expeditions such as that of Martin Frobisher, investigated the northern possibilities. In 1554 the Verrazano voyage, supported by Francis I, demonstrated that there was no passage through North America from Florida to Maine. French ambitions on the east coast of America, as well as an unsuccessful attempt to seize Sumatra, were foiled by the Portuguese, but in 1533 French activities resulted in Pope Clement VII modifying the Bull of 1493 so that it governed only known lands. In the following year Jacques Cartier showed that the St. Lawrence River was not a strait to Cathay. Thus both Britain and France were forced to use the southern routes to Asia.

In 1600 both of these countries granted charters (later amended) to East India Companies—two years before Holland.[11] The charter of the English East India Company, typical of others, gave the company the exclusive right to trade with any countries or islands between the Cape of Good Hope and the Straits of Magellan not already occupied by a friendly power, and also it was given the right to maintain order and to impose penalties. This proviso forced the British company to maintain a large army. Obviously it had a monopoly of all British trade in the Pacific Ocean.

The Dutch consistently foiled the early attempts of the English and French to establish themselves east of India. French expeditions for the annexation of Indo-China were repelled by the native rulers. The English and French were forced to concentrate their activities in India. However, the many European wars—from the naval wars with Cromwell in 1652 to the Napoleonic Wars—were a continuous drain on Holland, and its colonial power was whittled away. The Dutch lost Ceylon in 1763 and Capetown in 1806, both to Britain. After 1815 they were permitted to keep the East Indies, which they held until the Second World War, but they were dependent on protection by the British navy from possible French ambitions.

In 1763, except for a few French and Portuguese enclaves, the British won control of India. Meanwhile, without nearby bases, the British and French traders continued to visit China in search of tea, the major item of trade. They were forced to make their contacts through Portuguese Macao.

The increasing visits by foreign traders alarmed both Chinese and Japanese officials. This concern was accentuated by the activities of missionaries. In 1601 the Jesuit Matteo Ricci reached Peking and for some years the Jesuits were accepted, largely because of their knowledge of astronomy and mathematics, but their policies became suspect. In 1637 the Chinese excluded all foreigners and a similar action was taken by the Japanese in 1683. Jesuits continued to work secretly in China, however, and after a short period the ban was lifted and Catholicism revived. Because of their contributions to astronomy, science, and mathematics the Jesuits were eventually established at Peking. They gained added favour when they assisted in negotiating the Treaty of Nerchinsk with Russia. Unlike later treaties which China was forced to sign, the terms of this agreement were dictated by the Chinese.

CANTON

As early as 1635 an English trading expedition had reached Canton, but the venture had proved to be unprofitable. The trade did grow as other traders continued to appear. It became obvious to the Chinese that some trading was necessary and that, if this were so, the autocratic Chinese favoured trading with monopolistic trading companies rather than with individuals since the former had more control over their employees. In 1699 the East India Company, accepting the required submissive attitude, was permitted to establish a small trading post, the farthest outpost of British India for many years. In succeeding years other countries obtained similar concessions. Not until 1757 was Canton opened to the traders of all nations except Russia, which as late as 1805 was refused permission to trade through Canton because it already had entry through Kyakhta. The trade was subject to rigid Chinese rules and regulations. All vessels of war were prohibited from entering; neither women, guns, spears, or arms of any kind could be brought into the fort; foreigners could not row in the river for pleasure nor pass the night outside the factories; foreigners were not allowed to present petitions except to the Co-Hong.[12] Only the ports of Macao and Canton were open to foreign trade.

No contact was permitted with officials of the Chinese government. Merchants were considered to be of a low class, and foreign traders as barbarians from inferior nations were even lower. Trade was done through the monopolistic specially-licensed Co-Hong, a group of Chinese merchants which eventually totalled thirteen.[13] They in turn were responsible to the government for the good behaviour of their foreign customers. To both groups of traders profits depended on co-operation.

MID-POINT OF PACIFIC HISTORY

The Treaty of Paris, 1763, which ended the Seven Years' War (with Britain at the peak of its first mercantile empire), occurred near the half-way mark in the history of European influence in the Pacific. The power of China seemed to be invincible. The Portuguese empire in Asia had collapsed, although it still held some isolated possessions, especially strategic Macao. Spain, which had lost Manila for a short time to Britain during the war, was on the defensive and restricted to the Philippine Islands, where it opened Manila to foreign traders in 1789. Holland dominated the East Indies and had the only entry into Japan. French ambitions in India were ended.

In North America the French presence ended in Canada and rivalry intensified between the British colonies along the eastern seaboard and the great Spanish domain of the interior. On the west coast the Spanish still nominally claimed sovereignty and had a general idea of the coastline as far north as Cape Mendocino, but they showed no inclination to expand their settlements into the unknown regions north of Lower California.

The second half of the eighteenth century ended this period of inactivity in the North Pacific as Britain and France began a series of scientific and exploratory voyages from the Antarctic to the Arctic. At the same time Russia, which had crossed Siberia, had opened the fur trade, crossed to North America, and brought a new power to the Pacific. The threat of a new competitor from the north aroused interest and created alarm on both Pacific coasts. Another era of exploration was to begin.

3

Opening the North Pacific
(1750–1800)

The reputation of the sea-otter skin brought no inconsiderable body of the
Northern Chinese and Pekin merchants to Canton, a port which they had never
before visited. (Captain John Meares, 1790)

In the Spanish convention . . . restitution was offered to this country for the cap-
tures and aggressions made by the subjects of His Catholic Majesty; together
with an acknowledgement of an equal right with Spain to the exercise and
prosecution of all commercial undertakings in those seas, reputed before to
belong only to the Spanish crown. The extensive branches of the fisheries and
the fur trade to China, being considered as objects of very material importance
to this country. . . . (Captain George Vancouver, 1791)

RUSSIA REACHES NORTH AMERICA

During the thirteenth century the Mongol empire extended across Russia
to the borders of eastern Europe. Not until the reign of Ivan III, the Great
(1462–1505), was the Grand Duchy of Moscow freed from Tatar rule. As the
vast Mongol complex disintegrated, the Russian empire filled the resulting
vacancy by expanding in all directions. During the reign of Peter the Great
(1689–1725) Russia reached the Baltic Sea and became westernized. Meanwhile adventurers were advancing across the Urals and Siberia to the Pacific.

This movement eastward was in some ways similar to the westward movements of the Europeans in North America from the Atlantic to the Pacific.
The driving force was the search for richer fur lands—in Siberia primarily
the sable and in America the beaver—which forced traders to venture farther
and farther into unknown lands until the interior of the continent was opened.
The first exploratory traders were independent—the French *coureurs de bois*,
the English "pedlars," and the Russian *promishlenniki*. Competition and
government policies eventually displaced these individuals with powerful
monopolistic companies under royal charter.[1]

The movement eastward from Russia was led by bands of runaway serfs, criminals, and adventurers known as Cossacks. The first of these groups crossed the Urals in 1580 under Yermak, and soon bands of Cossacks had established themselves in the new lands. From the wilderness they sent back emissaries to the tsar with valuable gifts of furs, and in return they were granted pardon for their crimes. In small groups the independent Cossack traders, known as *promishlenniki*, pushed eastward, increasingly financially backed by merchants.

The traders on both continents faced vast wildernesses with unknown geographical challenges and extreme climates. In Russia there were no river systems such as the St. Lawrence and the Saskatchewan into the fur lands; portaging between tributaries extensively, the Russians were forced to cross river systems such as the Ob, Yenisei, or Lena, all flowing northward, and, before they reached the Pacific, they were forced to cross mountain barriers. Whereas American traders used canoes extensively, horses and oxen, sleighs, and wagons supplemented by barges for short distances were needed for the great trans-Siberian trek. The Russians never developed an efficient and acceptable method of river transport such as the North American canoe and used boats which were often towed against the current by horses.

On both continents the newcomers faced indigenous peoples who were sometimes peaceful but often warlike. In many cases the traders united with native women, leaving children of mixed blood who were more easily assimilated by the Russians than by the North Americans. As a general rule the French, British, and American traders were more dependent on the natives for furs and therefore more co-operative with them than the Russians who, nevertheless, did make alliances with certain chiefs. As traders and settlers advanced, the natives often rebelled and were subjugated by wars. The Russians were more ruthless and were not averse to the use of force or blackmail to obtain assistance in the search for furs. Although the Russian government stated that Siberian peoples were to be protected and treated as wards of the state, the officials, traders, and settlers in the region generally disregarded these instructions and continued to oppress and exploit the natives. The reduction of the fur animals along with epidemics resulted in the decimation of the native peoples—in Russia entire tribes were wiped out—and their eventual restriction to comparatively small areas.[2]

The traders of both continents were followed by officials, soldiers, and colonists who settled around the established posts and linked them with lines of communication. The first *promishlenniki* were sometimes authorized to act for the government in accepting oaths of allegiance and collecting tributes, called *yasak*, in furs from the native peoples. Sometimes friendly chieftains were appointed *yasak* collectors.

Whereas the North American traders took almost two centuries to cross the continent, the Russians reached the much farther Pacific coast sixty years after the first Cossacks crossed the Urals. By 1632 Yakutsk was established on the Lena River. Seven years later an expedition crossed the forbidding Stanovoi Mountains and reached the Sea of Okhotsk on the Pacific, where Okhotsk was founded in 1649. In 1642 a Russian overland expedition, led by the ruthless and cruel Vasily Poyarkov, reached the mouth of the Amur and probably saw Sakhalin. In this tragic venture, which lasted three years, the men, suffering from starvation and scurvy, were opposed by hostile natives. Finally the survivors sailed northward into the Sea of Okhotsk, from where they made their way overland to Yakutsk. Only about one-quarter of the 130 men returned. This was the same year that in North America the French established Montreal. On the east coast there were six English settlements, one Dutch (New York), and one Swedish (Delaware).

Poyarkov had reached the North Pacific overland, but he was not the first European to see those waters. The previous year the Dutch explorer Commandant Maerton Gerritsen de Vries is reported to have sailed as far as 49°, to have seen Sakhalin Island, and to have entered the Sea of Okhotsk. Probably because he saw little of trade value and also because trade with Japan was restricted to Nagasaki, the Dutch showed no further interest in the region.

At the same time traders seeking sables, beavers, and walrus teeth were probing northward towards a legendary river, the Pogicha. In 1648 an expedition under the trader Alexeyev started in search of this river. He was accompanied by a government representative, Deshnev, who was to collect *yasak*. With six boats and ninety men they followed the Kolyma River to its mouth and sailed eastward along the Arctic coast. Driven by storms, they were separated. Both apparently rounded East Cape to the mouth of the Anadyr, which empties into Bering Sea, and thus they had sailed between Asia and North America.[3] However, Alexeyev died of scurvy, and Deshnev alone is credited with this important passage. His report was sent to the commander of Yakutsk who, apparently, did not forward it to St. Petersburg, so that the separation of the continents remained unknown. The report was not discovered in the Yakutsk archives until 1736, eighty-seven years after it was made. By that time Bering had made his first voyage.

RUSSO-CHINESE TRADE

One of the aims of Russian expansion was to open a trade route to China which would be more direct than the roundabout overland route through Turkestan. As the Russians advanced eastward, they approached the Chinese territory of Sinkiang, after which they were separated from China by two buffer states, Mongolia and Manchuria. The first of these was struggling to maintain its independence from China; the rulers of the second were in the process of taking over the government of China. Having passed these two regions, the Russians reached the Amur River system and entered territory claimed by China.

At the time it would seem that the rulers of both Russia and China were ignorant of the extent of each other's territories. Each ruler expected the other to acknowledge his suzerainty, and both, especially the Russians, were surprised at the strength of the opposition. Both governments had very sketchy knowledge of the north-east coast, but China claimed it through its historical background, which had resulted in payment of tributes by the tribes of the coast and Sakhalin.

The Amur River is the natural outlet for Siberia. In 1658 Nerchinsk was established by the Russians on an inland tributary of the Amur but further expansion was stopped. Twice when the Russians attempted to establish a settlement farther down the river at Albazin, they were driven back by large Chinese forces who destroyed the post. This did not prevent the continued activities of Russian traders in the lower Amur and tension increased.

Moscow was more interested in establishing trade with China than in warring over an isolated unknown wilderness. In 1689 the two nations signed the Treaty of Nerchinsk, the first treaty China made on equal terms with a European power. It established the southern border of Russian claims as a line running from the Amur River north-east along the crest of the Stanovoi Mountains, thus cutting Russia off from the mouth of the Amur entirely. In return, Russian merchants were to have the right to travel and trade into China. Approximately forty years later it was agreed that the two Russian towns of Nerchinsk and Kyakhta were to be permanent posts for Russo-Chinese trade and that a trade caravan would be permitted into China every three years, and an agreement was reached that China was to have suzerainty over Mongolia, thus settling the Siberian–Mongolian border.[4] Within a few years China sent a mission to Moscow, the first Chinese embassy to be sent to a foreign country. These two agreements were to last for a century, during which time China signed no other treaty with a European nation. In the ensuing years China emphasized its authority by periodically closing the trade routes for a few years, with disastrous results for the Russian traders.

Cut off from the Amur, the Russians were forced to turn north-east towards the Kamchatka Peninsula, and for over a century Russian expansion followed a large arc extending around the Chinese territories to northern Japan, Alaska, and California. Exploration and expansion was carried on by the *promishlenniki* as the demand for furs continued. Prized by the Chinese, these were the basis of Russian trade; in return, China supplied tea and textiles as well as manufactured and consumer goods and luxury products such as porcelain, silk, and perfumes.

RUSSIA DISCOVERS ALASKA

The *promishlenniki* advanced rapidly to the north-east, but their trade was complicated by hostile and warlike natives. Not until 1697 did Vladimir Atlasov claim to have conquered Kamchatka, a region rich in furs. The natives remained aggressive and unreliable. In 1716 to avoid the warlike Chukchi and Koriaks, Sokolov sailed across the Sea of Okhotsk to Kamchatka. This became the common route to the few isolated posts on the Pacific where were found the valuable sea otter.

Peter the Great was concerned during most of his reign with gaining an outlet on the Baltic Sea and with converting Russia from an Asiatic to a European power. Peter spent some time in western Europe, supposedly incognito, studying European industrial and scientific advances, as well as European customs. Apparently, while in England, he became interested in the Hudson's Bay Company which, along with his scientific interests, led him to speculate that Siberia might be joined to North America and also that Russia might become a rival of the English company for the furs of North America. He visualized an eventual meeting of the Russian fur traders from the west with the Hudson's Bay Company traders from the east.[5] His last act before he died in 1725 was to appoint a Dane, Vitus Bering, to be leader of an expedition to discover whether Siberia was joined to North America.

Three years after Peter's death Bering reached Petropavlosk, on the east coast of Kamchatka, and launched the *St. Gabriel*, a vessel sixty feet by twenty feet with a crew of forty-four men. In two months they travelled to St. Lawrence Island, north of 67° N. latitude, before they turned back. Beset by fog, they had not seen North America. The following year a trader, Michael Spiridonovich Gvodzev, sailed as far north as East Cape, and on his return trip sighted North America, but he did not bother to report this until several years later.

Bering's report did not satisfy the scientists at St. Petersburg and a second expedition was planned. Eight years were spent in the preparation and the crossing of the continent before the *St. Peter* under the sixty-year-old Bering and the *St. Paul* under Captain-Lieutenant Aleksai Chirikov sailed from Kamchatka in 1741. Both vessels were eighty feet long, 108 tons burden, and carried seventy-six men. The two ships were separated, but both saw the coast of Alaska. Chirikov landed at about latitude 52° 21′ before sailing northwest; Bering made a landfall near Mt. St. Elias but did not land on the mainland. Chirikov, having lost twenty-one of his men, returned with news of the abundance of sea otters. Bering, beset by winds and fog on his return voyage, died of scurvy on Bering Island. After a miserable winter, forty-six of his crew returned to Kamchatka the following spring, bringing with them a wealth of blue fox, sea otter, and other furs.

Meanwhile, other Russians had been probing southward. Sakhalin had been discovered and much of the coastline south of Okhotsk explored. Martin Spanberg, who was with Bering on his first trip and was in the advance party of the second, explored southward and is credited with discovering thirty-four islands of various sizes.[6] He reached the Kuriles in 1738 and in the following year visited Japan.

The furs brought back from the Chirikov and Bering voyages lured the *promishlenniki* to new endeavours. By the following year traders were on their way to Bering Island and to farther islands in the Aleutians. The distances in small boats are almost incomprehensible—400 miles from Okhotsk to Petropavlosk, another 1,100 miles to the nearest Aleutians, which in turn extended 1,200 miles.[7] By 1763 Stepan Glotov had sighted the farthest of the Aleutians, Kodiak Island. Captain Cook comments: "The Russians have made several attempts to gain a footing upon that part of the American continent [near Unalaska] but have been repulsed by the inhabitants."[8] By 1768 there were fifteen active companies in the Aleutians and the numbers were increasing annually.

THE RUSSIAN-AMERICAN COMPANY

From the death of Peter the Great until the accession of Catherine II (1762) there were six tsars or tsarinas. In this corrupt period of confusion little government support was organized to follow up the explorations of Bering and others into the North Pacific and Japan. The government did continue to license the *promishlenniki* and to insist on the payment of *yasak*, but many traders acted independent of government controls. As the number of traders grew, competition was often ruinous and necessitated amalgamations of individuals and companies.[9] Although he received no encouragement from Catherine, Gregory Ivanovitch Shelikov was instrumental in forming a united company and in 1784 established a post on Kodiak Island (which Cook says the Russians reached eight years before).[10] From this headquarters traders were sent to the North American mainland. Shelikov's company gradually absorbed other companies and independent traders, and in 1788 was granted exclusive trading privileges in the land under its control. In 1797, after Shelikov's death, the United American Company was formed by his wife, Natalie, and Nicholas Petrovich Rezanov, who had married their daughter, Anna. The previous year Catherine II had died, and her son Paul was more favourable to monopolies. In 1799 the Russian-American Company was granted a charter under the direct patronage of Tsar Paul. It was similar to those of other trading companies of the time such as the East India Company and the Hudson's Bay Company and was comparable in wealth, prestige, and control of vast known and unknown territories to the latter.[11] A stock company, some of its shares were held by nobility, which brought it prestige and influence in Moscow. It held the trade monopoly and mineral rights for the eastern Siberian coast, the Aleutians, and an undetermined amount of the coastline of North America to 55 degrees. The company was responsible for law and order, the building of fortifications, colonization, and the establishment of missions.[12] It was to claim unoccupied lands, to trade with neighbouring countries, and to deal with foreign powers. Alexander Andreyvich Baranov, who had been appointed supervisor by Shelikov, became manager of the company in Alaska. Under his leadership the Russian-American Company was to become a powerful force in the history of the North Pacific.

Meanwhile, about twenty years after Bering's voyage to North America, news of the Russian discoveries filtered into Europe and eastern America. The rumours caused a revival of Spanish claims to the north-west coast and aroused interest in Britain, France, and the United States.

SPAIN EXPLORES NORTHWARD

During the Seven Years' (French and Indian) War (1756–63), Spain fought on the losing French side and lost Florida to Britain. With the elimination of the French in Canada, British traders began to push westward into the prairies and threatened the Spanish territories in the interior of the continent. More significant were the reports of Russian activities in the North Pacific. The Spanish ministers in St. Petersburg were continuously keeping their home government informed, as is shown in the following report in 1761: "Up to the present the Russian government cannot be said to have done more than sight the coast of America. . . . even though they have not taken possession of it they are in a position to do it at any time. . . . The mainland, according to what they say and believe here, is California, in which case it extends to 75 degrees."[13] As early as 1768 José de Gálvez was warned to watch for Russians on the coast.[14] At this time Spain was under the leadership of the enlightened Carlos III (1759–88), who attempted unsuccessfully to restore Spain's prestige and to revive its sea power. Almost thirty years had passed after Bering's death before, under Carlos's leadership, Spain took steps to forestall these advances and to reassert its claim to the entire Pacific coast. Missions, settlements, and exploratory expeditions were planned.

The driving force behind the move into California was that of the missionaries, led by the Franciscan Father Junipero Serra, a man who rightfully deserves an honoured place in California history. When the Spanish government exiled the Jesuits from both Spain and the colonies in 1767, Serra was chosen to take over from the exiled missionaries. At this time no settlements were in California although several of the harbours had been mapped. A man of poor health, Serra spent sixteen years in California baptizing the Indians, keeping peace, and opening new missions, where gardens were established.

Two expeditions were planned, one by sea, the other by land. Juan Perez's ship was the first to arrive at the meeting place of San Diego, followed almost three weeks later by Vicente Vila. The difficulties of sea voyages at that time can be appreciated by the fact that only sixteen of the ninety men aboard were fit to work on their arrival. The overland trip under Gaspar de Portolá was even more arduous—only 126 of the 300 survived. Upon their arrival the first California mission was established at San Diego.

The main objective of the expedition had been to establish a mission at the port of Monterey, which had been glowingly described by Vizcaino in 1603. Therefore Portolá continued northward by land. He missed the harbour at Monterey and reached San Francisco Bay, which he did not recognize as a great harbour and which was not explored until Pedro Fages reached it two years later. While returning, Portola found Monterey. A mission was established there in 1770, and in 1777 it was proclaimed the capital.

By 1823 there were twenty-one missions with friars and their neophytes. *Presidios*, or military posts, under a commandant, were built. Settlement and colonization were at first discouraged, but by 1780 the first *pueblo* (civic settlement) had been established.

The Spanish colonial institutions resembed those of old Spain. Strict regulations prevailed in the colony, which was controlled by an autocracy influenced by the mercantile theory. New posts were carefully planned and organized.[15] They were under rigid supervision, and since senior officers were required to make detailed reports of their activities at the end of their terms (reports which might mean promotion or demotion), they adhered carefully to regulations and showed little initiative. Throughout centuries a vast stream of regulations were sent out to the colonies dealing with matters of minute as well as of great importance. At one time there were at least 400,000 such regulations (*cédulas*). The reduction of these to some 11,000 laws which were published in 1681 was a most impressive feat.[16]

No trade was permitted with either foreign or Spanish vessels, and even the returning Philippine galleons calling for supplies were not allowed to trade in California ports. Although after 1781 settlers were granted land, they were forced to live where they were told, to produce required goods, and to sell any surplus to the *presidios* at prices set by the government. They were also subject to other regulations such as tithes, taxes, and military service in emergencies. People could not leave the colony without permission. In spite of these restrictions the population increased, augmented by settlers who trickled overland from the east.

By the 1780's Spain had found it impossible to maintain its monopolistic regulations and restrictions in trade in face of competition and the growth of illicit trade by Britain and others. The restrictions on inter-colonial trade established by the laws of 1681 were removed in 1790. Although still basically clinging to the mercantile theory trade was much liberalized.[17]

Besides settling California, Spain began a series of exploratory expeditions into the north. The first sailed in 1774 under Juan Perez. The account of this trip is described best in the diary of Fray Juan Crespi, who had accompanied Serra to San Diego and was the first friar to accompany Portolá to San Francisco Bay, as well as being chaplain and diarist for other exploratory expeditions to southern California. Perez was to sail as far north as 60°, to take formal possession of the coast, not to make any settlement, to report on the people and resources of the country and, if any foreign settlement or ship were encountered, to communicate with them as little as possible. The corvette *Santiago* left San Blas with eighty-eight men, stopped at San Diego for three weeks, and then sailed on a route which travelled far out to sea before reaching the coast at 55°, where fogs and storms prevented him from reaching the projected 60°:

> The pilots made observations, and they told us that we were in the latitude of 55° exactly, and so it is in this latitude that Point Sànta Margarita is situated.
> About one o'clock they turned the prow toward the land, but in two hours the wind changed to the west-southwest, and the prow was turned to the south. A little later the wind changed to the southwest.... The wind has been fresh all the time, and the afternoon very dark, with a heavy, thick fog, so that nothing could be seen.... For this reason, the contrary wind, the heavy swell, and the strength of the currents, which were driving us toward the land, a course was taken out to sea.[18]

Short of water, with a crew suffering from scurvy, Perez was forced to turn back. On Vancouver Island, possibly at Nootka Sound, another attempt was made to land but "the wind was driving towards the shore, dragging the anchor.... Seeing this, and the evident peril of shipwreck, the captain took the best course, losing the anchor and part of the stream cable, for he ordered the latter to be cut."[19] Perez was the first European to report on the north-west Indians and to see the Queen Charlotte Islands, Vancouver Island, and the Olympic Mountains before returning after almost a year to San Blas. He had not reached his objective of 60°, nor had he planted the cross to claim sovereignty, but nevertheless his expedition is one of the great exploratory voyages to the North Pacific.

In the following year a larger expedition, consisting of 106 men, was sent northward. It included the ship *Santiago* under Bruno Heceta with Juan Perez aboard and the schooner *Sonora* under Juan de Bodega y Quadra. They landed at approximately 41° N. latitude, made repairs to the ships, and claimed sovereignty for Spain. Farther north, near Port Grenville on the Washington coast, Heceta again landed and claimed sovereignty. The two ships parted. Heceta sailed as far north as Nootka Sound, failed to see the Strait of Juan de Fuca, but did report the mouth of a great river (the Columbia) before turning back. Perez died on the return voyage. Meanwhile the *Sonora* had landed seven men on the Washington coast to obtain water, but all were killed by the Indians. The *Sonora* continued north as far as 58°, within sight of Mt. Edgecumbe, before beginning the return voyage on which it stopped for a short time at Bodega Bay.

Another important northern expedition was made four years later under Don Ignacio Arteaga, accompanied by Quadra. They reached almost 60° and saw Mt. St. Elias, making formal possession at several points before returning. The three expeditions of Perez, Quadra, and Arteaga made claims of sovereignty in several places, but although they had travelled the coastline far enough to overlap Russian explorations, they had not seen any Europeans in northern waters.

Thus during the 1770's there had been a short revival of Spanish expansion during which San Diego, Monterey, and San Francisco (1776) had been established. For a few years after this short spurt, Spanish activity lost its drive towards the north-west coast. Carlos III died. In 1776 the Americans proclaimed their independence and in the ensuing years were joined, as allies, with Spain and France. From this war Spain recovered Florida and reasserted its claims to Louisiana. Here it now had a new aggressive neighbour, the American states, which resented its control of the Mississippi at New Orleans. Not until 1795 was the southern border established and New Orleans opened to American traders. In Louisiana, Spain pushed its posts north to the Missouri and, to forestall the British and Americans, entered the fur trade, for which it often hired experienced British and American traders.

Within a few years after Captain Cook's voyage in 1778 there was an increase of activity on the North Pacific coast. British and American traders, many arriving via Cape Horn and passing the Spanish California coast, cruised the coast in search of furs, while Russian traders were active in the north. From both Britain and France exploratory expeditions travelled to the North Pacific.

Threatened by the activities of four other nations, Spain realized that positive action was necessary to assert its claim to the entire coast. A number of expeditions were dispatched. In 1783 Captains Estéban José Martinez and Gonzalo López de Haro visited the Russians at Kodiak and from its commander gained the impression that the Russians planned to expand southward. Two years later three ships under Lieutenant Francisco Eliza separately charted and investigated the Strait of Juan de Fuca and the coastline to Alaska. Alessandro Malaspina, an Italian sailing for Spain, made a scientific voyage to Alaska. En route he visited California, where he left the first American settler, John Green. In 1791 Eliza returned to the north coast with José Narvaez and Juan Carrasso to study the Gulf of Georgia. The following year, Dionisia Alcala Galiano and Cayetano Valdéz met Captain George Vancouver off Spanish Banks in the Gulf of Georgia. Galiano noted the changed colours of the water off the mouth of the Fraser River, but failed to see the river. In the following year Martinez ascended the Columbia River for fourteen miles. Several other Spanish explorers who visited the north-west coast during these years added little new information.

FRANCE IN THE PACIFIC

The years 1756–1815 were a period of almost continuous European wars from which Britain emerged as the supreme colonial and naval power. The conquest of India and the annexation of colonies forced Britain to change the character of its empire. Whereas the Americas had been colonies for settlement, India was basically a commercial enterprise. Commercial policies were still based on the mercantile theory and the Navigation Laws, but these were being challenged by the liberal ideas of such men as Adam Smith and by the demands for freedom of the seas and trade by the United States. There was considerable diversity in the character of the British colonies, and this, along with the wide powers of the great trading companies, led to a variety of controls. Although Britain continued to expand its imperial interests in India and the Far East, after the Napoleonic Wars it retained only new colonies which had strategic values. During these years there were great improvements in navigation which enabled mariners to travel farther distances with less risk and with larger cargoes. Interest in science and the publication of many books resulted in a search for knowledge and an increasing awareness of the world as a whole. It was at this time that the American coast of the North Pacific was opened.

Two French explorers deserve mention. Louis Antoine de Bougainville sailed around the world (1767–69), visiting Tahiti and the Solomon Islands, the largest of which is named after him. Almost twenty years later Jean François de Galaup, comte de la Pérouse, spent four years in the Pacific. Rounding Cape Horn, he visited Chile and Hawaii en route to Lituya Bay in Alaska. Returning southward he reached San Francisco without stopping. At Monterey he received a warm welcome and alerted the Spanish to the threat of Russian expansion in the north. He returned to Hawaii and visited Macao, the Philippines, western Japan, southern Sakhalin, and Petropavlosk. La Pérouse returned to Botany Bay in Australia, but after leaving this port his ships and all hands disappeared. Forty years later it was established that both of his ships had been wrecked in the New Hebrides.

La Pérouse's comments reveal the interest of France in colonial expansion: "We had run along the coasts of Corea and Japan: but these countries inhabited by people barbarous towards strangers, had not allowed us to think of stopping at them."[20] He considered the conquest of Manila would be easy but believed that Formosa, where the Chinese had a garrison of 10,000 men, would not be worth the cost of occupation.[21] Of the north-west coast he stated: "Though the Russians are established at the north and the Spaniards to the south, many centuries will elapse before these two nations will meet; and there will long remain between them intermediary points, which might be occupied by other nations.... Spain would, doubtless, consider it as an usurpation, if the French were to possess themselves here of a few acres only, though the factory...might elude her search for years."[22] Of the sea otter trade he said: "I am of the opinion that it is by far too early to think of establishing a factory..." and suggested traders carry bars of iron and "a few barrels of charcoal, with a forge, and a smith capable of giving bars of iron any form which the Indians may wish."[23]

The voyages of Bougainville and La Pérouse were not typical of French activities in the Pacific. Early seventeenth-century moves towards Indochina were checked by the native rulers and the Dutch influence, while expansion in India was severely restricted by the success of the British in 1763. The greatest impetus for French activity in Asia came from the Roman Catholic missionaries, who were bitterly opposed by those from Portugal and later by Dutch and British traders and missionaries. It was the missionaries who encouraged the French in their unsuccessful attempts to control Indochina. Even after the Treaty of Paris, 1763, the French hoped to revive their Asiatic activities, as the voyages mentioned above illustrate. However, the lack of success in Indochina, the lack of a Pacific base, involvement in the American Revolution, and the disorders of the French Revolution all handicapped French imperial expansion. By 1800, except for the missionary activities, the French presence in the Pacific was negligible.

On the other hand, after 1763, British exploration, political influence, and trade expansion were active. British naval and commercial supremacy in southern Asia and the south Pacific were unchallenged. Britain enlarged its vision from the Antarctic to the Arctic. Two separate circumnavigations of the globe were made by Byron and Wallis between 1764 and 1767. The latter is credited with discovering Tahiti. The outstanding explorer of the era, however, was Captain James Cook.

CAPTAIN JAMES COOK

In Cook's two circumnavigations of the globe (1768–72 and 1772–75) he had explored the east coast of Australia and New Zealand, and he had disproved the theory of the great southern continent. On his third voyage, which began in 1776, he was not only to make scientific studies and claim undiscovered lands for Britain but also to survey the north-west coast of America in search of a western outlet for the North-west Passage (the Straits of Anian), which would give Britain entry into the Pacific without interfering with Spanish territories.

He sailed from Britain with two ships, the 462-ton *Resolution* and the 295-ton *Discovery*. With him were three other men who were to become famous, William Bligh, Nathaniel Portlock, and George Vancouver, as well as the excellent artist James Webber. Rounding the Cape of Good Hope, he visited New Zealand and Tahiti, and then, continuing north and east, he discovered and named the Sandwich Islands. Thence he reached the coast of New Albion near Cape Foulweather on the Oregon coast in 1778. Through rough weather, during which he was blown south 42°, he reached Nootka Sound on Vancouver Island, where he remained for several weeks resting and repairing his ships. Here he made a study of the friendly natives and received sea otter skins from them in return for paltry amounts of trade goods.

Continuing northward he visited the Asian coast north of the Arctic circle, where twice natives gave him letters in Russian, which he could not read, before he met the Russians at Unalaska. Here a co-operative chief trader promised to forward across Russia a letter which included Cook's charts of the northern coasts to the Lords of the Admiralty in London. These dispatches crossed the 8,400 miles successfully. He passed 70°N. latitude, much farther than Bering had been, before his progress was stopped in the ice of Bering Sea. His ships returned south for the winter to the Hawaiian Islands, where Cook was killed by the natives. The following year the ships returned north, calling twice at Petropavlosk, where again letters were dispatched. By these overland messages to London the news of Cook's death was learned eleven months after the event. The ice was still impenetrable, so the ships turned homeward calling en route (December 1779) at Macao and Canton, where they first heard that France and Britain were at war. "It was now three years since we had been in any port where we could converse any otherwise than by signs."[24]

At Nootka, Captain Cook had written: "The fur of these creatures [the sea otter] is certainly finer than that of any other animal we know of, consequently the discovery of this part of North America, where so valuable an article of commerce is to be procured, ought certainly to be considered as a matter of some consequence."[25] The truth of his statement became obvious at Macao, for "it afterward happened that skins which did not cost the purchaser six shillings sterling sold in China for 100 dollars."[26] Captain King, who completed Cook's journal, wrote:

> During our absence in Canton [from Macao] a brisk trade had been carrying on with the Chinese for the sea-otter skins which had everyday been rising in value. One of our seamen sold his stock alone for eight hundred dollars: and a few prime skins...were sold for one hundred and twenty each...the whole amount in both ships, I am confident did not fall short of two thousand pounds sterling.... The rage with

which our seamen were possessed to return to Cook's River, and by [*sic*] another cargo of skins to make their fortune at one time, was not far short of mutiny.[27]

Captain Cook had ended the myth of a navigable North-west Passage from Hudson Bay. He introduced scientific details about the geography and peoples of the north-west coast. Britain had a strong claim for the coast north of California. Cook's voyages alarmed Spain and reactivated exploratory voyages north of California. The profits made by his crews from the sale of the sea otter pelts in China aroused interest in the possibility of the fur trade on the north-west coast and resulted in development of the maritime fur trade.

THE MARITIME FUR TRADE

The maritime fur trade was based on the fur of the sea otter, a marine animal whose habitat formed a huge arc from northern Japan to Kamchatka, the Aleutians, and south along the North American coast to northern Washington, where it became scarce until another populated area appeared off California. The Russians had been hunting it for a number of years, sending the pelts across the sea to Okhotsk, overland to Yakutsk, by barge on the Lena River to Irkutsk and then overland to Kyakhta, a distance of over 3,000 miles. From here the furs were sent by camel caravan to Peking. Two or three years might pass between the time when the sea otter was caught and when its pelt reached its destination.[28]

The Spanish knew of the California sea otters but at first, according to La Pérouse, "scarcely imagined the fur of the sea otter to be of more value than that of the rabbit," although he states later, "they, at present, are better informed of the subject." He did not realize that Perez and other Spanish explorers had picked up a few furs on their voyages, that missionaries were buying them from the natives, and that a few had been sent on the Manila galleons to China.

Numerous individuals recognized from the accounts of Cook's voyage that profits could be made from the sea otter trade, and within a few years vessels were scouring the inlets of the north-west coast searching for furs. The first arrival was the Englishman James Hanna (1785–87), sailing under the Portuguese flag, who, according to Dixon, procured 550 sea otter skins which he sold at Canton for $20,000. Dixon himself sold 2,552 sea otter skins plus fox, beaver, fur seals, and others to the East India Company for $50,000.[29] The first traders were British who came both by Cape Horn and the Cape of Good Hope, but they were joined within a few years by Americans as well as by a few traders from France, Sweden, and Portugal.[30] Some vessels made several trips between China and the north-west coast; others exchanged their furs for tea and continued homeward. "In the year 1788 there were on the North West Coast the ships *Prince of Wales, Princess Royal, Felice, Iphigenia, Columbia* and *Washington*."[31] Rickard estimates that in one summer 15,000 sea otter skins were obtained by the north-west traders plus possibly 10,000 by the Russians for a year's total of 25,000.[32]

Space does not permit a detailed account of the many traders who, while probing the inlets of the coast during these years, discovered and named numerous geographical features. One of the more interesting is the twenty-five-year-old Englishman Charles Barkley, who brought with him his seventeen-year-old bride Frances Hornby—the first white woman to see this region. The Barkleys discovered Clayoquot Sound, Barkley Sound, and the Strait of Juan de Fuca, which they recognized and named but did not enter. Several places are named after Mrs. Barkley. They picked up John Mackay, who had been left on the coast the previous year by Charles Stuart Strange and who was the first white man to live with the Indians on the coast. The Barkleys typically flew Austrian or Portuguese colours. Although their voyage was not a great success as they lost most of their profits through legal problems when they reached Calcutta, they did return to the north-west coast a few years later.

Five years after Captain Cook reached the North Pacific the American colonies had gained their independence and within a few years were to form the United States of America. The new nation was an Atlantic state confined at the north by Britain and at the west by Spain. With independence the strong commercial interests of the Americans were free to expand throughout the world without the previous restrictive British regulations.

With Captain Cook on the *Discovery* was a young American, John Ledyard. On the long voyage he had journeyed to the South Sea Islands and the north-west coast, had met the Russians, may have been one of the three men who had escaped when Cook was killed, and had shared in the profits from the sea otter skins sold in Canton. His book, *A Journal of Captain Cook's Last Voyage to the Pacific Ocean*, was published before Cook's *Journal*. Ledyard was an enthusiastic romantic who saw the possibilities of Pacific trade but who lacked money. The rest of his life was spent travelling throughout the world unsuccessfully trying to obtain financial backing for his various schemes. Hard-headed businessmen listened but would not support him. Nevertheless, his visions of Pacific opportunities did not go unnoticed.

Formerly, prospective American traders to the Far East had been hampered by the monopoly of the East India Company, but now these restrictions no longer applied. Within a year after independence the *Empress of China* sailed from New York via the Cape of Good Hope to Canton, the first successful American trading expedition to China. The next few years saw an increasing number of ships sailing from Salem, Boston, and New York.

As newcomers in the area the Americans were handicapped in the competition for trade. The earlier nations had established ports where they could stop for supplies and rest on the long journey to the East. They also had comparatively close bases for trade—Spain in Manila, Holland in Batavia, Portugal in Macao, and Britain in India. The Americans, without such ports, were dependent on the good will and co-operation of the other powers, a condition which was subject to cancellation in times of war or during disputes. At first the English and French were friendly towards the newcomers, but as competition increased so did suspicion and hostility. During the Napoleonic Wars, British warships in Asiatic waters asserted the "right of search" in American ships for deserters, a claim which was one of the causes of the War of 1812.

Meanwhile, inspired by the accounts of Cook, the propaganda of Ledyard, and the successes of British traders, American merchants began sending ships to the north-west coast in search of furs. The first of these were the *Columbia Rediviva*, Captain John Kendrick, and the *Lady Washington*, Captain John Gray. As they were short of supplies the captains changed ships and Kendrick, who planned to purchase land for a trading post, remained on the coast for some years before being killed accidently in Honolulu in 1794. Gray, with the collected furs, called at Honolulu (the first American visitor) on his way to Canton. Here he sold the furs, took on a load of tea and other merchandise and, after a three years' absence from Boston became the first American to circumnavigate the world. In 1791 Gray returned to the north-west coast with the *Columbia* and *Adventure* and established Fort Defiance on Clayoquot Sound.[33] The *Adventure* went north while the *Columbia* traded southward. Gray entered the Columbia, which he named after his ship, and followed it fifteen miles.[34] Several other place names reflect Gray's explorations, including the state of Washington, which was named after his earlier ship.

The maritime fur trade was a precarious venture. Trade goods acceptable to the Indians varied from year to year, and with the increase in trade their demands became more selective. Thus Captain Joseph Ingraham, who arrived three years after Gray, discovered that the Indians did not want trinkets or iron bars. He had his blacksmith convert the latter into iron collars, which became profitable "best sellers." While the British traders were handicapped by the restrictions of the East India Company, the Americans had no such handicap. Soon after the trade started, the French Revolution and the Napoleonic Wars curtailed British trading activities in the Pacific, while at the same time the British blockade of Europe encouraged more Americans to go to the Pacific. Within a few years American traders had almost displaced the British on the north-west coast.

FOUR NATIONS

Although Spain had been alarmed by the threat of Russian expansion in the north, it had come to an understanding with the Russian court and accepted conditions as a *fait accompli*. Now both Russia and Spain were alarmed by the influx of British and American traders, and both planned expansion of their own trading activities. Russia moved closer to North America by establishing a permanent base on Kodiak Island in 1783. Spaniards in California developed a plan for collecting furs from the local Indians through the missions, who would in turn pass them on to officials for shipping to China by the galleons. This plan, hindered by government bureaucracy in Mexico and the Philippines, collapsed after seven years of bickering because of the powerful opposition of the monopolistic Philippine Company.

With its position in the North Pacific becoming precarious, Spain determined to assert its sovereignty by establishing an outpost at Nootka Sound as an extension of its *presidios* and missions in California.

In 1789 Don Esteban José Martinez was sent from San Blas to Nootka Sound with the Spanish ship-of-war *Princesa*, mounting twenty-one guns, accompanied by another similar vessel. The year before, a post had been established by Captain John Meares, who used this as headquarters for a number of vessels trading on the coast. Whether this post was still standing, as Meares claimed, is doubtful. Meares had been involved in the north-west trade for several years but, according to witnesses such as Portlock, Dixon, and the Barkleys, he was dishonest, scheming, and evasive. Thus his reports of later actions are questionable, especially as Meares was not present at Nootka.

When Martinez arrived at Nootka he discovered there Meares's vessel the *Iphigenia* and the two American ships *Lady Washington* and *Columbia*. For a week relations were peaceful, but suddenly Don Martinez seized Meares's ship with its crew. "As soon as the *Iphegenia* had been seized, Don Martinez took possession of the land belong to [Meares], hoisting thereupon the standard of Spain and performing ceremonies...declaring at the same time that all the lands comprised between Cape Horn and the sixtieth degree of north latitude did belong to his Catholic Majesty; he then proceeded to build batteries, storehouses, etc...."[35]

The *Iphigenia* was released and left for Hawaii. However, as the *North West America* (the first vessel built on the north-west coast), the *Argonaut*, and the *Princess Royal* returned to Nookta each was seized. The crew of the *North West America* was permitted to accompany Captain Gray on his departure to China. The other two vessels with their crews were taken to San Blas along with a number of Chinese whom Meares had brought as labourers.[36] The American vessels were not involved in these incidents except that the *Columbia* carried the crew of the *North West America* to China. Possibly there was a common dislike of the British stemming from the Spanish–American alliance in the recent War of Independence. Spain might have thought that the newly-formed American states were too weak to offer any threat to the north-west coast.

For a quarter of a century, through the Seven Years' War and the American Revolution, the rivalry between Britain and the French–Spanish alliance had been intense. The publication of Meares's report in England resulted in outraged anger fanned by the press. Both sides prepared for war, but in France, where revolution was fast approaching, the States-General refused to support Louis XVI's proposal to increase the navy. The unsettled conditions of its ally, combined with the assembly of the "Spanish Armament, the noblest fleet that Britain ever saw," caused Spain to modify its position. By the Nootka Convention of 1790 Spain agreed to repay Meares's damages and further accepted the policy that the "subjects [of both countries] shall have free access and shall carry on their trade without any disturbances." In other words the convention gave Spain and Britain equal rights on the coast. Each side was to send representatives to Nootka to complete the arrangements formally. Spain sent Don Quadra and Britain sent Captain George Vancouver. They did not agree on the terms of reference, but in 1795, three years after their meeting, the Spanish flag was lowered at Nootka in a formal ceremony, and the post was destroyed. Spain gave up its claims of sovereignty to the entire coast along with expectations of expansion and withdrew to California. The Nootka Convention also simplified trading for the Americans. Technically, Gray and Kendrick had been poaching in nominally Spanish waters, but now the north-west coast was open to all.

CAPTAIN GEORGE VANCOUVER

The British representative sent to Nootka, Captain George Vancouver, left Britain with two ships, the *Discovery* and the *Chatham*, in April 1791 for the north-west coast via the Cape of Good Hope and New Zealand. Almost a year later he sighted the coast south of Cape Mendocino and proceeded northward. South of Cape Flattery he met the American Captain Gray, who told of discovering the Columbia River, which Vancouver had missed. Continuing northward the two British ships entered Juan de Fuca Strait and surveyed Puget Sound. Many name places reflect the voyage of Vancouver: Lt. Puget and Mr. Whidbey were officers on the *Discovery*, Rainier was a rear-admiral of the British navy, Townshend was a marquis. As he continued, Vancouver missed the Fraser River and off Spanish Banks met two Spanish explorers, Galiano and Valdez. After travelling with them for a short time, the two British ships completed the circumnavigation of Vancouver Island (for some time called Vancouver and Quadra's Island) to Nootka Sound.

Here Vancouver met the Spanish representative, Don Quadra. Although negotiations between the two men were very friendly, they agreed that since their instructions were not clear they could not conclude the terms of the Nootka Convention without further instructions from their governments.

Leaving Nootka, the British were welcomed by the Spanish at San Francisco and Monterey, who gave them "very cordial reception and hearty welcome" before they left for the winter in Hawaii. The following year Vancouver returned to his survey of the north-west coast, but at the end of the year the attitude in California was cool: Vancouver received a letter from the commandant: "that he was without orders for the reception of foreign vessels into the ports under his jurisdiction, excepting in the cases where the rights of hospitality demand his assistance: and requesting that I would communicate to him the objects that had brought me hither.... He could not permit any persons to come on shore, excepting the commander of foreign vessels, with one or two officers."[37] After another winter in Hawaii, Vancouver returned for his third year of surveying, which was done as far north as Prince William Sound. In August the ships turned southward, and passed Nootka, Monterey, and San Blas en route to Cape Horn and England, where they returned after an absence of four years.

Captain Vancouver has been criticized for missing the Columbia, Fraser, and Skeena rivers, but nevertheless he made a thorough survey of the coast. He had proven undisputably that there was no north-west passage south of the Arctic Ocean. Today the coastline from California to Alaska bears permanent reminders of his voyages. The performance of these two ships exemplified the outstanding characteristics which made the British navy the most powerful of the era.

In later years Captain Vancouver's explorations and acts of possession were among the strongest British claims to the north-west coast. They ensured that Canada would become a transcontinental power and not one tied to the Atlantic coast. Had Gray not preceded Vancouver's entry into the Columbia River, Britain's claim to the land north of this would have been much stronger.

RESUMÉ

The last years of the eighteenth century had opened the North Pacific. The entire west coast of North America was surveyed and the Russians were active in Alaska and in north-eastern Siberia, but the coastline from Kamchatka to southern China was almost unknown to Europeans. The maritime fur trade was flourishing in American waters, and numerous vessels were sailing from them to Hawaii and China. Europeans were not able to penetrate into the mainland of China nor to trade into any of its ports except Macao and Canton. Britain was the undisputed naval power in the Pacific and had established itself in Australia. Spain continued to send its galleons across the ocean to Manila, but its weakening influence in the Americas was indicated by its withdrawal from the coast north of California as well as by the increasing restlessness in its colonies in both Americas. The United States, still east of the Mississippi, was becoming a serious rival in Pacific trade. The nineteenth century was to see the arrival of new forces, the development of new rivalries, and the partition of the North Pacific Rim.

4

The Fur Trade Era
(1800–40)

Yet it is a well known fact that the East India Restrictions has operated against us as a premium in favour of the Americans and has hitherto secured to them the Trade of a Great part of the North West Coast. (John McLoughlin, October 6, 1825)

Our natural boundary is the Pacific Ocean. (Francis Bayliss, Member, U.S. Congress, 1822)

In Europe, the first forty years of the nineteenth century saw political, economic, and social changes which were reflected throughout the world. The century opened with the Napoleonic Wars, which directly affected the power structure of the nations and had revolutionary effects on commercial and trading patterns. Victorious Britain controlled the seas and added strategically to its world-wide empire. Russia had become an important member of European alliances, Metternich's Austria led a strong reactionary movement and dominated central Europe, while declining Spain sought to gain support through an alliance of monarchs. France, after a short period under the restored monarchy, attempted to revive its lost prestige under Louis-Philippe. The United States, handicapped during its formative years by the repercussions from the French Revolutionary and Napoleonic Wars, was to expand territorially and commercially.

Probably more significant than the changing status of nations and their attempts to maintain peace through international agreements was the influence of the Industrial Revolution, which strengthened the domination of Britain in the financial, commercial, and colonial fields. The Industrial Revolution brought technical improvements, an increased use of power-driven machines, and major changes in transportation. The *laissez-faire* policies supported by such men as Adam Smith marked the decline of mercantilism in favour of free trade, freedom of the seas, opposition to monopolistic trading practices, and the spread of democratic ideas. Closely related to these were the growth of humanitarian organizations with their demands for social reform, and the rise of politically influential Catholic and Protestant missionary societies. All of these factors were to transform the earlier attitudes towards colonization. There was no enthusiasm for, in fact there was often definite opposition to, the acquisition of new colonies. Any that were established were the results of local conditions or the requirements of commerce.

THE SOUTH PACIFIC

The prospect of trade with China was still an attractive challenge to merchants, but its expansion continued to be restricted by Chinese regulations. Until the nineteenth century monopolistic control was suitable for trade with China and Japan, which still retained their own cultures and maintained state regulations on trade. The new economic theories of the United States and Britain, which opposed monopolies, were both to destroy the European monopolies and to end the restrictions imposed by the governments of China and Japan as well as to disrupt the ancient cultural patterns. At first independent British traders were handicapped by the East India Company monopoly and used various devices to overcome it. John Meares established a post in Macao and flew Portuguese or Austrian flags. Later, the North-west Company used American ships in their trans-Pacific trade. Tea was the major trade commodity, but textiles, silks, lacquers, porcelain, and other luxury goods all served to fill the ships. Unfortunately, foreigners had few goods suitable to exchange with self-sufficient China, and payment was demanded in silver. Near the turn of the century the East India Company, through middlemen, began to ship opium from India into China in order to relieve this heavy drain on silver. By the 1830's opium had become the major trading commodity, and the direction of the flow of silver had been reversed. The abolition of the company's charter in 1834 was followed by an increase in the number of independent traders. The sale of opium increased. However, these new traders, although freed from the company's monopoly, were still restricted by Chinese officialdom and were still only permitted to trade through either Macao or Canton. These limitations on trade and the attitudes of Chinese officials were a constant source of irritation, which resulted in increasing demands on the home government to force a relaxation of Chinese policies.

The domination of the British navy extended into south-east Asia and the Pacific islands. The British interest in the north-west coast was also shown in 1813 when H.M.S. *Racoon* entered the Columbia River. Following the Napoleonic Wars, Britain's territorial gains had been slight, and colonies were acquired more for their strategic values in protecting the shipping lanes than for colonization or settlement. There was no challenge from declining Portugal, Spain was restricted to the Philippines, and Holland was limited to Indonesia. During the 1830's, affected by the ambitious policies of Louis-Philippe and pressures from Roman Catholic missionaries, there was a revival of French activity. As France was trying to encourage British friendship as a counterbalance against other European powers, it did not challenge Britain's control in the Pacific. Although often rivals, the two countries would support each other in major crises.

The expulsion of missionaries gave France an excuse for annexing Tahiti. Three French expeditions under Petit Thouars, La Place, and de Mofras visited San Francisco. A French consulate was established in Manila. The threat of France caused Britain to annex the islands of New Zealand in 1840.

The French and British navies were active throughout the South Pacific region, usually co-operating but at the same time remaining competitive. The navies were not seeking new territories to annex. They patrolled the region protecting friendly chieftains, controlling the excesses of traders and whalers, and assisting in protecting missionaries against natives or sometimes settling intermissionary disputes. The main purpose was to uphold the national prestige by "showing the flag."

Even before the rise of the opium trade attempts were made to introduce trade goods which would relieve the drain on silver into China. Two of the most successful of these, although of comparatively little value in the total trade, were ginseng from the Hawaiian Islands and furs from Siberia and North America. Thus, the maritime fur trade, exploiting the sea otter, was an important factor in the Chinese trade pattern. Ships were loaded with trade goods in Britain or the United States for voyages which would last over two years. British and American vessels were to be seen from California to Alaska searching all the coves and trading with native peoples. Thence they sailed for China, usually stopping at Hawaii for supplies, rest, and entertainment as well as for picking up other trade goods, especially ginseng and sandalwood. By 1830 the ruthless search had practically wiped out the sea otter, and, with no other resources suitable for the China trade, the maritime fur trade faded out.

HAWAII

The wind-driven vessels of the early navigators were dependent on wind systems and ocean currents. In the North Pacific the North Equatorial current, usually below 20°N latitude crosses the ocean from Mexico to the Philippines and the Asiatic coast. Here the Kuro Siwo moves north-easterly past Japan to approximately 30°N towards Oregon, where it divides—one part returning south while the other moves northward until it meets the cold Kamchatka current from the Bering Sea, resulting in the fogs and storms typical of the Aleutians. Paralleling the trans-Pacific currents are the North-East Trade winds in the south and the Westerlies in the north. Within the circle formed by these currents and winds are the Hawaiian Islands at latitude 20°N. The flow of currents and winds explains the routes of the Spanish galleons and why they missed the islands. Improvements in navigation enabled later sailing vessels to overcome some of the earlier problems but even into the nineteenth century currents and wind systems were significant factors in ocean travel. Vessels from the north-west coast sailed south to catch the trades towards Hawaii and from Hawaii they headed north-east to catch the westerlies.

Eight years after Captain Cook discovered the Hawaiian (Sandwich) Islands the first maritime fur traders, Portlock and Dixon, visited the islands on their return voyage to China.[1] These were the first of a steady stream of traders who stopped at the islands en route to China either from the north-west coast or Cape Horn. To them the islands offered a haven for overhauling their ships, for obtaining provisions and supplies, and for relaxing from their long arduous voyages. From 1810 to 1830, when the forests had been decimated, the traders supplemented their cargoes with sandalwood, which was used by the Chinese for carving, incense, and oil.

At this time Hawaii was divided among a number of chieftains who welcomed the traders not only for their trade goods but also for their arms, which enabled them to continue their wars. White men were often employed for their technical knowledge—it is estimated that the great chief Kamehameha, who eventually united the islands, had fifty whites working for him.[2] Early in the nineteenth century the first whalers and missionaries appeared, the first American missionaries, the Reverend Hiram Bingham and the Reverend Asa Thurston, establishing themselves in 1820. The relaxed attitudes of the traders, whalers, and naval crews brought a holiday atmosphere to the islands, which was bitterly but unsuccessfully opposed by the missionaries.

The islanders themselves were adventurous travellers and often joined the traders as crewmen or tourists. Captain Meares tells of taking a Hawaiian to China. Captain Vancouver, who carried a Hawaiian home from London in 1792, returned two Hawaiian women from a north-west trader to their homes.[3]

> The partners [of the *Tonquin*] of Canadian experience aboard the *Tonquin* now proposed to enlist thirty or forty Hawaiians, because they had never seen watermen to equal them, not even among the voyageurs of the Northwest. Captain Thorn signed 12 for the company and 12 for the ships. The tradesmen were to serve three years, were to be fed and clothed and at the end of the term were to receive $100 in merchandise.[4]

"The name of Sandwich Islanders was dropped, and they were called by the whites, all over the Pacific Ocean, 'Kanakas,' from a word in their own language, which they apply to themselves and to all South Sea Islanders, in distinction from whites, whom they call 'Haole.'"[5] Throughout his journal Dana continuously remarks on the Kanakas both in the ships and in the settlements. In 1843 John McLoughlin wrote from Fort Vancouver, "I must send to the Sandwich Islands to make up the numbers of hands we require, or we cannot go on with our work" and three weeks later, "I find it necessary to order fifty Sandwich Islanders from Woahoo for the Columbia."[6] A chronicle on John McLoughlin "makes no less than twenty references to Hawaii and Hawaiians."[7] Many Hawaiians participated in the California gold rush, and others made their homes in Victoria.

For a century the islands remained independent, but there were various early indications of annexation. Captain Vancouver raised a British flag and Kamehameha agreed to be a subject of Britain, but this cession was not recognized by the British government. During the War of 1812, American vessels used the islands as a haven from British warships. In 1815 the Russian, Schaeffer, attempted to raise the flag but was prevented by British and American opposition.

The threat of Russia worried the islanders, who believed that their safety from annexation was through British support. Unfortunately, when King Kamehameha and his favourite queen visited London in 1822, hoping to have Britain make Hawaii a protectorate, both died—the queen from measles, the king from abscess on the lung. Both bodies were returned in state on a ship of war. Britain was not anxious to annex the islands but did agree that a selected commercial agent would be its authorized representative.

By 1840 the threats to Hawaiian independence were critical. French naval vessels were actively showing the flag throughout the Pacific Islands and often, by threats, were establishing Roman Catholic missions. France had annexed Tahiti. As early as 1827, although only six of the two hundred foreigners in Hawaii were French, a Roman Catholic mission was established. Because of the influence of the other Europeans the French missionaries were expelled after only four years.[8] However, in 1839, a French naval vessel under La Place forced Hawaii, by threats, to grant complete freedom of worship to persons of the Roman Catholic faith. In 1843 Lord George Paulet took possession of the islands for Britain, but again, the British government, fearing French and American reactions, did not verify the action. Instead, Britain convinced France to make a bilateral declaration that both countries would never take possession of any part of the territory.

The United States welcomed this agreement. It had had a commercial agent as well as missionaries in residence since 1820. Six years later the first American naval squadron visited the islands. The United States, however, recognized that Britain had a line of bases stretching from New Zealand and Fiji to the north-west coast, and that British annexation of Hawaii could establish a barricade across the strategic travel lanes from the United States to Asia. Thus, although the United States would not sign the Franco–British agreement on non-annexation, they agreed to participate in its essence. Fear of British annexation was to worry the United States into the 1870's.

By 1850 the fur trade was finished and whaling was nearing its peak. Businessmen and plantation owners had become firmly established. The United States annexation of California, combined with the increased population from the gold rush, opened new markets for Hawaii and brought closer commercial relations with regular shipping services. Thus, although the monarchy might be friendly towards the British, the islands were becoming increasingly dependent on the United States economically.

These changes, along with the uncertain policies of foreign governments, disturbed King Kamehameha III, who was also worried about the influx of troublemakers from the declining California mines. The king was favourably disposed towards Britain and applied to the British consul-general for protection, only to discover that Britain and France had signed the secret convention in 1843 not to annex the islands. Kamehameha III then approached the United States to propose the annexation. Probably because the Americans recognized that such a step would be opposed by Britain, the negotiations dragged on until 1854, when Kamehameha III died and was succeeded by his adopted son, who did not favour the proposal. The islands were to remain independent until their formal annexation by the United States in 1898.

THE RUSSIAN FUR TRADE

In the north the Russian–American Company was active under Baranov. An ambitious commoner, Baranov was an excellent leader and organizer. A disciplinarian, he kept strict control and established rigid regulations. Generally he was successful with the natives, respecting their rights and gaining their co-operation. In spite of the early problems of distance, poor ships, lack of equipment, and shortage of funds he struggled on to success. Baranov early became aware of the British and American traders. In 1799, to forestall these, Sitka (called Archangel by the Russians) on Kodiak Island became the headquarters. Basically a trading centre, it had numerous industries, which included sawmills, flour mills, a tannery for California hides, and a metal foundry. In 1841 the first steamer on the Pacific coast was built there. Among its exports were bells which were used in the California missions.[9]

The British and American traders were often welcomed, and peltries were exchanged for the much needed supplies which they brought. Unfortunately, some of the traders added to Baranov's problems by supplying the warlike Tlingits with arms and ammunition, and their sometimes ruthless actions caused the natives to turn against all white men. In 1802 the Tlingits destroyed

Sitka, massacred some of the inhabitants, and held others for ransom. With arms and tools obtained from the Americans, Baranov was able to recapture and rebuild the post, which for a while became the only major settlement north of San Francisco.

Russia's interests were spreading throughout the world. Nicholas Rezanov, a Russian nobleman, envisioned Alaska as a great colony expanding southward along the American coast at least to 55°. In fact he contemplated Russian control of California and the Hawaiian Islands, which would give Russia undisputed control of the North Pacific. In 1803 he joined Krustenstern on the first Russian expedition to circumnavigate the world.[10] Rounding the Cape of Good Hope, Rezanov visited Hawaii and Kamchatka before going to Japan, where he hoped to make a trading agreement. Here he was courteously received, but after six months' delay he was unable to convince the Japanese to change their exclusion policy. From Japan he returned to Petropavlosk, where he embarked on a Company brig to Kodiak. The miserable conditions of that settlement came as a shock. Seeing the slaughter of the seals, he became one of the first to support conservation. He recognized that the American trade was necessary for supplying badly needed goods. Having visited Unalaska and the rebuilt Sitka, he continued southward and after considerable hardship reached the Columbia River. His crew were so weakened by scurvy that they could not cross the bar. The voyage continued to San Francisco where, although Rezanov was cordially received, Governor Arillago was hesitant at first to allow trade with a foreigner. The governor's daughter, Concha, fell in love with Rezanov, whose first wife, Anna, had died in 1802, and the two agreed to marry when he returned. This unexpected development resulted in more friendly relations, and trade proceeded briskly. Rezanov returned north but died on his return trip across Siberia. Concha entered a convent, where she spent the rest of her life.

These expeditions, along with the increasing British and American activities in the North Pacific, aroused Russian interest in the possibilities of increasing sea commerce. The Alaskan furs to China were still being carried overland to Kyakhta and thence along the established routes to Peking. Under their second and third charters the Russian–American Company had obtained practically a monopoly of the very profitable tea trade.[11] In the early nineteenth century tea had become the major import to Russia from China but by the 1840's it was cheaper for Moscow to buy this from Europeans who carried it by sea than to obtain it by the slow overland Russian route. As a result two ships were sent to Canton in 1805, but they were refused permission to trade by the Chinese, who claimed that the Russians already had entry through Kyakhta. Nevertheless, Russia increased its maritime activities in the North Pacific.

Rezanov's ambitions for southern expansion were shared by Baranov, who hoped to extend the sea otter trade. In 1803 he made an agreement with the American Joseph O'Cain by which O'Cain, instead of trading in Russian territory, would be supplied with Aleut hunters to exploit the California coast, although this was Spanish territory, and would share the profits equally with Baranov. This collaboration also enabled Russian furs to enter Chinese ports. The venture was so successful that similar agreements were made with a number of Americans for several years until in 1816 the Russians stopped buying supplies from foreign merchants (mostly American) and took over the California hunting by themselves. The reaction of the Spanish officers in California was predictable; they closed the ports to foreign traders. Americans and Russians were forced to hunt away from the coast, but surreptitious trading continued with the natives in isolated bays. Eventually, in 1811, the Russians occupied Fort Ross on Bodega Bay, near San Francisco Bay, ostensibly to provide provisions for the northern posts but also to be near the California sea otter colonies. In spite of Spanish protests, within three years strong fortifications had been built, settlers (including some Aleuts) were established, and gardens planted. The settlement did not provide as much food as had been expected and the sea otter trade declined, so this Russian outpost became unprofitable. Meanwhile, the arrival of overland traders and explorers from Canada and the United States drove a wedge between the Russians in Alaska and the fort. In 1841 Fort Ross was sold to the German–Swiss American Johann August Sutter, for $30,000.

Baranov, who maintained a friendly correspondence with King Kamehameha through the visiting traders, hoped to establish a permanent post in Hawaii as early as 1809, but he feared British opposition. His first emissary was arrogant and was dismissed. Baranov attempted to appease Kamehameha for this unfortunate misunderstanding, and in 1815 another expedition was sent to restore good relations and, if possible, to gain a share of the sandalwood trade. Unfortunately, again, Baranov's representative, George Anton Schaeffer, exceeded his instructions. When he attempted to raise the Russian flag on land obtained from Kamehameha, British and American protests forced him to leave. On Kauai Island, which was not under Kamehameha, he made an agreement with the local chieftain, who gave him land and concessions. He proceeded to build a fort and to raise the Russian flag. Not only was Kamehameha angry, but he was supported by the traders of other countries. The Russian was forced to withdraw, and the flag was hauled down in 1817. This incident, although it did not have the sanction of the Russian government, ended any hopes of Russian influence in Hawaii.

The Russian–American Company had proven successful as a profit-making venture but had spent little towards improving conditions in the colony. With its charter coming up for renewal, changes and reorganization were necessary. Baranov, now seventy, was dismissed in 1819 and died at sea on his homeward voyage to Russia. From the time of Krustenstern and Rezanov naval officers had recognized the importance of expansion in the

North Pacific as a check to the expansion of the British and Americans in that region. With Baranov's removal and the reorganization, high-ranking naval officers rather than civil administrators were in control. Under their leadership extensive surveys of the coast were made, and exploratory and scientific expeditions were sent into the interior of Alaska. Russian–American Fur Company activities became extensive, and trade was carried on with the United States, Canada, China, Japan, Hawaii, and Chile.[12] The new administration appointed a new governor and staff to Alaska and planned to establish churches, schools, and medical services in the colony. The new policies proved to be successful, and the charter was renewed with the support of Tsar Alexander I.

Sitka was remodelled and became a city rather than a backward outpost. Most of the Russians were transient officials rather than being permanent settlers, and the colony was therefore predominantly male. The result was a considerable number of half-breeds, called Creoles. In 1863 Sitka had 978 Russians and Creoles, of whom 418 were Russian men and 50 were Russian women. Creoles were considered to be Russian subjects, were educated, and held responsible positions. Some of the more promising were educated in Europe at the company's expense, in return for which they were required to serve the company for at least ten years. As Russia did little penetration inland most natives remained independent, but those who settled in Russian territories were considered to be a special class of Russian subjects. Although not required to pay taxes they were expected to work for the company and to sell their furs to it. Thus when Alaska became American the organization of the colony was not disrupted either by a large emigration of Russians or by the presence of a large alien population.[13]

THE AMERICAN MARITIME TRADE

While Captain Vancouver was reinforcing Britain's claim to the north-west coast by sea, the first Europeans crossed the continent by land. In 1793 Alexander Mackenzie, a North West Company employee, after an arduous journey from Great Slave Lake, reached the coast near Bella Coola. Other Nor'westers followed, investigating possible overland routes to the Pacific: Simon Fraser followed the Fraser River to its mouth in 1808, and three years later David Thompson descended the Columbia, although he was disappointed to find the American post, Fort Astoria, at its mouth.

When the American colonies won their independence in 1783 only the wildest speculators could envisage them as a united Pacific power. Their commercial interests were tied to Britain and Europe, ties soon to be disrupted by the French Revolutionary and Napoleonic wars. Within a year after independence they were trading with China, and shortly they were to enter and eventually dominate the maritime fur trade of the north-west coast.

The United States had few trade goods to offer the Far East and China. American ships loaded with furs, tobacco, or iron would often take a circuitous route, exchanging their cargoes for products suitable for sale later during their voyages, probably arriving on the Pacific Asiatic coast with ebony, cloth, or ginseng. In time, to compete with the British, they picked up opium in Turkey and thus entered the Chinese opium trade. In the Far East their ships loaded spices, tea, and exotic products such as porcelain and lacquered furniture. Within fifty years American clipper ships were competing with the British for the tea trade.

The Americans had not developed imperialistic ambitions in the Pacific and were less aggressive than other nations. They hoped to gain trade by good will and friendship rather than by force, a preview of America's later support for the Open Door policy. When a seaman, Francis Terranova, was accused of killing a woman, the Chinese demanded that he be turned over to them for punishment, and when the Americans hesitated, the Chinese stopped all trade with them. Terranova was surrendered and strangled. The Chinese had discovered an effective weapon against foreigners—the stopping of trade— but foreign traders became more insistent on extraterritorial rights. Within a few years similar "insults to the national honour" would be reasons for bloody reprisals, but in 1821 the American position was still uncertain and the policy to maintain trade through friendship was dominant.

On the Pacific shores of North America the American fur traders had displaced the British. American traders visited numerous islands in the Pacific, including Hawaii, seeking trade goods. They entered into agreements with the Russians, selling them necessities and illegally helping them to poach furs off the California coast, although the Californians were not averse to some under-the-table trade. About 1830, since the sea otters were almost exterminated, the traders broadened their activities and accepted seal and land furs. Meanwhile, events on the mainland were reaching a critical stage.

SPAIN LOSES A COASTLINE

The Napoleonic Wars dealt the death-blow to the Spanish–American empire. During the war Spain veered from one side to the other until the occupation of the homeland by France resulted in the collapse of Spanish control in the Americas as one province after another rose in revolt. In 1800 Napoleon demanded retrocession of Louisiana to France, and once again Spanish America, as well as the United States, had a French neighbour. This short-lived phase ended three years later when Napoleon sold Louisiana to the United States for $15,000,000. During the War of 1812-14, Spain was allied to Britain, and in 1819, during the uncertainty of the postwar years, the United States forced Spain to sell Florida.

California was almost a self-contained unit. Although technically controlled by the regulations promulgated in far-off Mexico City, or the even more distant Madrid, the life of the people centred on the missions, with their gardens, vineyards, poultry, and farm stock. The immense cattle ranches were a source of hides, which became the major export. After the early years a few skilled artisans arrived and began local industries. At first regulations restricted trading, but gradually external pressures overcame the restrictions and some trade was carried on illegally.

Communication between California and the east was still difficult, and almost all contacts came by sea. On the defensive against the increasing number of British and Americans in the Pacific, as well as fearing the Russians from the north, the Spanish governors were suspicious of foreign visitors. Captain George Vancouver and Rezanov had both received cool receptions. As early as 1796 the American vessel *Otter* was known to be hunting sea otters off Monterey. Especially worrisome were the unknown plans of the Russians, as Baranov's Aleuts hunted off the California coast and Fort Ross was established.

The Californians welcomed the smuggled trade goods which the "Boston Men" (Americans) brought from the eastern states and were only too willing to exchange furs, hides, and food for them. The trade gradually became established, especially for California hides, which found ready markets in the eastern states. By 1820 British and American merchants were settled in California, and trading was an accepted fact.

> In Monterey there are a number of English and Americans . . . who have married Californians, become united to the Catholic Church and acquire considerable property . . . they soon get nearly all the trade into their hands. . . . The people are naturally suspicious of foreigners, and they would not be allowed to remain, were it not that they become good Catholics, and by marrying natives and bringing up their children as Catholics and Spaniards, and not teaching them the English language.[14]

Alexander Simpson noted the same:

> By the Laws of the Republic of Mexico, land can be granted to no Foreigner except he become a Citizen of that Republic, which in California involves also the necessity of marrying a native and becoming a catholic; these conditions however, it is possible to evade by holding land in the name of a citizen. . . . I am of the opinion that an Establishment in the Port of San Francisco would be productive of much profit and advantage.[15]

Thus American seamen, whalers, merchants, and settlers began to infiltrate the California establishment. While this insidious influence was taking place more dramatic events were to affect the colony. In 1810 Mexico rebelled against Spain and by 1822 had proclaimed itself a republic, ending more than three centuries of Spanish rule. In the same year the United States recognized an independent Mexico. California, controlled by the military and missionaries, supported the Spanish monarch, with the result that during the years of revolution it was the prey of Mexican privateers and blockade. When Mexico announced the annexation of California in 1822, the people were forced to submit.

The native population had decreased considerably during the Spanish years, paralleling the decline of the missions. In 1832 these were secularized while their lands, gardens, and ranches were confiscated, so that they ceased to be significant in later developments. The years of Mexican rule saw the end of mercantilist restrictive trade policies, the breakdown of the establishment, a period of disorder, and a steady increase of American settlers and traders.

With the American acquisition of Louisiana, Spain and, later, Mexico found themselves with a long American border stretching from the mouth of the Mississippi north and westward to the Pacific coast. In 1822 by mutual agreement the boundary was established and this set 42° N. latitude as the northern limit of Mexican claims to the coast. This dividing line was to last for twenty-six years.

JOINT OCCUPANCY

Within a year after the purchase of Louisiana two Americans, Meriwether Lewis and William Clark, had crossed the continent and on a piece of pine carved: "William Clark, Dec. 3, 1805, By Land from the United States in 1804 and 1805." A new era of American history had opened.

Alexander Mackenzie and Simon Fraser were the forerunners of a plan by the North West Company to establish a transcontinental trade pattern. An American, John Jacob Astor, planned a grandiose competitive operation. He would tap the western trade by developing both an overland route and a coastal trade with ships. The project soon ran into difficulties. One vessel, the *Lark*, was wrecked on the Hawaiian Islands; another, the *Beaver*, was blockaded by the British in Canton when war broke out. The third ship, the *Tonquin*, successfully reached the mouth of the Columbia, and there Fort Astoria was established on the south bank. The overland expedition, led by Wilson Price Hunt, after a disastrous trip in which the men were forced to eat their dogs and horses, barely reached the fort, some after almost a year's travel. Shortly afterwards, when the *Tonquin* was blown up by the natives, the only two survivors were made the slaves of Chief Maquinna for a year before they were rescued.

Meanwhile, in 1811 the North West Company, still hoping to find a practical route to the Pacific, sent David Thompson down the Columbia River, at the mouth of which he found Fort Astoria already built. The British traders had been challenged in the west for some time by American activities, and this was further proof of the threat. The War of 1812 gave the North West Company an opportunity to send a number of men to the coast who forced the Americans to sell their company, and thus American land competition in the area was temporarily eliminated.

The establishment of Astoria alarmed the British government, which had shown its concern for the north-west coast by the expedition of Captain Cook, the Nootka controversy, and the work of Captain Vancouver. Hearing that the American frigate *Essex* was threatening British shipping in the Pacific and determined to forestall American occupation of the north-west coast, Britain dispatched four ships. Only one, the *Racoon*, with twenty-six guns, arrived at Astoria—the first British warship in the region not concerned with exploration. On its arrival the *Racoon* found the fort already controlled by the North West Company. Nevertheless, orders are orders and the commander insisted on a formal ceremony of lowering the American flag and raising the British and renaming the post Fort George. This petty formality was to prove costly. At the peace treaty it was agreed that all occupied territories were to be returned to their original owners, and the Americans claimed Astoria, ignoring the fact that it had been sold before the ceremony. Although the post was returned to the Americans in 1818, they were in no position to use it and as Fort George it was leased to the North West Company and became its Columbia headquarters for a number of years.

John Jacob Astor's plans were not ignored by the North West Company.[16] For several years its western posts were supplied by goods sent by ship from England to Fort George. In 1814 goods from the *Isaac Todd* were delivered as far inland as Fort St. James. However, the Pacific route was seldom used by the inland posts for some years, trade goods continuing to arrive via the long overland route from Canada. The ships continued to sail to China, but because the East India monopoly prevented them from loading tea, this part of the venture proved to be unprofitable. In an attempt to circumvent these restrictions, American traders were sometimes employed for the China trade.

Following the Treaty of Ghent (1814) a number of border agreements were made between the United States and Britain. In 1818 the two countries agreed that for ten years the land west of the Rocky Mountains was to be held in "joint occupancy." This agreement was renewed in 1827 for an indefinite period.

The ruinous competition between the North West Company and the Hudson's Bay Company forced the two to amalgamate in 1821 under the latter's name. The new company was completely reorganized under the dynamic governor, George Simpson.

American traders had penetrated into the mountains but the War of 1812, which had ended Astor's ambitious scheme, was followed by an economic depression. This, along with the uncertainty of sovereignty in the Far West, resulted in a period of comparative inactivity in the American fur trade. By the 1820's several companies and individuals were planning to revive the mountain trade. Simpson took steps to eliminate both American and Russian competition. Traders such as Peter Skene Ogden travelled south into the Snake River country. Inland forts were established, and in areas threatened by American traders fur-bearing animals were decimated to establish a waste land before their advance.

Although the North West Company traders had used Fort George at the mouth of the Columbia, most of their activities were in the interior and they had not challenged the American maritime fur traders nor the Russians. Simpson determined to expand the trade along the coast. He believed that the boundary might be established along the Columbia River and therefore Fort George, on the south bank, was abandoned for new headquarters on the north bank farther inland at Fort Vancouver. To counter the threat of American maritime traders, forts were established along the coast from the Columbia to Alaska. The first steamship on the coast, the *Beaver*, was brought from Scotland in 1836, and, until it was wrecked near Vancouver harbour in 1888, it symbolized British influence on the coast and restored British control as the American maritime traders withdrew with the decline of the sea otter. Simpson, who was a worldwide traveller, was vitally concerned with these coastal forts and not only visited them but also travelled to California in 1841 and expressed the hope that eventually Britain would obtain San Francisco, which he believed to be one of the best ports on the coast. The Hudson's Bay Company extended its trade from furs to other goods such as salmon and timber which were exported to Hawaii, England, and across the Pacific. The company established an agency in Hawaii in 1833 and Simpson was an early supporter for an international guarantee of Hawaiian independence.[17]

Meanwhile, the Russians were turning against the American traders and whalers off Alaska, who were not only taking Russian furs but were also providing the natives with firearms and rum, a policy forbidden to Russian traders. In 1821 the tsar issued a ukase proclaiming Russia's southern boundary to be 51°, just north of Vancouver Island, and also forbidding foreign ships to come within one hundred miles of the shores of that region. As earlier the South Pacific had been the "Spanish Sea," now the North Pacific threatened to become the "Russian Sea." This territorial claim and the closing of the ocean raised protests from both Britain and the United States, who were joint occupants north of California.

Concurrent with these developments were the attempts of Ferdinand VII of Spain to gain support of the other monarchs in the Holy Alliance for the recovery of the Latin American colonies. Britain officially remained uncommitted to Spain or the rebellious colonies, but nevertheless, hoping to open Latin America to trade and always desirous of weakening Spain, it unofficially encouraged the colonies by supplying aid. To check the expansion of both Russia and Spain, Britain approached the United States with the suggestion that they make a joint protest, but the United States decided to act on its own. The result was the Monroe Doctrine of 1823: "We should consider any attempt to extend their system to any portion of this hemisphere as dangerous."

The opposition to Russia's advance resulted in a flurry of diplomatic discussions in which the Russians used the British–American rivalry to advantage. Two separate agreements were signed by Russia. In 1824, in the treaty with the United States, Russia accepted 54°40′ (Dixon Entrance) as its southern boundary and promised not to establish posts south of this line. Freedom of navigation with rights of trading and fishing were promised. Britain had wanted 60°, but the following year, influenced by the Hudson's Bay Company, it accepted these terms with additions. The eastern boundary of Alaska was stated, the basis of the present boundary. Britain was also to have the right to navigate the rivers so that it could pass through Russian territory to its inland posts. During the 1840's, as foreseen by Peter the Great a century before, Hudson's Bay Company explorers had reached their farthest western limits as Robert Campbell explored the Pelly River to where its junction with the Lewes formed the Yukon River. Here Fort Selkirk was built in 1847. On the Yukon River the Russian and British fur traders were in direct competition.

Before 1834 Russia had lifted its ban against foreigners in its possessions. With the increasing number of traders on the coast and the fact that Hudson's Bay Company traders ascending the rivers were cutting off the inland furs, the Russian company was put in serious financial difficulties. The Russian–American governor, Baron Ferdinand von Wrangell, attempted to stop British ships using the Stikine River, refusing the *Dryad* permission to enter. The resulting British protest led to a new agreement in 1839, which, although originally made for ten years, lasted until the sale of Alaska. The Hudson's Bay Company was to lease the coast as far north as Cape Spencer and in return would supply food from its southern forts, pay a rental in sea otter skins, and provide manufactured goods from England. This agreement was the foundation for the agricultural economy of Fort Langley, which became a major supplier of foodstuffs.[18] Co-operation between the Russian and British companies became so successful that even in wartime they respected each other's territory. As the agreement made Fort Ross, which was in difficulty because of the expansion of neighbouring settlements, of little value it was sold to John Sutter. Sutter never paid for the land, which was to become famous later when gold was discovered.

RÉSUMÉ

By 1840 few of the present-day boundaries of the North Pacific Rim had been established. Japan was closed to foreigners but was becoming alarmed by the southward movement of Russia. Between Russia and China the boundary was unsettled. The Alaska boundary and the northern limits of California had been set. Between these two the land was technically shared by "joint occupancy" of the United States and Britain, but the Hudson's Bay Company dominated the north and American settlers were increasing near Fort Vancouver. Russians, British, Americans, and other Europeans were active along the coasts, and whaling ships were scouring the sea, but the only settlements were isolated trading posts. Although the trans-Pacific voyages of the Spanish galleons had ended, traders continued to cross from the American coast to Hawaii, Macao, and Canton. The activity of the American coast was in contrast to that of Asia, where western traders were frustrated by their inability to penetrate the restricted markets of the empires of China and Japan.

Except for minor clashes between the traders and the native peoples, no major military confrontation had occurred. The next decade, however, was to bring wars and threats of wars.

5

The Decisive Decade
(1840–50)

The presentation of letters was forbidden and he [Admiral Frederick Maitland] dared to present a letter without the character *pin* [petition] at the city gates! Such conduct was most outrageous! (Teng Ting-Cheng, Viceroy of Canton, 1838)

But the most valuable branch of commerce, which is offered spontaneously by the North West Coast, is the Whale Fishery. (John Meares, 1790)

THE WHALERS

The maritime fur traders had established trading patterns between the north-west coast of America and China. As the number of sea otter traders declined, another type of marine hunter appeared in the North Pacific. This was the whaler.

Organized whaling began in Europe in the twelfth century and by the 1700's had extended to the open seas and had become pelagic. As the whales in the North Atlantic became scarce, the whalers were forced to venture into the South Atlantic and Arctic. The first whaleship to enter the Pacific was the *Emelia* of London, which rounded Cape Horn in 1789. Many others followed it from both Europe and the United States, entering the ocean from east and west and scouring the south seas. In 1819 the first whaler reached the Hawaiian Islands, and for forty years whaling was the most important factor in the economic life of the islands. During the twenty-year period 1822–42 the number of arrivals of whaling ships at Honolulu was about 1700, an annual average of 85; nearly 1,400 were American, slightly more than 300 were British. During the last five years of this period, of the 880 arrivals, 789 were American and 52 were British.[1] By 1824 the traders and whalers were urging President Monroe to establish a naval force in the Pacific for protection against mutineers, deserters, and natives and an American naval squadron made its first visit to the islands in 1826. This period marks the growing domination of American interests in the islands.[2]

Whaling had been done by the aborigines on both the Asiatic and North American North Pacific coasts. Early visitors to the north-west coast were impressed by the seamanship and courage of the natives as they hunted the whales in sixty-foot canoes.[3] As early as 1790 both Meares and Portlock had recommended that the waters off the north-west coast were potential whaling grounds, but their opinions were disregarded at that time.[4] Not until 1821 did the *Maro* of Nantucket and the *Syren* of London sail to the rich fishing grounds off Japan, and almost another twenty years passed before the whalers reached the north-west coast and Kamchatka on their way to Bering Strait, which they reached in 1848.[5]

The Napoleonic Wars almost destroyed the whaling fleets of Britain and the United States, but with postwar recovery the American whalers, based in New England, became dominant. "In the year 1835 commenced the period which might be termed the Golden Age of Whaling for during the next decade the whale-fishing assumed its greatest importance."[6] In the year 1846 the United States had over 700 vessels, while the foreign fleet numbered only 230 vessels. From 1855 to 1861 the gross value of products from the whaling fleets was over three million dollars annually.[7]

During the Civil War the Confederate raider *Shenandoah* scoured the North Pacific as far as the Arctic, destroying twenty-four Union whalers and merchantmen. In 1871, thirty-three ships were trapped in the ice floes north of Bering Strait. The ships and cargoes were left to be destroyed by the ice while over five hundred crewmen escaped safely south in small boats to seven rescue vessels anchored in free waters. In 1859 an oil well was brought into successful production in Pennsylvania, inaugurating the use of a substitute for whale oil. These three events, combined with the reduced whale population, were to destroy the Hawaiian whale industry, which was by far the greatest in the history of the Pacific.

The whalers reached the Gulf of Georgia about 1868 and for four years there was considerable activity in this new field. After this short flurry there was a lapse of systematic hunting on the British Columbia coast until 1905, when the Victoria Whaling Company was formed. Numerous whaling stations such as those at Rose Harbour and Naden Harbour were active for forty years, in the peak years processing as many as 1,200 whales. By 1942 only 163 were caught, and in 1967 the last B.C. whaling station was closed.[8]

At first whales were hunted only for their oil, which was important for lamps and lubricants, and for whalebone for corsets. In more recent times whales supply constituents for soaps and perfumes, materials used in explosives, bone meal for fertilizer, and food for animals, and in Japan whales are a major source of food. In their search for whales the whaleships discovered and charted hundreds of Pacific islands heretofore unknown. Hawaii became the major centre of the whaling fleets, while other centres, especially San Francisco and Sitka, became ports of call. The whalers were the first Europeans to visit many native tribes, sometimes with favourable results but often leaving a legacy of distrust and hatred. Melville's comment would also apply to them: "There is many a petty trader that has navigated the Pacific whose courses from island to island might be traced by a series of cold-blooded robberies, kidnapping and murders," and later, discussing missionary mismanagement: "The demoralizing influence of a dissolute foreign population, and the frequent visits of all descriptions of vessels, have tended not a little to increase the evils."[9]

By approaching the coasts and often collecting seal skins as a sideline, the whalers angered and alarmed the Mexicans in California and the Russians in the north, whose seizure of their vessels caused numerous minor international disputes. Nevertheless, in their long dangerous voyages the whalers strengthened the vision of the North Pacific as a single geographical area from west to east.

THE MISSIONARIES

Missionary activities contributed significantly to the exploration and settlement of the North Pacific; in fact, in numerous cases missionaries were the first Europeans to penetrate unknown regions. For the Portuguese and Spanish the propagation of the Roman Catholic religion was a duty imposed by papal bulls, and every significant exploratory expedition had its church representative whose records are often the foundations of historical research. In North America the Franciscan Serra was instrumental in the establishment of missions and settlements in California, and a Roman Catholic mass was held by the Spaniards at Nootka Sound in 1789. In south-east Asia the church penetrated into China and Japan in very early times; it was the success of their activities which led to the expulsion of Christian missionaries from Japan in 1587 and from China after 150 years in 1724. Roman Catholic activity did not revive in these two countries until the mid-nineteenth century and then it was sponsored by the French following the First Opium War and Perry's visit to Japan.

Protestant missionaries followed the penetration of the Dutch and British into the Far East. By the close of the eighteenth century missionary activities became more organized and widespread. The undenominational London Missionary Society was formed in 1795, and within thirty years similar groups were formed in the United States, Switzerland, Denmark, Germany, and France.[10] The missionaries spread throughout the world from the Near East to Africa, India, and by 1807 Robert Morrison, a Presbyterian Englishman, refused passage by the East India Company to India, was forced to reach Canton via the United States, the first Protestant missionary to China. The first Americans, Elijah Coleman Bridgman and David Abeel, went to Canton in 1829. During the nineteenth century China became a major field for missionary work.

The missionaries were active in Indochina and the islands but were forbidden to enter China. To overcome this handicap they used various subterfuges to justify their presence in Macao and Canton. Robert Morrison, ironically, became interpreter for the East India Company. The American medical missionary, Peter Parker, opened a hospital in Canton. Missionaries' work consisted mainly of publishing and distributing printed material, much of which was translated into Chinese, through contacts made outside of China or in the trading posts. After 1840 they moved into the newly opened treaty ports. Not for another twenty years, after the Second Opium War, would they be permitted to move inland. In 1871 the Canadian Presbyterian missionary, G. L. Mackay, was sent to Formosa and two years later the first two Canadian Methodist missionaries, Dr. George Cochrane and the Reverend Davidson McDonald, were sent to China.[11]

Supported by influential church organizations, the societies had strong political influence. In such countries as Britain and the United States, the governments adopted a *laissez-faire*, neutral attitude towards missionary activities, and the societies handled their own affairs. Other governments associated missions with imperialistic prestige. France was more interested in propagating the Roman Catholic religion than in commercial expansion, as can be seen in the China treaties. The German Empire used the killing of missionaries as an excuse for the occupation of Shantung. Any country would send naval vessels to protect its nationals.

Missionaries played a significant role in opening north-western America. Baranov brought missionaries to Kodiak as early as 1794. The first Protestant missionaries to reach the Columbia River were Jason Lee and Cyrus Shepard in 1836. They were followed in 1841 by the Roman Catholic, Father Demers, who visited Fort Langley in that year. The Hudson's Bay Company arranged for the Reverend Edward Cridge to serve as clergyman on Vancouver Island in 1854. From these beginnings both Roman Catholics and Protestants spread inland and along the coast. By 1861 the Church of England missionaries reached Fort Yukon and in the 1870's a variety of missions was established in Alaska. By 1903, of the eighty-two missions in Alaska only sixteen were Russian. In the north-west, missions continue to have a strong influence, especially in isolated communities scattered throughout the region.

In Hawaii, Japan, China, and Korea the Protestants of Britain, the United States and, later, Canada, co-operated in their efforts. In 1890 the following figures represented the deployment of Protestant missionaries: China: total 537; Great Britain 301, United States 198, Germany 29, Canada 8; Japan: total 175; United States 146; Great Britain 20, Canada 9.[12] Three general phases of missionary policies have become apparent over the last 175 years.

In the early 1800's the objectives were to make converts as rapidly as possible and to teach the gospel. About 1875, "the Christian conscience, already awakened to social abuse at home, was becoming more sensitive to the conduct of westerners abroad," and a period of humanitarianism with educational and social reform was undertaken.[13] By the early 1900's nationalism was undermining the missionary efforts and attempts were made to organize national churches and to interpret Christianity as a social gospel. Unfortunately, the first phase left legacies which could not be erased. It was during the second phase that organized Canadian missionary efforts began in China, Japan, and Korea, but these were handicapped by the prejudices established earlier.

In summary, missionaries in the western Pacific faced five major handicaps:

(a) Other whites, such as traders, whalers, and derelicts, undermined their teachings and often opposed them. As Mark Twain said of the Sandwich Islands: "The missionaries are sorry that most of the whites are there, and the latter are sorry the missionaries don't migrate."[14]

(b) The different branches of the Christian churches—not only Catholics and Protestants but also the many subdivisions within these groups—confused the converts with their varying doctrines and were also often antagonistic among themselves.

(c) Differing opinions as to whether Christianity should be rigidly based on the infallibility of the Bible or whether it should be adapted to the cultures of the peoples were a continuous source of disagreement.

(d) The missionaries faced strenuous opposition, not only from other whites, but also from the ruling and wealthy classes as well as the leaders of other established religious beliefs who saw their authority challenged. Supplementing these were the nationalists, who increasingly opposed the spread of Western authority and customs.

(e) The missionaries themselves were often from poorer classes with minimal educations and were the products of civilizations which were convinced that it was their "burden" to enlighten the inferior peoples by imposing Western ideas and customs as well as to convert the heathen to Christianity. These idealistic, dedicated individuals were not trained to appreciate the centuries-old native cultures and religions upon which the economic and social stability of the peoples were based. Melville said:

> Against the cause of missions in the abstract no Christian can possibly be opposed; it is in truth a just and holy cause. But if the great end proposed by it be spiritual, the agency employed to accomplish the end is purely earthly; and, although the object in view be the achievement of much good, that agency may nevertheless be a production of evil. In short, missionary undertaking, however it may be blessed of Heaven,

is in itself but human; and subject, like everything else, to errors of abuse.[15]

If the people could not be converted by reason or a peaceful approach, then Christianity could be imposed by force. When the British slaughtered some Chinese soldiers, a missionary's wife, Henrietta Shuk, stated: "I regard such scenes...as the direct instruments of the Lord in clearing away the rubbish which impedes the advancement of Divine Truth."[16] Of the Second Opium War, Samuel William said, "I am sure that the Chinese need hard measures to bring them out of their ignorance, conceit and idolatory."[17]

With attitudes such as these, supplemented by extraterritorial rights obtained by imposed treaties, backed by military force, the opposition of nationalists is not surprising. "There was not a single province or area during all this time when the common man, as well as the mandarin, did not make it clear that the missionary was an unwelcome intruder.... Not a single year passed without violent manifestation in some town or other against missionary activity."[18] In the Boxer Rebellion, 189 Protestant missionaries, including 52 children, were killed.

Appraisals of the value of Christian missions in the North Pacific are still matters of controversy. Established economic balances along with skills and crafts were destroyed. Educational systems, whether based on primitive rituals or on other religious beliefs, were displaced. Political systems were changed. Social patterns, built over the centuries and founded on tribal or family bases, were destroyed. On the other hand were the many contributions, especially beginning in the late 1800's when a better concept of cultural identities and an attitude of humanism rather than "anti-heathenism" were adopted: the ethical teachings of Christianity, schools, colleges, hospitals, health services, orphanages, the freeing of women, the opposition to opium, the administration of famine relief, the improvements in agriculture, and the use of scientific information for better living conditions. China alone, in 1914, is estimated to have had almost two million Christians, consisting of 1,500,000 Roman Catholics, 300,000 Protestants and 5,000 Russian Orthodox. Christians must have had considerable influence, although they comprised only .5 per cent of the population.[19]

The missionaries played a significant part in opening the North Pacific. Their reports revealed new lands and peoples. As interpreters for both traders and government officials, they did much towards assisting in mutual understanding. They were probably the best carriers of information between the Chinese and Occidentals: explaining the West to the Chinese and sympathetically portraying China to the West. They contributed much to the education and health of their followers. On the other hand, they were often the cause of unrest and in some cases the immediate cause of war. "It is now widely taken for granted that, whatever may have been the beneficial intentions of the missionaries, they were in fact the tools of governments, and missions may be classed as one of the instruments of western infiltration and control."[20]

During the twentieth century missionaries have attempted to establish church groups which are self-supporting and self-governing, with the result that there are now national Christian organizations, and the demand for missionary work has lessened. With the Communist takeover of China in 1949 most governments advised their nationals to leave the country and most did. However, they have left a core of Chinese Christians who continue to worship within the state's regulations.

Missions have played a prominent part in the history of the North Pacific for almost two centuries, but how important have they been? How many of the social changes would have been achieved without their leadership? How many of their ideas led to political and social revolutions? How many of the doctrines of modern Communist China are an outgrowth of early Christian teachings? These are some of the questions which have not, as yet, been answered. Nevertheless, it is a fact that Christianity continues, with varying degrees of success, throughout the entire North Pacific.

THE FIRST OPIUM WAR

During the 1830's European traders were still restricted to the port of Canton, where they were subjected to the whims of the Co-Hong. The traders protested to their home governments, who in turn were irritated by the attitude of the Chinese government, which would have no direct communication with them. Attempts by Britain to open negotiations with the Chinese had been unsuccessful. In 1793 (the same year that Captain Vancouver was surveying the north-west coast), Lord Macartney visited Peking in an attempt to open an embassy, to open more ports to trade, and to obtain other concessions.[21] During the elaborate approach to Peking, "I shut my eyes upon the flags of our yachts, which were inscribed 'The English Ambassador bringing tribute to the Emperor of China'."[22] On being asked to perform the kowtow, he insisted that he would only kneel on one knee: "I was willing to conform to their etiquette, provided a person of equal rank with mine were appointed to perform the same ceremony before my sovereign."[23] After a short visit in which he was courteously received but in which he received no successful responses to his requests, the mandarin indicated that he should leave: "He answered me that China never sends Ambassadors *to* foreign countries; that Ambassadors *from* foreign countries were only occasionally received, and, according to the laws of the Empire, allowed but forty days residence."[24] Besides obtaining a glimpse of Chinese life, although restricted, the journey was not altogether a failure: 'We are masters now of the geography of the northeast coasts of China, and have acquired a knowledge of the Yellow Sea, which was never before navigated by European ships."[25]

Another approach in 1816 was also courteously received but failed to make any progress in opening diplomatic relations. These setbacks had been of minor consequence during the East India Company régime, for the company and not the British government was the power in the Far East. Being self-sufficient, and willing to abide by Chinese regulations, the company did not seek assistance from the home government. Not having this strength or wealth, the independent traders, after the cancellation of the company's charter in 1834, needed the support of their governments. Many people believed that the recognition of foreign diplomatic representatives by the government of China, which was a requisite to the expansion of trade, could only be achieved by force.

The climax came in 1839. The Chinese government, alarmed by the outflow of silver and by the effects of opium on the people, determined to stop the illegal opium trade. Opium had been banned in China in 1729, with little effect; and an Imperial Edict in 1808 condemned smuggling. In 1839 Lin Tsê-hui was sent to Canton to institute a rigid prohibition of the opium trade. The "thorough" Lin immediately took a firm position, censured Co-Hong merchants, and demanded that all foreign merchants deliver "every particle of opium" within three days for destruction. A token delivery of 1,037 chests was not considered to be enough, so the factories were blockaded and the British inhabitants became virtual prisoners. The promised surrender of another 20,283 chests resulted in an easing of regulations. The seized opium was all destroyed.

Tension was intensified when a shore party of British and American sailors fought with the villagers and killed one of them. Although the British official, Captain Elliott, offered restitution and promised to punish offenders, this was not enough for Commissioner Lin, who demanded that the murderers be surrendered to him. This Captain Elliott refused to do. Lin now demanded a bond for future good behaviour. The American traders agreed, but the British refused and were forced to withdraw from Canton and Macao to the inhospitable Hong Kong. Gradually some independent traders posted bonds and returned to trading.

Lin was not only demanding the posting of bonds but was also asserting his right of trying foreigners in Chinese courts for crimes. He insisted on boarding British ships in search of opium and increased his military forces. When two British frigates entered Whampoa, shots were exchanged with the Chinese men-of-war, but which side began firing is controversial. Lin provocatively ordered the stoppage of all trade with Britain. As Britain could not communicate with the Chinese government through diplomatic channels, there was no alternative but force and the First Opium War began. This first imperialistic war fought in Asia by the British government (others had been by the East India Company) was fought to obtain indemnity for British losses, to protect the independent traders, and to force China to grant diplomatic recognition to British officials. The war resulted in the downfall of Lin. A sincere man, he had been unable to evaluate the situation. He was dismissed and sent to exile in Ili.

The war consisted of several consecutive phases. As all agreements made by the Chinese governors were subject to verification by the emperor, who could not envisage Chinese defeats, any concessions were nullified. The delays and uncertainties infuriated the British, who extended their campaigns from Canton into the ports farther north. When Nanking was threatened by the fall of Chinkiang, the Chinese were forced to capitulate and to accept the Treaty of Nanking (1842), which was signed on the British ship *Cornwallis*.

Four more ports, Amoy, Foochow, Ningpo, and Shanghai, were opened to trade; British consuls were to be established in each port and foreign merchants were to be permitted to bring their families; the Co-Hong was abolished; China paid a large indemnity of twenty-one million dollars for the opium seized and for the costs of the war; Hong Kong was ceded to Britain in perpetuity and was made a free port; the opium trade continued and Chinese and British officials were to meet on a basis of equality.

A supplementary treaty guaranteed most-favoured-nation treatment for Britain, granted extraterritorial rights, and established a tariff schedule. By this last clause, Britain was to set the rate of maritime customs duties and British were always selected as commissioners of customs, although, later, other foreign nations obtained a share. Foreign goods entering the country paid customs duties only once, but internal Chinese trade was subject to taxes at numerous "likin" stations throughout the country. This system was obviously detrimental to domestic goods by raising their costs. In return for all these concessions, Britain agreed to co-operate with the Chinese authorities against smuggling.

American ships were held in Canton with those of the other traders, but the Americans did not share in any military operations, preferring to maintain a neutral position. Nevertheless, two years later, the first American commissioner to China, Caleb Cushing, negotiated the Treaty of Wanghia. This treaty included the first clear statement of extraterritoriality: "Citizens of the United States who may commit any crime in China shall be subject to be tried and punished only by the consul or other public functionary of the United States." Other nations quickly followed these two leaders. The French obtained the Treaty of Whampoa, the Portuguese demanded more concessions in Macao, and in succeeding years Belgium, Norway, and Sweden gained the right to trade. The French treaty resulted in an imperial edict permitting the admission of Roman Catholic missionaries and tolerance for the religion. This edict was extended the following year to other Christian sects.

The dictated Treaty of Nanking had opened the Chinese Empire to foreign penetration. The British commercial interests not only had made an important step in opening China to trade, but they had also extended British influence far north along the coast to Shanghai. The British navy, which was covering Australia, the Pacific Islands, and the Oregon coast, now expanded its protection along the Asiatic coast. Furthermore, the British were now approaching the expanding Russians, who were to sign a new trade agreement with China.

MANIFEST DESTINY

Even with the purchase of Louisiana the Americans were limited to a narrow band across the continent through which the scientific expedition of Lewis and Clark passed to the mouth of the Columbia River. Six years later Astor's overland expedition, led by Wilson Price Hunt, opened a route which later became the Oregon Trail. North of these routes was land controlled by the British fur companies, first the North West and later the Hudson's Bay. South was California controlled by Spain and, after 1822, by Mexico.

The Spanish territories were a magnet drawing the Americans. As early as 1807 adventurers such as Pike were probing westward, seeking southern routes. Against these intrusions the Spanish maintained rigid opposition, arresting any interlopers they could catch. These Spanish policies of restriction proved untenable against the numerous infiltrating traders searching for gold, silver, or furs, and the persistent Americans increasingly established routes such as the Santa Fé trail into the south-west.

At the same time British and American traders, who were competing in the joint-occupancy territory of the north, were penetrating into California. In 1829 Peter Skene Ogden, of the Hudson's Bay Company, who made numerous trading trips into the Snake River and Salt Lake country, was the first to travel overland north to south from the Columbia River to the Gulf of California. In 1826-27 Jebediah Strong Smith had travelled through the desert lands of Utah as far as the Colorado River, searching in vain for beaver. Hungry, with his few remaining horses emaciated, Smith decided to seek relief in California. At San Gabriel Mission the expedition was well treated but officials were suspicious that Smith was a spy, mapping the country. Smith was taken to San Diego for questioning. He was told to return on the same route by which he had arrived, but instead he went to San Francisco and continued thence northward inland, leaving some of his men. In the following year he returned to California, but his former associates had already travelled northward safely. Probably not without reason, the officials were even more suspicious. After being imprisoned for several months, Smith was again permitted to leave, and eventually he reached Fort Vancouver.

When Captain Louis F. Bonneville was sent in 1831 to explore the American territory west of the Rocky Mountains, his travels took him as far south as Monterey. Numerous trails led through Mexican territories north-south or east–west to the Pacific. As early as 1832 Thomas O. Larkin of Boston had opened a branch in Monterey, and soon other American trade centres were established in California. By this time some Americans were envisioning a United States extending from Panama to the Arctic Ocean, from Atlantic to Pacific. This dream was summed up in the phrase "Manifest Destiny." Agricultural and commercial interests that were already considering the possibilities of the Asiatic markets were loud in their demands that San Francisco should become an outlet for American goods.

The American government responded by sending two exploratory expeditions. In 1833–34 Charles Wilkes in the *Vincennes,* along with other ships, not only mapped parts of the South Pacific but also surveyed the west coast of North America from Puget Sound to San Francisco as well as exploring inland. In 1842–45 John C. Fremont was in the western mountains north of San Francisco.

Thus, when James Polk, who was an ardent expansionist, successfully ran for president in 1844, the United States was straining to extend its boundaries. Texas has proclaimed itself an independent republic from Mexico in 1836, and there was a strong move in the United States to annex it. The harbours of the Pacific were seen as natural outlets for the expanding agricultural interests of the mid-continent. In the 1840's with the opening of Chinese ports following the First Opium War, San Francisco could be a base for Pacific trade as well as for increasing American influence in British-dominated Hawaii. When California successfully rebelled against Mexico in 1844, the weakness of Mexican control became apparent, and the American appetite was whetted. The ambitions of the United States both in Texas and California were opposed by Britain and France, which preferred numerous weak buffer republics rather than an enlarged United States. "By the end of 1843 Great Britain and the United States appeared to be moving into open conflict on the southern frontiers of the Union."[26] In 1839 Britain had made unsuccessful approaches to Mexico, suggesting that it would cancel its debts in exchange for California. In 1843 the French foreign office appointed a consul to Monterey.

OREGON

The land between California and Russian America was technically under the joint occupancy of Britain and the United States, but in reality the United States had influence only as far as the Columbia River, while north of that the territory was dominated by the Hudson's Bay Company. By 1840 the threat to the company's control was becoming serious.

The American Nathan J. Wyeth had hoped to establish a colony on the Columbia and, reviving Astor's scheme, planned to have a major portion of his supplies sent by ship. The return trip would carry furs and salmon.

Wyeth reached Fort Vancouver overland in 1832, but his brig the *Sultana* was wrecked on a reef. His project was apparently a failure. Two years later he resumed his salmon/beaver plans, which again did not succeed, but with him on his return to Oregon were two Methodist missionaries, Cyrus Shepard and Jason Lee, who established missions in the Willamette valley. Two years later Mr. and Mrs. Marcus Whitman began another mission. "The American missionaries are making more rapid progress in the extension of their establishment and in the improvements of their farms, than in the ostensible object of their residence in the country... the country is studded with Missions."[27] Other settlers began to establish homes and claim land: "Besides missionary establishments there is a population at Willamette of 65 persons, Americans and other, and 61 retired servants of the Company, in all, 126 men, principally heads of families, making a population of about 500 souls."[28]

By the end of the 1830's the fur lands of the mountains had been decimated, the beaver hat was no longer fashionable, and the price of beaver skins was steadily falling. The mountain trade declined and the fur traders were displaced by settlers and missionaries. In the first large body of immigrants to the Columbia were eighty British people who left Fort Garry in the Red River Settlement in 1841. Mostly retired Hudson's Bay Company servants, they settled in the Cowlitz and Williamette valleys. However, no other British immigrants arrived for almost a decade and meanwhile the Americans were arriving in increasing numbers. The first large group of over one hundred men, women, and children reached the Columbia in the following year under the leadership of Dr. Eliza White. In 1845 over three thousand arrived along the "Oregon Trail." "In the Willamette [Dr. Elijah P. White] called a meeting of the Settlers to whom he shewed his Commission from the Government of the United States supporting him as Indian Agent for the West Side of the Mountains, and told them the United States intended to take them under their protection, which information was received with pleasure by the American Citizens, but with great coolness by the Canadians. It is also reported that American troops are to be here next year."[29] Sir George Simpson stated in 1842: "I collected from a very intelligent and confidential member of the expedition that it was the intention of Captain Wilkes to recommend strongly to his government, to claim the whole of the territory on the shores of the Northern Pacific, from the Mexican boundary in Latitude 42° to the Russian southern boundary in Latitude 54°40'."[30]

In 1843 the settlers drafted a local constitution. In that year their pleas were answered by President Tyler in Congress: "After the most rigid, and, as far as practicable, unbiased examination of the subject, the United States have always contended that their rights appertain to the entire region of the country lying on the Pacific and embracing within 42° and 54°40' of north latitude."[31] It was but a small step for Polk to endorse as an election slogan "fifty-four forty or fight," and to follow this by stating in his inaugural speech of 4 March 1845: "Our title to the country of Oregon is clear and unquestionable." This was part of the programme of a group of extreme Democrats, who were also demanding the annexation of Texas as well as the eventual seizure of Canada.[32]

After the jingoism of the election year and the threats of imminent war had subsided, moderation prevailed. France had no real interests in Texas or California. Britain was involved in expansion into Chinese ports and with the threat of French annexation of Hawaii. The Americans were becoming more involved in the Texas controversy. Britain disliked the American threats to Texas and California, but it was not concerned enough to bring about a confrontation with the aggressive Americans, although Governor-General Lord Metcalfe proposed that a force consisting of Europeans and native troops from India occupy Oregon territory. However, it did not intend to surrender its foothold on the north-west coast. H.M.S. *America* made a short visit to Victoria and the coast. In 1846 five of Her Majesty's ships happened to be doing routine patrols and surveying duties in the region.[33] Both sides were willing to compromise, and Britain was desirous of restoring good relations.[34] By the terms of the Treaty of Washington (Oregon Treaty) in 1846 the boundary west of the Rocky Mountains was set at 49° to the middle of the straits separating Vancouver Island from the mainland. Vancouver Island remained British. Oregon Territory was proclaimed in 1848 and included Washington, Oregon, Idaho, and parts of Montana and Wyoming, but in 1853 Washington became a separate territory.

Britain had hoped to establish the Columbia River as its southern boundary, but the Hudson's Bay Company was pessimistic and in 1842 built Fort Victoria which, being on Vancouver Island, remained British and became the company's headquarters. To strengthen its claims to the coast, Britain proclaimed Vancouver Island a colony in 1849, thus bringing it under the direct control of the British government, with Victoria as its capital. The Hudson's Bay Company retained special privileges, but a governor was to be appointed by Britain. Richard Blanshard, a British career diplomat, resigned after two years of frustration, and was succeeded by the chief factor of the company, James Douglas.

Douglas laid the foundations for British Columbia. Coming to Canada as a North West Company trader in 1819, he joined the Hudson's Bay Company with the amalgamation of the companies and worked in numerous interior posts until 1830, when he was posted to Fort Vancouver under Dr. John McLoughlin, whom he succeeded as chief factor in 1846. Douglas was responsible for selecting the site of Fort Victoria. As chief factor, he had almost absolute authority, but as governor he found great difficulty in sharing his power with the elected assembly demanded by the independent settlers. When he was appointed governor as well of the newly formed colony of British Columbia in 1858, he was forced to relinquish his position with the company. Douglas retired in 1864, but before his death in 1877 he had seen British Columbia change from being a wilderness of isolated trading posts to become a province of Canada. Throughout his career he had forestalled the threat of Russian expansion as well as the pressure of the Americans in Oregon, San Juan, and during the gold rush. Throughout the many crises Douglas had been a powerful force in maintaining British control and it was his efforts more than those of any other person which assured the British presence on the west coast.

CALIFORNIA

Events in California were developing towards the boiling point, with representatives of Britain, France, and the United States established. "The whole population of California does not exceed 7,000 of whom 600 are foreigners...about 400 are American and 100 British."[36] Most Americans were seamen or traders, but some settlers had arrived—the Bartleson–Bidwell party of 69 immigrants, for example, crossed the mountains into California in 1840. At this time the Californians, who had opposed Mexican control from the beginning, were dissatisfied with the inefficiency and corruptness of the Mexican government. The Californians blamed the basic economic weakness of the country on Mexico's unconcern for its needs. Adding to the condition of uncertainty was the influx of American settlers. They in turn did not wish to face a repetition of Mexican opposition as seen in Texas and were disgruntled by the incompetence of the Mexican government. There were rumours that Britain intended to seize the colony if a suitable occasion arose. George Simpson wrote: "The presence of a British cruiser on the coast with a private assurance of protection from Great Britain...would be a sufficient inducement to declare themselves independent of Mexico and claim the protection of Great Britain."[37] Lord Stanley's attitude, reflecting the British government's feelings towards colonies, was cool to this sugges-tion: "I am not anxious for the formation of new and distant colonies; all of which involve heavy direct, and still heavier indirect expense, besides multiplying the possibilities of misunderstandings and collisions with Foreign powers. Still less am I prepared to recommend the adoption of a plan whereby the soil...should be vested in a company of adventurers."[38] The Californian Americans were probably encouraged in their expectations of American support by Manifest Destiny, the increasing interest of the United States in Pacific trade possibilities, and by the knowledge that President Polk favoured annexation.

The American settlers proclaimed an independent republic under the Bear flag and easily defeated the Mexican force sent to suppress the revolt. John C. Fremont had been travelling through California with sixty-two men and, when the Mexican government had asked him to leave, had withdrawn to

Oregon. The original objective of his expedition was to find an overland route to the Pacific, as is shown by his statement before the Oregon Treaty: "...the Columbia, which stands alone as the only great river on the Pacific slope of our continent which leads from the ocean to the Rocky Mountains, and opens a line of communication from the sea to the valley of the Mississippi."[39] Hearing of the revolt, he returned to assist the rebels. It was about this time that news of the Mexican War with the United States reached California, and the United States navy and army moved in from the sea. Commodore John D. Sloat was unopposed as he seized Monterey and other ports with his Pacific fleet.

Commodore Sloat was succeeded by Commodore F. Stockton, who left fifty men to hold Los Angeles. The Californians rebelled, and this led to a general uprising against the Americans. The Americans were forced to return in force and successfully crushed the revolt.

The Mexican War ended with the Treaty of Guadalupe Hidalgo, 2 February 1848, which reduced Mexico to less than half of its original size. The United States paid $15,000,000 for the entire south-west, including California with its valuable Pacific ports. The conquered land remained under military rule until the state constitution was written in 1849.

SPANISH CONTRIBUTIONS

The empire which Spain had established on the mainland of North America was ended after three and one-half centuries, but its influence remained. Today from Alaska to Cape Horn place names remain as memorials to the early Spanish explorers, although many of the early Spanish names have been displaced by later European explorers. Spain had discovered and explored many islands on both sides of the Pacific as well as the entire North American coastline as far north as Alaska. The Spanish were the first to establish regular trade routes across the Pacific, and they had expanded their horizons from Mexico through the Philippines as far as Japan. With their explorers went the Roman Catholic missionaries, keeping records, establishing missions, and zealously spreading and establishing their beliefs.

Whereas most European governments were encouraging scientific organizations such as the Royal Society (Britain, 1662) and the Academy of Sciences (France, 1666) and supported the dissemination of knowledge acquired from voyages, the Spanish government for political and religious motives unfortunately did not publish its great accumulation of charts, maps, and records. Throughout the years many were lost or destroyed. Even today unpublished documents remain in numerous archives still to be researched. Because of the lack of publicity, many of the Spanish explorations have been unrecognized until modern times, although the rich cultures of Portugal and Spain were transplanted throughout the world, especially to Mexico and South America. As Franklin D. Roosevelt pointed out, much of the Spanish and Portuguese culture of the world now comes from the Americas.[40]

Except for Nootka there were no Spanish settlements north of California, so it is in that state that the Spanish heritage on the north-west Pacific coast remains strongest. Most obvious are the unique architecture of the missions and the political divisions, such as counties, with their Spanish names. Words such as rodeo, adobe, canyon, ranch, and plaza are part of the Spanish heritage. The missions began the vineyards, orchards, and ranches which have remained basic to California's economy.

The defeat of Mexico opened a new era in the history of the North Pacific. Most immediate was the discovery of the California gold fields at Sutter's Mill in January 1848, two weeks before the peace treaty was signed. In that year between eight and ten thousand miners arrived. The following year saw the great rush which eventually brought probably eighty thousand adventurers. San Francisco, which had been a town of about eight hundred inhabitants with two hotels and two wharves, became overnight a colourful boom town which was to dominate the west coast and draw the United States to the Pacific.

RÉSUMÉ

By the middle of the nineteenth century the Europeans were moving northward along the coast of China, the Russians were moving southward, but Japan still maintained its policy of isolation from the Western world. In North America the political boundaries along the Pacific shores were almost finalized between the United States, Britain, and Russia. The following years were to see the closing of the unknown gap in Asia, the opening of Japan, the settlement of the west coast of America, and the clarification of boundaries.

6

New Rivals in the North Pacific
(1850–70)

The Slav Russian Empire now stands on the Pacific and an alliance with the
United States, previously a Platonic idea, now becomes a reality. (Michael
Bakunin, 1857)

JAPAN

Japan consists of four main islands and innumerable small ones. From
north to south it extends approximately the same length as the United States.
Japan's area is comparable to the province of Newfoundland or the states of
Montana or California. Like the United Kingdom it is close enough to be
affected by a large continent but far enough away to make invasion difficult,
which has enabled it to develop a highly individual culture. However, it has
twice the population of the United Kingdom in an only slightly larger area.
Only 17 per cent of the land is arable, and, except for some copper, there
are few mineral resources. Much food is obtained from the sea. Like the
British, the Japanese are maritime people, and in modern times they have
become dependent on a trade which imports raw materials and exports manufactured goods.

Japan is an empire headed by an emperor who traditionally traces his
ancestry back to the Emperor Jimmu in 660 B.C. By the twelfth century the
emperor had become a semi-deified figurehead controlled by powerful feudal
nobles known as shoguns. During the 1600's the Tokugawa family was the
dominating power in the country, a position which it was to hold for 250
years. Early feudal Japan was centred in the island of Honshu, with its capital
at Edo (Tokyo).

The early Japanese had some knowledge of their borderlands. From the
seventeenth century they nominally annexed the Ryukyu Islands and accepted tributes from the individual rulers. A Japanese expedition discovered

the Bonin Islands in 1593, and they were annexed almost a century later. From early times there were spasmodic contacts with the mainland and some trade. From these contacts with China the Japanese derived some cultural aspects such as religion (Buddhism), art forms, costumes, and writing, which they modified to their way of life. Early attempts by the Chinese to invade the islands were repulsed. Similarly, an attempt by Japan to invade Korea (1592-98) was a failure. When the first Europeans arrived, Japan was a self-contained, isolated group of islands still in the throes of power struggles among the feudal nobles.

In surveying the penetration of Europeans into China and Japan, a significant contrast becomes obvious. China was an immense empire, and although Westerners controlled the ports along the coast they did not penetrate the inland farming regions for many years, and much of China was unaffected. The control of a few Japanese ports, on the other hand, could give foreigners a stranglehold on the economy of the entire country if countermeasures were not taken.

The first Europeans to contact the Japanese were the Portuguese, who arrived in 1542 during a period of feudal anarchy. The Portuguese introduced firearms, a commodity which became a necessity for trading into Japan in succeeding years. Within a decade of the first arrivals numerous other European traders appeared, and in 1549 Francis Xavier established a successful Roman Catholic movement. After thirty years (1587), the authorities were alarmed by the increasing influence of the missions and Christianity was nominally prohibited. Later, stricter regulations were enforced, and a number of Christians were cruelly executed. The persecution reached its peak in 1625, although twelve years later a revolt "which assumed a Christian character" resulted in thirty thousand peasants being massacred after three months of fighting.[1]

Other visitors followed the Portuguese. The first Dutchman to visit Japan was Direk Gerritsz, who spent eight months there in 1585-86. In 1611 the Spaniard, Sebastian Vizcaino, from Mexico, paused in his search for legendary islands reportedly rich in gold. A British trading post was unprofitable. The famous Dutch explorer, Abel Tasman, called into Japan on a voyage northward from Batavia. Thus, through numerous scattered contacts, Japanese were introduced to Europeans.

The obvious strength of the Portuguese, Spanish, and Dutch alarmed the Japanese. Spanish activities in the Philippines led to fear in Japan that a similar fate might befall its islands, and Spanish ships and traders were banned in 1624. In 1637, almost a century after the first Portuguese arrivals, complete seclusion was enforced; not only were foreigners prohibited from coming to Japan but also Japanese were forbidden to leave. The former extensive trade with south-east Asia was restricted. Any Japanese who left the country was forbidden to return on pain of death, and to strengthen this decree all junks were to be built with open sterns to prevent them travelling in open seas.[2] The only contact with the outside world was through a rigidly controlled Dutch port at Deshima (1641) on an island near Nagasaki. All attempts by foreigners to gain trading or other rights were rejected. Japan had not only closed her doors to the spread of western ideas, but she had also ended her trading contacts with the mainland. The result was internal unity but at the cost of retarding international relationships.

By 1850 Japanese isolation was being threatened. The Russians were intermittently visiting Hokkaido (Yezo). Britain and France had become the two great rivals for Pacific prestige, and by the First Opium War they had extended their trade to the northern coast of China. The United States had extended its coastline on the Pacific, and American competition with the other western nations in Asia was increasing. Whaling ships, which often touched on the coasts of Japan, were resulting in clashes. Japan was on the great circle route from California to China and was a logical stopping place for rest and the replenishment of supplies for the trans-Pacific traders as well as whalers. The development of steamships had not only improved ocean transportation but had also made strategically located coaling stations desirable. Townsend Harris could see Britain or Russia using Japan as a base of operations against each other.[3]

The approach of the great powers from the south, west, and north made the Japanese seclusion policy untenable. The only question was which nation would break this barrier. By a matter of weeks it was the United States.

Commodore Matthew C. Perry of the United States navy arrived in Japan in 1853 with four men-of-war (the four black ships) and a letter to the emperor from President Fillmore suggesting a treaty. Perry stated that he would return with more ships for an answer the following year. The Japanese leaders were not unaware that similar British demands in China had led to the First Opium War. The subsequent Treaty of Kanagawa was supplemented four years later by Townsend Harris, the first United States consul-general to Japan, who showed great skill and patience in dealing with the shoguns. These treaties arranged for a United States diplomatic agent to be posted in Tokyo. American residents were to be permitted in treaty ports, to have extraterritorial rights, and to be permitted freedom of religion. Three supply ports—Yokohama, Nagasaki, and Hokodate—were opened. There was also provision for an agreement of friendship with the United States, which was to act as a mediator between Japan and other powers. The American treaty became a model for later treaties negotiated by Britain, France, and Russia, whose navies "showed the flag" in Japan during the following decade. For example, when Admiral Stirling visited Nagasaki Bay in 1854, with four warships, he was able to secure a similar treaty.

RUSSIA LOOKS SOUTH

For many years Japan had feared Russia. Since 1700 the Russians based on the Kamchatka Peninsula had been active in the Kurile Islands, but it was not until the end of the century that the expansion of the Japanese northward met the Russians moving southward. By 1785 the Japanese had surveyed the coast of Hokkaido and the following year Yamaguchi Tetsugoro and Mogami Tokunai landed in the southern Kuriles, and a settlement was established on Etoforu Island.

As yet the occupation of these islands was not a matter of concern. The Russians hoped to establish friendly trading relations with Japan. In 1792 an expedition under Adam Laxman to Hokkaido had been courteously received by the Japanese, but he was told not to return. In 1803 Nikolai Rezanov had received the same treatment in Nagasaki, but as he continued his northward journey he destroyed the Japanese settlement at Etoforu. Three years later Krustenstern pillaged the coast of Sakhalin. Between these voyages the British corvette *Providence* under Captain William Broughton (1796–97) also visited Hokkaido. In the succeeding years Russian visits to Hokkaido continued.

The Russian depredations forced the Japanese to venture northward in support of their claims. The Kuriles remained a source of dispute, but Sakhalin was to become the meeting place. Very little was known of this region; some believed Sakhalin was a peninsula of the mainland while others believed that it was a group of islands. To Japan it could be a threat in alien hands. In 1807 Japan claimed Sakhalin, and two years later the Japanese explorer Mamiyo Rinzo claimed that it was an island. This statement was disregarded for fifty years while the accepted belief that it was a peninsula continued.

The First Opium War had shown the weakness of China, but to the Russians the important result was British expansion northward. Afraid of losing China trade, the Russians had adhered to the century-old Treaty of Kyakhta, which closed the Amur River to them. Although they had been infiltrating the Amur region, there had been no flagrant breach of the treaty, but now the situation had changed. What if the British should occupy the mouth of the river? Russia was forced to enter the international power struggle for Chinese concessions.

With the unofficial support of the tsar, Nikolai Muraviev, the governor-general of Eastern Siberia, determined to extend Russia's Pacific territories. Muraviev believed that if Russia did not move, Britain or France would occupy the east coast, and, to forestall this, he planned military and naval forces for the Siberian coast as well as the southward extension of Russia's boundaries to include Mongolia and Manchuria. This would not only check the British and French, but would also add to Russia's influence on China.

Muraviev's methods were simply to send a large "protective" force into Chinese territory and, once established, to present a weak and disorganized China with a *fait accompli* that China would be forced to accept.[4]

No one actually knew what was at the mouth of the Amur, which was believed to empty into an unnavigable shallow delta behind the peninsula of Sakhalin. In 1849 Lt.-Commander G. P. Nevelskoi not only proved that Sakhalin was an island but also found that the mouth of the Amur contained navigable channels. This information was kept a closely guarded secret. The following year he sailed past the Chinese posts and raised the Russian flag sixteen miles from the mouth at Nikolaevsk, following this by establishing posts. When the tsar heard of this unauthorized occupation of Chinese territory, he accepted it in the famous sentence, "Where the Russian flag has once been raised, it must not be lowered."[5] China was informed that this move was to protect both countries from the occupation of the region by a third power. The new aggressive attitude against a weak China was further illustrated two years later when the Russians occupied Emperor Harbour (Soviet Harbour), which was an excellent coastal port south of the Amur. In the same year the Russian flag was raised on Sakhalin.

The fears of British action were not unfounded, and the Russian measures had not been too early. In 1854 Britain and France faced Russia in the Crimean War. The major campaign centred in the Black Sea, but the war, nevertheless, had significant repercussions in the Pacific. The Russian Admiral Paniutin had been informed of the serious complications in Europe, but before he knew that war was declared, he entered Manila with his fleet. His objectives are not clear. He may have considered this to be an excellent location for observations of British/French activities; he may have thought that it would be a suitable place from which to raid India and China. There is also the possibility that Paniutin was reconnoitering places of refuge in case of disaster. The governor-general of the Philippines, however, suspected that this visit was an advanced southern move of Russian expansion, and, as he refused to permit the fleet to remain it sailed away for an unknown destination.[6]

Meanwhile the British and French fleets, having left Callao and having paused at Hawaii, steered northward towards Sitka and Petropavlosk, "where the Russian fleets will doubtless be."[7] On reaching Petropavlosk the fleet bombarded the town for three days and silenced the batteries, but, in an attempted landing, the attackers were driven back in hand to hand fighting with heavy casualties. A Russian account stated: "Besides the dead and wounded on board his ships the enemy lost 300. We have 37 killed."[8]

The allies withdrew to the warm south, where they scattered into independent patrols for the winter, with apparently no firm agreement on the 1855 campaign. Meanwhile, on 16 April, the Russian fleet had sawn a channel through the ice at Petropavlosk and sailed south. A report that it had been seen by three small British vessels in Castries Bay, latitude 51° 17', resulted in attempts to assemble the disorganized allied forces, a part of which arrived at Castries Bay a week after the Russians had left. Believing that the Russians had sailed north, the allies returned to Petropavlosk, which they found almost deserted. The allies were convinced that the enemy was "snugly ensconced" somewhere in the Sea of Okhotsk, but although they searched as far as Alaska, the Russian fleet could not be found.[9] Actually, the Russians had sailed south and had disappeared into the Amur River, which the searchers still believed to be unnavigable.

The activities against the Russian fleet in the Pacific alarmed the residents of Vancouver Island. Victorians feared Russian retaliation, especially as news of the war was not received until three months after its declaration. The colony had no military force, and Governor Douglas suggested that an irregular militia force of whites and Indians be formed, but the council refused since it feared to arm Indians.[10] The colony chartered the Hudson's Bay Company's steamer *Otter*, which was armed, as a defence measure. Douglas appealed to the British government for naval protection. What Douglas did not know was that the Russian Fur Company and the Hudson's Bay Company had reached an agreement in the Treaty of London, 1854, which ensured that their North American posts would be neutralized and safe from each other. The British government knew of this agreement and therefore sent only the odd token warship to Vancouver Island to quell the uneasiness. Britain also refused to pay for a defensive force. The neutrality agreement was honoured by both sides during the war and business continued to be carried on between the companies as usual. The colony was asked to co-operate with the Pacific Squadron by supplying provisions, coal, and a temporary hospital for the expected wounded from the attack on Petropavlosk. In 1855 the fleet did pick up supplies, but after the Petropavlosk expedition only one casualty arrived for the hospital, an engineer suffering from scurvy; the other wounded had been sent to San Francisco.[11] However, the British navy had been searching for years for a sovereign naval base north of South America—it had considered San Francisco before the American annexation—and now it used Esquimalt, which was finally accepted as a major naval base.[12]

THE ARROW WAR

Events in China saw more co-operation among foreign nations as they seized opportunities for further demands. The Taiping Rebellion (1850-64) threatened to overthrow the empire, and at times the Taiping controlled large areas of the country. The beleaguered government was unable to prevent the British from insisting on the right to collect customs in 1854, part of which were returned to China. This was a comparatively small concession since, although the foreigners controlled a number of ports, they also wanted to trade inland, to have the right to export Chinese labourers, and to establish diplomatic relations with Peking, and the French desired to expand their missionary efforts. As these requests were strongly opposed by the Chinese government the belief increased that force would have to be used against it.

In 1857 Chinese authorities seized a wanted pirate from the *Arrow*, a Chinese vessel which had been formerly under British registration. In the same year a French missionary was killed. The Chinese viceroy refused to apologize or make amends, and the Second Opium War, or Arrow War, began. British and French troops seized Canton and captured the viceroy. The United States, although not actively engaged, supported the aggression. Russia offered to mediate. The Chinese government agreed to discuss the problems but refused to admit foreign envoys to Peking. At this point Britain was diverted by the Indian Mutiny. In the following year military activity was renewed when Britain and France captured the protective forts at Taku and forced their way into Peking, where the British vindictively burned the summer palace.

The four treaties of Peking (1858) were signed by Britain, France, the United States, and Russia and were followed by the Convention of Peking. Within ten years further treaties were also signed with Germany, Portugal, Denmark, Spain, Holland, and Italy. Eleven more ports (and later Tientsin), including some inland rivers, were opened. Sizable indemnities were levied. Kowloon was added to the British territories at Hong Kong, missionaries were permitted to move freely through the country, extraterritoriality was granted, and foreign powers were permitted to establish legations in Peking. Britain, France, and Russia established legations in 1861; the Americans arrived a year later. In return the allies agreed to help the Chinese government against Taiping rebels. Foreign traders, who had been divided on the question of supporting the rebellion and thus overthrowing the Manchu régime, had concluded that the established government was preferable to the uncertainty of the Taipings. With limited foreign assistance the rebellion was crushed, and the Manchus were restored to control over the whole country. The reactionary and anti-foreign governing bureaucracy was faced with western control supported by military force. This problem it was unable to solve.

For the next forty years China was completely dominated by foreign powers claiming special rights and privileges, while missionaries, especially French and American, moved freely through the country. Spasmodic incidents against foreigners were met by a united western front, supported by naval units and usually followed by the payment of an indemnity. In 1870 when France and Prussia were at war in Europe, both nations joined the force which was sent as the result of an uprising against the French church in Tientsin.

By the Treaties of Tientsin, Britain had reasserted its predominance in the

1. Drake's Plate of Brass, discovered near
   Drake's Bay, California about 1930.
   The inscription reads: BEE IT
   KNOWNE VNTO ALL MEN BY
   THESE PRESENTS/ IVNE 17 1579/
   BY THE GRACE OF GOD AND IN
   THE NAME OF HERR/
   MAIESTY QVEEN ELIZABETH OF
   ENGLAND AND HERR/
   SVCCESSORS FOREVER I TAKE
   POSSESSION OF THIS/
   KINGDOME WHOSE KING AND
   PEOPLE FREELY RESIGNE/
   THEIR RIGHT AND TITLE IN THE
   WHOLE LAND VNTO HERR/
   MAIESTIES KEEPEING NOW
   NAMED BY ME AN TO BEE/
   KNOWNE VNTO ALL MEN AS
   NOVA ALBION./ FRANCIS DRAKE

2. Vitus Bering sailed through Bering
   Strait and was the first European
   to visit the northwest coast of America.
   He died on his return voyage.

3. Mission Santa Clara de Asis, Santa Clara, California, c. 1777. The first California mission was established at San Diego ten years earlier.

4. The early maritime fur traders on the northwest coast of America frequently stopped at Hawaii en route to China.

5. An early view of Sitka, Alaska.
   Baranov's castle and the
   Orthodox church are at the left.
   At one time Sitka was the most
   important port north of San
   Francisco.

6. Juan Francisco de la Bodega y
   Quadra, explorer of the north-
   west coast and Spanish emissary
   who met Captain Vancouver
   at Nootka, 1792. For many years
   Vancouver Island was known
   as Vancouver and Quadra's
   Island.

7. Meeting of the Russian explorer Otto von Kotzebue with King Kamehameha at Oahu, 1816.

8. Whaling was the most important industry in the North Pacific during the mid-nineteenth century. This fanciful painting illustrates the whaling ship, the methods of whaling, and the dangers.

9. Chinese barges carrying Lord Macartney's mission to Peking, 1793.

10. The approach of the Emperor of China to receive Lord Macartney. After a month of delays Macartney was sent away from Peking.

11. Canton was the only port in China open to foreign traders until the Treaty of Nanking, 1842.

12. British ships attacking the Chinese fleet during the First Opium War.

13. A missionary preaching to the natives in Hawaii, 1826. The first missions were established in 1820.

14. Commodore Matthew C. Perry arrived in Japan in 1853 with four men-of-war and a letter from President Fillmore suggesting a treaty. Japan was unable to hold to her seclusion policy any longer.

15. French troops marching from Peking following the Treaty of Peking, 1838. *Illustrated Times*, 2 February 1861.

16. Following the Treaty of Peking, 1858, foreign powers were permitted to establish legations in Peking. A crowd of Celestials contemplates the barbarians in Peking. *Illustrated London News*. 5 January 1861.

17. Foreign ministers being received at Peking. *Canadian Illustrated News*. 22 November 1873.

Pacific. The British navy, with bases at Singapore, Hong Kong, and Esquimalt, patrolled not only the ocean but the Chinese rivers as well. Although France had co-operated in most ventures, its objectives were different. Nevertheless, there was always an underlying rivalry. Britain was basically interested in commerce. France, under Louis Napoleon, was seeking prestige and recognition as a great power and was interested in spreading Roman Catholicism. After the war France withdrew territorially from the North Pacific (leaving Canton in 1861) and diverted its attention to Indochina, which it took over in the 1870's and 1880's. The French withdrawal did not rid Britain of competition. The United States was becoming more commercially aggressive, and within a few years Germany and Japan were to join the imperialistic rivalry.

The Treaty of Paris, 1856, which terminated the Crimean War, denied the Black Sea to Russia for the use of her battleships, with the result that Russia became more interested not only in Pacific naval activities but also in expanding its influence southward. For a short decade, from the seizure of the Amur until the establishment of Vladivostock, Russia had revived its interest in China. In 1855 Japan agreed by the Treaty of Shimodesto to permit Russia three ports of call, to accept the division of the Kurile Islands between the two nations, and to accept "joint occupancy" of Sakhalin. Twenty years later it was agreed that Russia was to have all of Sakhalin and Japan kept all the Kuriles.

During the Arrow War, Russia, hoping to win Chinese friendship, disassociated itself from the Anglo–French military activities (although maintaining contact and supplying them with information) and at the ensuing peace conference acted as mediator. In spite of its claims to be sympathetic towards China in the negotiations, Russia did manage to pressure China into accepting the Treaty of Aigun (1858). By this Russia obtained both banks of the Amur with the right of navigation as well as the east coast of Manchuria as far as the border of Korea. Here Russia proceeded to build the port of Vladivostock just north of the peninsula. Soon after the Treaty of Aigun the Russian–Chinese treaty at Tientsin gave Russia commercial rights similar to other powers, the right to trade by sea and to use open ports. In Vladivostock not only had Russia gained a port far south of its previous possessions, but it had also checked the possible northward expansion of Britain and France. It had also moved towards further isolating Japan from the mainland. Three years later Russia established a post on Tsushima Island at the southern entrance to the Sea of Japan, an island generally understood to belong to Japan. As a further check to Britain and France, Russia continued its friendship with the United States, supporting the north in the Civil War and sending six warships on visits to San Francisco in 1863–65.

In spite of these advances, the Crimean War had convinced Russia that protection of the North Pacific from the sea was almost impossible and interest in the region declined. The Amur Valley proved to be a disappointment since its agricultural production was minimal and it could not be depended upon as a food base for Pacific military posts. For twenty years naval forces in the North Pacific were limited, mainly patrolling the sealing and fishing industries. Seeing no immediate future profitable expansion in the North Pacific, Russia continued its policies of withdrawing from one region to exert pressure on another. Its attention now turned towards the annexation of Central Asia, which brought it to the boundaries of Afghanistan and Persia where, once again, it became a challenge to British ambitions. For the last half of the nineteenth century Russia was Britain's most persistent rival, a condition which lasted until the two nations, threatened by the rise of Germany, settled their differences and formed the Triple Entente of 1907 with France.

ALASKA

Contemporary with its increasing interest in the Asiatic coast was Russia's disillusionment with Alaska. The Russians were not a colonizing people in the same sense that the western Europeans were. The headquarters of the Russian–American Company were in St. Petersburg, and the stockholders were more interested in stock manipulation and profits than in developing a colony. Comparatively few Russians came to Alaska, and most returned after their term of duty. Instead of settlers the Russians parsimoniously supplied missions and schools for the native peoples. Thus, the true Alaskans were the natives who became administrators, artisans, and traders. There were few cultural or ethnic ties between Russia and Alaska.

Far from St. Petersburg, unprofitable and almost impossible to defend from the encroaching British and Americans, Alaska was a burden. The Crimean War had shown the vulnerability of Russia in the North Pacific and there was always the danger that in some future war Alaska might become a British threat to the Russian Pacific coast. Possession by the United States was preferable to such a possibility. In 1859 negotiations began for the sale of Alaska, but they were delayed by the American Civil War. In 1867 Russian America was sold to the United States for $7.2 million.

The reasons for the sale are complex but some facts are obvious. Because the Russian government was not happy with the Russian–American Company, which was doing little colonization and was often on the verge of bankruptcy, there were doubts about the renewal of its charter. There was a growing belief that the aggressive American policy of Manifest Destiny would lead to the takeover of British Columbia, with a resulting move towards Alaska. The gold rush in British Columbia brought many Americans to that colony, and they could conceivably claim the land as earlier Americans had occupied and then annexed Oregon, Texas, and California. It was known that William Seward, the American secretary of state, was an expansionist who would probably not be averse to annexing British Columbia. The friendship of Russia and the United States was encouraged by a common fear of France and Britain, which was shown in the attitude of the United States during the Crimean War and by the visit of the Russian navy to San Francisco and New York during the American Civil War. "The knowledge that the Russian fleet . . . could winter in safe American waters attracted international attention."[13] In fact, if the United States should control the entire west coast, British naval power in the North Pacific would be negligible.

The sale caused protests in both Russia and the United States. Russia had a policy of not relinquishing any land which it once possessed, and this reversal of policy was criticized in many quarters. Similarly the purchase of "Seward's Ice Box" was bitterly attacked in the American Congress. In neither case was the opposition effective.

For two centuries Russia had been a force in the history of the north-west coast, but now this period was ended. Russia had been the first to discover the coast and had dispelled many of the legends about the North Pacific. It had opened the maritime fur trade and, in time, had adopted policies of conservation. Some of its dedicated leaders had envisioned the possibilities of expanding Russian control as far as California; in fact, during the period of Mexican unrest, control of San Francisco was contemplated. Political intrigues, indecision, misunderstanding, and distance limited the scope of Russian expansion. Little remains of Russian America—a few settlements, the missionary influence, numerous place names, and the Alaska–Canada boundary.

In the decade before the sale of Alaska, Russia had discontinued exploration in the north-east Pacific. Leases of exploitation rights in the northern waters were granted to foreign powers. An American company was given whaling rights in the Sea of Okhotsk, and in 1871 another American company received the sealing rights in the Kommander Islands for twenty years. These leases terminated at the expiry date but not before the Americans had almost exterminated the animals which Baranov had tried to preserve. The Kommander Islands remain as one of the few places where the sea otter still survives, protected by strict government regulations.

Relieved of their responsibilities in the American North Pacific, the Russians concentrated on the Asiatic coast and offshore islands. In 1872 the main naval base, which had been moved in 1854 from Petropavlosk to the mouth of the Amur, was established at Vladivostock. By the 1875 treaty, the first which accepted Japan as an equal to a European power, Russia surrended the Kurile Islands in return for Sakhalin. Six years later, following a dispute in Turkestan, Russia forced China to permit navigation rights on the Manchurian rivers. Russia had become a serious participant in the international race for Korea and northern China.

MINERS AND SETTLERS

The Oregon Treaty made little immediate change to the life of the people. The economy was still based on the fur trade. During the 1840's and 1850's settlers flocked in thousands to Oregon, settling in the Columbia and Willamette valleys and expanding to Puget Sound. Concentrations of peoples were laying the foundations for the future cities of Portland, Tacoma, and Seattle. Oregon Territory became a state in 1859, but another thirty years were to pass before Washington achieved statehood. These were years of steady expansion in Oregon except for the short flurry which drew many men to the California gold rush.

The British possessions, except for Vancouver Island, were still Hudson's Bay Company territories, dotted with trading posts. Victoria was still dominated by the company officials. For its privileges on Vancouver Island the company had agreed to bring settlers to the island, a chore which it performed with little enthusiasm. Nevertheless, the colony grew, and the independent settlers forced Governor Douglas to accept an assembly, a development which he considered a nuisance.

Vancouver Island was connected to Britain by the annual supply ships of the Hudson's Bay Company. There was little interest in trans-Pacific affairs except for the limited amount of export trade in salmon and timber, mainly destined for the Hawaiian islands. This disinterest was shaken by the Crimean War, when British naval vessels used Esquimalt and increased their patrols in the North Pacific.

The California gold rush brought the first dynamic change to the west coast. For four years, until it passed its peak, thousands of goldseekers arrived to change the life of the new state. The adventurers poured into San Francisco, making it a booming restless city. Although many came around Cape Horn and others crossed Panama, most arrived by land and transportation patterns developed connecting the coast with the east. The newcomers were a new type to the west. Instead of fur traders, seamen, or farmers these people were from all stratas of society and were interested not in acquiring land for cultivation but in making money fast. From this group remained an aggressive capitalistic nucleus interested in an urban rather than an agrarian society. San Francisco commercial interests dominated the entire coast, and their influence spread to Hawaii. Even Vancouver Island and the British territories inland were drawn into the San Francisco orbit. Transportation and communication joined Vancouver Island by sea to San Francisco. Mail from the island carried Vancouver Island and United States stamps.

Within ten years another gold rush was to bring a second great influx, this time to the Fraser and Cariboo districts in British territory. The Fraser River gold rush started slowly after the news of gold reached San Francisco in 1856. However, within a few years thousands of miners, mostly from the

United States, had penetrated far up the Fraser River to the rich creeks of the Cariboo. Here rose the town of Barkerville, at one time the largest city north of San Francisco. The invasion resulted in the building of the Cariboo Highway, an amazing road over three hundred miles long, joining Yale at the head of navigation to Barkerville. Along this highway streamed traffic to and from the mines—by foot, horse, stagecoach, and even camels. By it came the gold en route to Victoria on its way to San Francisco.

An alarmed Governor Douglas took immediate steps to control the influx of miners. The British navy was called upon to patrol the mouth of the Fraser and to collect mining licences. As a result of the governor's frantic appeals, the British government proclaimed the colony of British Columbia in 1858. In the following year, on the advice of Colonel R. C. Moody, New Westminster was selected as the capital of the new colony, partly because of its defensive possibilities. At the same time, with memories of the Crimean War still fresh, as well as the constant threat of the United States, surrounding lands were reserved for military and naval purposes.[14] The Royal Engineers were sent to the colony to establish settlements, build roads, and keep order. A judiciary was established by Chief Justice Begbie, a man whose reputation for impartiality and severity maintained law and order throughout the colony.

The gold rush lasted only a few years. Most of the miners left and a period of depression, caused by the rapid expansion along with high public debts, set in. In 1866 the two colonies of Vancouver Island and British Columbia were united as a single colony with the capital eventually established in Victoria.

THE SAN JUAN DISPUTE

During the British Columbia gold rush occurred an incident which brought the British and American military forces face to face for the first and last time on the Pacific coast. This is known as the San Juan dispute.

The source of this disagreement originated in the Oregon Treaty, which had set the international boundary as "the middle of the channel which separates the continent from Vancouver Island." There are over 170 islands in this channel, most of which created no problems of sovereignty, but in the middle of the gulf the ownership of one group was disputed. The largest and most western of these is San Juan. Agents of the Hudson's Bay Company had taken formal possession of the island in 1845, before the Oregon Treaty. In 1850 the company had established a fishing station from which it shipped barrels of salmon to the Hawaiian Islands. A few years later a sheep farm was begun from which sheep were also exported. Governor Douglas appointed a Hudson's Bay Company servant, Charles J. Griffin, as magistrate on the island and sent Captain Sangster, the Victoria collector of customs, to the island. Meanwhile Washington Territory had been created and San

Juan was included as part of Whatcom County in 1854. The Americans also sent the collector of customs for the Puget Sound district, Isaac N. Ebey, to San Juan, and thus there were two customs officials established in tents on the island with their respective flags flying.

Ebey notified Governor Douglas that the sheep were liable to seizure for the non-payment of customs duties. With the officials of both countries claiming jurisdiction over the island, there began a series of incidents which became known as the "Pig War" because at one time an American settler had killed a Hudson's Bay Company pig which had wandered into his garden. Tension increased when the Americans, with the threat of force, seized thirty sheep for non-payment of customs.

Reports were sent to both London and Washington, but both governments had more serious problems than a dispute about a group of distant islands, so were content to defer discussion. The British faced the Crimean War; the Americans had domestic problems. A strong anti-colonialism spirit was prevalent in England. On the other hand, Manifest Destiny was strong in the United States and there was some feeling that the Oregon Treaty had been a concession to Britain. The Americans were determined to control Puget Sound with its ports, and San Juan, to them, was a strategic military location for the defence of the sound. On the west coast, at this time, Vancouver Island was facing the influx of miners to the goldfields, while Washington Territory was being threatened by minor Indian troubles, which led to a strengthening of military forces and defences.

Tension continued to mount and correspondence became more and more acrimonious. In 1858, Brigadier-General William S. Harney was appointed to Oregon. Harney had a violent temper, was impetuous, and had been in trouble for acting on his own initiative and disregarding army regulations. Undoubtedly he was a brave man, popular with his troops, and supported by the more aggressive citizens of the region. Now, far from the controls of Washington, he adopted a belligerent attitude, determined to ensure American control of the islands. Opposed to him was the autocratic governor, Douglas, who could be "furious when aroused" and who was determined to retain the islands, which he believed to be unquestionably British.

In 1859 Harney sent Captain Pickett with a small force to occupy the island. Douglas, who had no army, called upon the British navy and sent the sloop-of-war *Satellite* to protest the American action. This was followed by the thirty-one-gun steam frigate *Tribune* under Captain Phipps Hornby, and later by the warship *Plumper* with 125 men. Douglas instructed Hornby to land marines on the island, but, after surveying the situation, Hornby decided against landing. For a short time three naval vessels and 775 men faced sixty determined Americans on the island. A landing would undoubtedly have resulted in hostilities, deaths, and possibly war between the United States and Britain.

Fortunately, Hornby's actions delayed confrontation and cooler heads prevailed. Admiral Baynes arrived in Victoria and, against Douglas's advice, supported Hornby. Washington, which had been unaware of Harney's actions, dispatched General Winfield Scott, who had Harney recalled and who began discussions with Douglas. Governor Douglas was very aware that the vast majority of people in British Columbia, as a result of the gold rush, were Americans. It was quite feasible that should a shooting war start these miners would seize control of the colony and that the United States might use this as an excuse for annexation, a policy previously adopted in American expansion. On the other side, the United States had become involved in the Civil War and could not be expected to become entangled in a war over some isolated islands far away.

Eventually a temporary compromise of joint occupancy was accepted. Each country was permitted to place a force of one hundred men on the island. The occupation of this small island by the two opposing military forces lasted for thirteen years, during which the two camps established a friendly relationship. Ultimately the problem was referred to the German emperor for arbitration, one of the first instances of an international dispute being settled in this manner. In 1873 the emperor drew the line through Haro Strait, thus upholding the American claims and giving them all of the disputed islands. The British troops were withdrawn, but most of the settlers remained to become American citizens.

The arbitration award was an outcome of the Washington Treaty of 1871. For years British–American relations had been deteriorating, especially during the civil war and the period of Fenian raids, with a resulting series of crises. Britain needed its resources to check the possible aggressions of Bismarck in central Europe and the North Sea coast, as well as those of the Russians in the Balkans. The necessity of maintaining sizable forces in North America handicapped its influence in Europe. The Treaty of Washington solved many of the British–American problems and, by restoring a spirit of amity between the two countries, enabled Britain to withdraw its garrisons from North America.[15] However, the Pacific coast for many years was to fear an outbreak of hostilities between Britain and Russia and remained dependent on the British navy.[16]

RÉSUMÉ

By 1870 the Asiatic Pacific coast was in a state of transition. European nations had opened the ports of China, and the race for concessions was beginning. To counter the pressures from foreign powers, Japan was entering a period of reforms which were to make her a contender in the power struggle. The territories bordered by China, Russia, and Japan were sources of growing rivalries among the three nations, a struggle which the United States and

Britain watched with concern as it could result in loss of trade. On the North American coast the United States had consolidated its control, had purchased Alaska, and had established a definite northern border with Canada (1873). San Francisco, joined to the east by a railroad, dominated the economy of the coast and controlled the growing Pacific trade. The colony of British Columbia was in a state of depression and was considering joining the newly formed Dominion of Canada (1867). This union would bring Canada to the Pacific Ocean.

7

Across Continent and Ocean
(1870–1914)

The Pacific Railway would form an Imperial Highway across the Continent of America entirely on British soil, and would form a new and important route from England to Australia, to India and all the dependencies of Great Britain in the Pacific, as also to China and Japan. (Sir Charles Tupper, 1879)

You will have coolie labour in California some day. You will not always go on paying $80 or $100 a month for labour you can hire for $5. (Mark Twain, 1866)

The Franco–Prussian War of 1870–71 caused a reassessment of international alignments and policies. Not only did a new military power, Germany, threaten to dominate central Europe, but Austria–Hungary had been relegated to a secondary status and France was in a state of disorganization. Britain, following a policy of "splendid isolation," was facing the challenge of Russia in a number of places. Now Germany threatened to become an energetic rival in trade, in naval power, and in the colonial field. The United States, following the Civil War, had emerged a stronger and more aggressive nation and had consolidated its Pacific holdings by purchasing Alaska. The Dominion of Canada had been formed and was soon to extend from ocean to ocean. On the Asiatic side of the Pacific the Manchus still refused to recognize the threat of foreign pressures. Japan had just started on its age of reform.

The thirty years after 1870 have been called the Age of Imperialism or the New Imperialism as imperialistic ambitions in Africa and Asia became more aggressive and European domination approached its climax. The Industrial Revolution had expanded from Britain and other powers, especially the United States, Germany, and France, were challenging British trade supremacy. With protective tariffs and modern machinery, Britain's competitors were closing former export markets and invading new commercial fields. Britain, unwilling to forsake the *laissez-faire* policies which had brought it leadership and prestige, sought alternatives to protection for the maintenance of its financial and economic leadership. Assured sources of raw materials, along with preferred markets by an expansion of colonial possessions would seem to be logical means of keeping British exports competitive. The dependence on worldwide territories necessitated protected trade routes through an efficient navy and by the control of strategic bases.

As other nations expanded industrially they, too, sought for protected sources of raw materials and wider, protected markets. Improved technology meant that control was possible over larger areas. Improved weapons enabled the western nations to assert domination over native peoples with their obsolete equipment. Railways and steamships, burning coal and oil, enabled troops and materials to be moved quickly to unsettled or insurgent regions. Where formerly home governments had been forced to leave decision-making to isolated traders, missionaries, naval officers, or other government representatives, now, with the rapid communication through wireless, telephone, or cable, the central governments had more direct contacts with their outposts. Control of strategic positions on the trade routes, such as Cape Horn, the Suez Canal, the Straits of Malacca, and (later) the Panama Canal, became essential for the preservation of sovereignty and the protection of trade.

Combined with these factors was the increasing prestige connected with trading success as well as the extent of colonial possessions. Even Germany, which had heretofore shown little interest in colonies, was becoming actively involved by the end of the century. The increasing awareness of colonial possessions as a measure of success intensified national pride. Improvements in education, followed by the development of the popular press, brought awareness to the people of distant lands and military successes. The relief of besieged cities in South Africa or China was hailed with celebrations. Classrooms were adorned with world maps showing the British Empire in red. The increasing popular support for colonial expansion influenced the attitudes of politicians and governments.

Along with the pressures for colonial expansion was an awareness that colonies were expensive and that the cost of maintenance was often greater than the financial returns. Thus Britain was not averse to giving limited self-government with increasing taxing powers to its more advanced colonies. In China, the westerners preferred to maintain China as a unit and, by controlling specified spheres, to take profits from investments in railway or business expansion rather than to undertake the heavy costs of governing a far-distant alien land.

TRANSCONTINENTAL COMMUNICATION

In 1860, although telegraph and railway lines were common in the east, the west coast of North America was still isolated by land and most transportation was by sea. Regular steamship services rounded Cape Horn, but the more common route was across Panama, where regular steamships from New York and San Francisco met both ends of the road.

The California gold rush increased the demand for transportation, and stage coaches maintained regular schedules on the arduous journey from Missouri to the west coast, a distance of 1,900 miles which took about twenty days. The heavy traffic hastened the building of a railway across Panama in 1855. In the United States, for nineteen months the Pony Express, which covered 1,600 miles in six days, shortened the time for messages until the completion of the telegraph to San Francisco in 1861 finally gave a direct connection with the east. The telegraph line was extended northward to Oregon and made it possible for that state to have direct contacts with the Atlantic. During this same period the Russians were building a comparable telegraph line from St. Petersburg to the mouth of the Amur.

THE COLLINS TELEGRAPH

Three attempts to connect North America to Europe by a trans-Atlantic cable failed. As an alternative to the apparently impossible Atlantic cable, Perry McDonough Collins, among others, looked westward. Collins proposed to join the trans-Russian telegraph line to the line in Oregon by building northward from the Amur, across the Bering Strait with a cable and thence southward through Alaska and British Columbia. By this route Europe could be joined to eastern Canada and the United States.[1]

Collins was born in Hyde Park, New York, and eventually moved to San Francisco. He outlined his Bering Strait plans to President Pierce and was appointed commercial agent for the United States for the Amur River. In this capacity he visited St. Petersburg and travelled down the Amur. In 1860 he presented his plan to Congress and followed this with missions to Russia, London, and Russian America. Three years later he obtained a thirty-three-year imperial concession from Russia to operate a telegraph line from Nikolaevsk across Bering Strait and through Russian America. Further permissions were received from the governments of Britain, the United States, and British Columbia. He was granted a preliminary amount of $50,000 from the American Congress and $100,000 from the Western Union Telegraph Company. Other funds were raised by public subscription. The proposed route, cable terminals, and surveys were organized by an American, Captain C. S. Bulkley. Surveys under the Americans Robert Kennicott and Dr. William H. Dahl resulted in the first systematic exploration of what was still Russian America (Alaska), although the land north of the Yukon remained largely unknown.

Cold and permafrost handicapped the building of the line from the north, but construction from Oregon proceeded rapidly. By April 1865 New West-minster was reached, the first message to arrive being the news of the assassination of President Lincoln. The line was built along the Fraser River, the Cariboo Highway, and north to the confluence of the Kispiox and Skeena rivers. Soon after its arrival at this point came news that Cyrus Field had completed the laying of the Atlantic cable. The work on the Bering Strait route was abandoned, as were all the construction supplies. British Columbia had direct contact with Canada and Britain through the United States. The Russians eventually extended their line from the Amur to Shanghai and Hong Kong, which was joined to India by a British line.[2]

THE RAILWAYS

The Civil War, with its demand for military equipment, was followed by a period of great industrial expansion in the United States, and plans for a transcontinental railway were revived. In 1869 the Union Pacific from San Francisco and the Central Pacific from Omaha met at Ogden, Utah, joining the west coast to the eastern lines. Within three years the exports and imports with Asia had doubled, although they were still an insignificant part of American total trade. Other transcontinentals followed: the Northern Pacific from Lake Superior to Puget Sound, 1883; the Southern Pacific from New Orleans to Los Angeles, 1884; the Atchison, Topeka, and Santa Fé from Chicago to Los Angeles, 1884; The Great Northern from Duluth to Seattle, 1893. Within a quarter of a century five transcontinental railways had crossed the nation.

These railways tied the Pacific to the Atlantic, but they also revolutionized the settlement and economy of the west. Inland regions were opened, new resources were tapped, orchards were extended, and financial and trading organizations became powerful. After the short early spurt trans-Pacific trade did not develop as rapidly as had been expected—Americans were exploiting their own new lands. San Francisco continued to dominate the coast from Mexico to Alaska as well as Hawaii, but the railways enabled other cities such as Oakland, Los Angeles, Portland, and Tacoma to establish themselves as rivals.

Along with the settlements came demands for political reform. Oregon was made a state in 1859 and Washington in 1889. Within ten years the Klondike gold rush was to make Seattle one of the most important ports on the Pacific coast.

Between 1865 and 1870 numerous constitutional reforms were made in a number of countries—Switzerland, The Netherlands, Austria, and Britain. More significant, internationally, was the unification or strengthening of national federations. The German Empire was formed, the Kingdom of Italy was established, the Japanese emperor was restored to power, the United States was strengthened by the Civil War, and four eastern colonies became the Dominion of Canada. To Britain the costs of maintaining a large naval and military establishment in North America was a major financial burden. In Europe, Britain was faced with the uncertainty of Prussian ambitions, including the possible threat to Belgium, as well as the continued threat of Russia in the Black Sea. Relationships with the United States after the Civil War were at a low ebb and the Fenian raids into Canada aggravated the tensions. A more independent Canada would reduce Britain's obligations in North America, would lessen tensions with the United States, and would permit Britain to strengthen its position in Europe and the Mediterranean.[3]

The newly formed Dominion of Canada was still separated from the colony of British Columbia by thousands of miles of sparsely populated wilderness. Whereas American settlers had expanded rapidly westward into the Great Plains across the Mississippi, the Canadians had been blocked by the rocky, inhospitable land north of Lake Superior. The vast territory between Canada and British Columbia was under the jurisdiction of the Hudson's Bay Company, a fur trading organization which did not favour settlement. British Columbia itself was separated from the prairies by a series of formidable mountain ranges.

Nevertheless, the British and Canadians envisaged transcontinental expansion and watched with trepedation the Americans filling their inland plains and moving northward towards British territory. To Britain, Canada was a possible link with its interests in the Pacific and Asia. To Canadians, the central plains offered great potential for commercial development. The spread of American settlement threatened to separate irretrievably the western and eastern colonies in North America.

British Columbia, isolated and economically depressed, faced a dilemma. It could remain a separated British colony, insular, beset by debts, with no foreseeable prosperous future. It had no military forces and depended on the British navy based at Esquimalt for defence. This harbour remained important to British strategy. After the last British troops had left and the buildings were formally transferred to Canada in 1911, it was on condition that the facilities be maintained efficiently for the use of the royal navy.[4] From the time of the Crimean War the British Pacific coast feared Russia. The sale of Alaska partially reduced this threat but fear of American expansionist policies were increased. British Columbia was not threatened by the Civil War but did have its own worry with the continuing San Juan dispute. The colony was dependent on the United States not only for communication with the outside world but also for its commerce, which suffered from American tariffs. Because of its vulnerable position, the fact that there were no foreseeable eastern markets, and the presence of American immigrants, a strong faction believed that the natural development was to join the United States, a step which would end the hopes of Britain becoming a power in the North Pacific. The third choice was to join Canada, but this option had little to offer without direct communication and transportation.

Steps were taken to unite the British possessions. The Hudson's Bay Company charter was cancelled, the Dominion of Canada took over the North-West Territories, and the small settlement at Red River became the nucleus of the new province of Manitoba. When British Columbia approached Ottawa to discuss union it requested a railway, which was to begin within two years and be completed in ten, along with other concessions. After bitter debates British Columbia became the sixth province in 1871.

The transcontinental railway, which was completed as the Canadian Pacific, was built from both ends. Political disputes, scandal, and the shortage of money retarded construction. The persistence of Prime Minister John A. Macdonald and a small group of dedicated officials eventually overcame the problems. The two lines met in 1885, and by the following year trains were reaching the Pacific at the newly formed port of Vancouver. The railway tied the nation together, countered the threat of American settlers, stopped American railways from penetrating the country, opened the west to settlement, made practical the development of agricultural, mineral, and forest resources, and made possible the "all-red line" by which Britain could send goods and soldiers by a more direct and less vulnerable route to Asia, Australia, New Zealand, and its other Pacific possessions.

As in the United States, other transcontinental railways were built, the Canadian Northern to Vancouver and the Grand Trunk Pacific to Prince Rupert, "the expected centre of a future golden trade with the Orient."[5] These were completed during the First World War and were amalgamated with other lines after the war to form the Canadian National Railways.

Largely as a result of the efforts of Sandford Fleming, another "all-red route" between the British colonies was opened for business on 1 January 1903 when the trans-Pacific cable was completed from Canada to New Zealand and Australia. The "all-American Pacific cable" from Point Lobos near San Francisco to Honolulu opened a day later.

The Pacific Mail Steam Navigation Company, with a government subsidy, had maintained a monthly schedule between San Francisco and Hong Kong since 1866, the year before the Union Pacific transcontinental was completed. In Canada, George Stephen, first president of the Canadian Pacific, stated: "The railway will not be complete until we have an ocean connection with Japan," and, in the same year that the first transcontinental trains reached Vancouver, chartered steamships began operating across the Pacific.[6] The expansion of trans-Pacific steamship services increased the demands for coaling stations, resulting in the occupation of islands which had little of value otherwise. Thus, in 1867, the United States annexed Midway and pressures for a coaling station in Hawaii increased.

In the same year that the Canadian Pacific was completed, Russia began to plan its own military transcontinental railway. For centuries Siberia and the Pacific coast had been isolated regions connected to European Russia by overland trade routes. A railway, it was believed, would not only open Siberia for colonization and the exploitation of its resources but would also strengthen Russia's position on the Pacific, as the Canadian Pacific strengthened that of Britain, by providing a faster and more direct route for military personnel and supplies. European activities in the Pacific were becoming more threatening, especially after the opening of the Suez Canal and the opening of northern Chinese ports. Britain's threat to build Port Hamilton off Korea in 1885 (although it was cancelled when faced by protests from Japan, Korea, and China) emphasized the vulnerability of Russian ports, and a railway would allow these to be supplied by land. Trade with the newly opened ports of China and Japan could be expanded. The railway would also establish better connections with the friendly United States.

The Trans-Siberian Railway (1891-1905) ranks among the greatest of construction feats and strengthened the economy of Russia as well as accentuating its Pacific influence. Seventy per cent of the financing was done by the government. It was constructed simultaneously in five sections using almost entirely Russian materials. The workers were all Russian, and convicts were used extensively as cheap labour. The railway, when completed, joined St. Petersburg with Vladivostock which, although the most southern Russian port, was not entirely ice-free. An ice-free port could be obtained by branch lines through Korea or Manchuria. The Trans-Siberian Railway offered an alternative to the maritime route for goods from the Pacific to Europe. The possibilities of profitable commerce, the opportunities of ice-free ports, and the Sino-Japanese war combined to end the thirty years of inactivity and indifference by Russia to Pacific events.

The United States, Britain, and Russia now had transcontinental railway routes to the Pacific to strengthen their aspirations in eastern Asia. Within a short time Russia was planning branches southward, and thus it became one of the international groups vying for the rights of railway construction in China. Its ambitions were to meet strong opposition from other nations, including the United States, which had aspirations for Manchurian trade and investment, but the strongest opposition came from Japan.

THE MEIJI OR RESTORATION PERIOD (1868-1912)

The concessions granted by Japan to Commodore Perry were followed by subsequent agreements to other foreign demands which resulted in a decade of dissension in Japan. The pragmatic Tokugawa Shogun had recognized the weakness of the country in the face of foreign threats and had, unhappily, accepted the treaty requirements. Other clans, who were strongly opposed to this submission as well as to the resulting increase in the number of foreign visitors and the return of the Christian religion, encouraged resistance against the foreigners. In 1862 when an English merchant, C. L. Richardson, was killed, Britain demanded an indemnity and enforced this by a naval shelling of Kagoshima. The following year when some Japanese fired on a number of foreign vessels, American ships retaliated by shelling their forts and French troops landed to destroy them. In 1864 anti-foreign demonstrations led to warships from Britain, France, Holland, and the United States shelling and destroying forts protecting Shimonoseki Strait. It was obvious that, as in China, the powers would act in concert to enforce the treaties, and, after this display, they did not again need to threaten force. In 1873, when Japan negotiated a treaty with Italy, the treaty was successfully opposed by the other powers, which were intent on maintaining their special positions.

Even before Perry's visit there had been signs of growing unrest and a weakening of the shogunate. The rigid classification into classes, the large number of unemployed *samurai* (professional warriors) and others, the growing wealth of merchants whose positions were unrecognized, the ambitions of rival clan leaders, the disruption caused by the introduction of western technology, and the miserable conditions of the peasants all served to keep the country in turmoil. The divisions among the ruling classes caused by disagreement over the foreign treaties brought all these factors of discontent to a climax and resulted in far-reaching reforms.

These had started soon after Perry's visit. The Dutch were asked to give technical guidance. Education, especially in the sciences, was encouraged. A mission was sent to the United States to report on western customs and was in New York when the immense *Great Eastern* arrived on its maiden voyage. Steamships were bought and manned by Dutch-trained Japanese crews. The country was preparing for the reform period which began in 1868.

The "Era of Enlightenment" (1868–93) had several underlying objectives. The "spirit of Japan," the pattern of Japanese life and national unity, was to be maintained. Japan would accept western material techniques but would preserve its own way of life as much as possible. Foreign domination must be ended. At the same time Japan must become recognized as an equal of the great powers. To its leaders this not only meant that Japan must become strong militarily but also that it must adopt those extrinsic ways of life which prevailed in Europe and the United States. Such objectives could be achieved most quickly by establishing friendly relations with other nations. The United States was sympathetic to Japanese efforts to modernize their country and in 1873 signed a convention which recognized Japanese equality, a move which aroused resentment from the other powers.[7]

Revolutionary changes were introduced into Japan over the following years. In 1868 the power of shogun was ended and the emperor was restored as the head of state with an assertion of his divinity and sacred origin. He was the head of the armed forces and had the power of veto over the cabinet, which was responsible to him. A constitution inaugurated a government of two houses. At first the suffrage was narrowly limited to landowners, but it was progressively extended until 1928 when universal manhood suffrage was granted. The constitution was modified over the years, but in the end was similar to that of Prussia, by which the power of the assembly was limited. Serfdom was abolished and peasants were encouraged to own land. The army and navy were reorganized—the army on French and German patterns, the navy on that of Britain. Conscription was introduced. New codes of law were established. Foreign scientists and experts were employed to build Japanese industry and to train the Japanese. Japanese steamship companies with government subsidies eventually controlled the coastal trade and expanded into overseas markets. Factories and railways were built and the mechanics of international trade studied. Compulsory education was introduced and universities were established, although these were controlled so that the curriculum would indoctrinate students with loyalty to the state. With government support students were sent abroad to study western technology and sciences. Religious toleration (as a sop to foreigners) was nominally accepted. Western modes of living were adopted in dress, social customs, entertainment, and food.

The Japanese had again shown their ability to adjust to outside pressures, as they had done many years before when faced with Chinese influences. Whereas the refusal of the Chinese in the nineteenth century to accept innovations from industrial societies had resulted in forced subjugation, the Japanese had accepted western advances to their own lives and encouraged western assistance in change. Although this ability to adjust was probably the major reason for Japan's escape from the domination of foreign powers as had occurred in China, other factors also may have had an influence in checking foreign aggression. The distraction of the Indian mutiny, the Franco-Prussian War, the American Civil War, and the rivalry of Russia and Britain may have diluted and diverted the attention of Europe and the United States from Japan during these critical years of adjustment.

JAPAN TESTS EXPANSION

During the years of reform, tentative trials of military strength were made. The Ryukyu Islands had their own king, who considered himself to be independent but who had historically paid tribute to China and, for some time following the conquest of the islands by a Japanese baron, to Japan. The king signed his own treaties with foreign nations, such as the one he had signed with Perry. In 1872 the Japanese proclaimed ownership, abducted the king, and forced him to accept Japanese rule.

In 1873 when two shipwrecked seamen were murdered in Formosa, an expedition was sent against the island. Foreign nations protested, Britain mediated, China agreed to pay an indemnity, and Japan withdrew. Included in the agreement was indemnity for damages to Japanese in the Ryukyus, a clause which China did not realize the Japanese would use to claim sovereignty of the islands. The Japanese continued to administer the Ryukyus, but they remained a source of contention with China. In 1875 the Bonin Islands, which had at times been claimed by Britain and the United States, were recognized by the western powers as Japanese.

For over three centuries Korea had been largely ignored by China, although the rulers admitted the suzerainty of China and sent annual tribute to the emperor. The Koreans were a proud people, determined to maintain their independence, who remembered that the peninsula had been occupied by the Japanese for a short time in 1598. A French invasion in 1866 was repulsed. After the crew of the wrecked American bark *Rover* had been murdered by the Koreans in 1867, the United States sent two ships of the China squadron in reprisal, but they were driven off. The ensuing suggestions that Korea should be invaded were cancelled.[8]

In 1872 Japanese envoys who attempted to negotiate a treaty were insulted and dismissed. The Japanese approached China hoping to make an agreement on Korea, but the appeal was refused. The Japanese believed that some agreement on Korea was important not only because of its economic potential and its proximity to Japan but also because they feared that Russia, in its search for an ice-free port, might seize one in Korea. This fear was not unfounded, since the Russians did try to obtain Port Lazaroff until they were discouraged by protests from both China and Japan. Japan decided on "gunboat" diplomacy and sent a naval force to the Korean coast, which was fired upon. China vacillated. In the face of force the Koreans unwillingly signed their first treaty with a modern power, the Treaty of Kanhwa, in 1876. Japan was to have two ports with extraterritoriality and would recognize the independence of Korea.

China had lost all of its dependencies, including Burma and Annam, except for Korea, so it refused to recognize Korean independence and to accept a treaty signed by Korea. The United States offered to mediate and signed the first western power treaty with Korea (1882), providing for peace and friendship but admitting Korea's dependence on China. As the treaty was signed with Korea it would, in fact, seem to indicate that the United States in reality recognized its independence. In the following four years Great Britain, Germany, Italy, Russia, and France signed similar treaties, in each of which was a clause recognizing Korea's dependent position on China. With the treaties the persecution of Roman Catholic missionaries ended, and in 1885 the first Presbyterian and Methodist missions were established.

Anti-Japanese riots broke out in the peninsula and revolution threatened. The king apologized to Japan and paid an indemnity. Chinese–Japanese relations over Korea continued to deteriorate until 1885 when a compromise (the Li–Itō Convention) was negotiated. Both sides withdrew their troops and agreed to warn the other if either had any intention of sending soldiers to Korea.

THE SINO–JAPANESE WAR

The anti-foreign demonstrations, largely against the Japanese, expanded into rebellion. In 1894 the Korean government appealed to China for aid, and a small force was sent. Japan claimed that China had broken the previous agreement and therefore Japan intervened, resolved to drive the Chinese out of Korea. The Sino–Japanese war was short and decisive. The Chinese fleet was destroyed, and Japanese forces successfully invaded Manchuria and occupied Port Arthur on the Liaotung Peninsula.

The Treaty of Shimonoseki (1895) was severe. Korea became independent. Japan annexed Formosa, the Pescadores, and the Liaotung Peninsula and received a large indemnity. Four Chinese ports were opened to the Japanese.

The European powers viewed Japan's success and especially the threat of territorial annexation with mixed feelings. Britain did not want to take any action which would result in a Japanese–Russian entente. The United States remained uninvolved, although Theodore Roosevelt had warned Germany and France that if they made any move against the Japanese he would support Japan.[9] Although German traders and whalers had appeared in the Pacific Islands and Hawaii before 1850, and German traders had been increasing rapidly after that time, Germany did not extend its economic interests to political involvement until the 1890's and therefore remained aloof from this conflict. France was occupied in Indochina. Russia had problems in interior Asia and at the time of the war was adjusting to changes brought about by Tsar Alexander III. Moreover, the Trans-Siberian Railway was far from complete, garrisons were small, and the Pacific fleet had been allowed to disintegrate. Thus the western powers did nothing.

The war, combined with the Russian setbacks in the Balkans and central Asia, resulted in a revival of Russian naval interest in the Pacific. In 1894 Japan had passed a regulation that only two foreign vessels could stay in a Japanese port at one time, which meant that the Russian fleet, which had regularly used Japanese ports during the winter when Vladivostock was frozen, had lost its winter bases. The need for an ice-free port became more pressing. Such a port could be in Korea or Manchuria; hence it was to Russia's advantage to have an independent Korea while at the same time expanding its influence in Manchuria. To advance these plans Russia enlarged its Pacific fleet. Before the peace treaty was signed, with the support of Germany (which was interested in diverting Russia from the Balkans and Europe) and France (with which it had just signed a defensive entente), Russia demanded that Japan return the Liaotung Peninsula and Port Arthur as well as agreeing on the independence of Korea. For these concessions Japan would receive a larger Chinese indemnity. Faced by these three powers Japan was forced to agree.[10] The importance of the decision on Korea was seen in the following years when its trade increased with Japan, England, the United States,

Germany, and China. Foreign capitalists invested in railways and electrical industries, and gained concessions in the resources—for example, an American company held 500 square miles of gold-mining territory. The great majority of concessions were in Japanese hands.

The Sino–Japanese War marked a turning point in the history of the North Pacific. An Asiatic nation had defeated China and had become one of the imperialists. Within a short time most of the foreign concessions in Japan were ended. The British had terminated extraterritoriality and had restored tariff control before the end of the century. On the other hand, the easy victory of the Japanese in 1894 marked the national awakening of the Chinese to their own helplessness. An embryonic patriotism stirred within the Chinese people.[11]

The war had united the political factions of Japan and had inspired an enthusiastic nationalism. Success had enflamed this spirit. The loss of territories gained by the war but lost by the intervention of three distant nations intensified the anti-foreign sentiment. Russia was especially blamed and condemned for the withdrawal. Japan realized that recognition of its position as a nation of equal status to others depended on even greater military strength, thus beginning a militaristic nationalism which it was to foster for half a century. Japan indicated its entry into imperialistic ambitions by supplying one-half of the international force which relieved Tientsin during the Boxer Rebellion, for which contribution it received a share of the Boxer indemnities.

Following the Treaty of Shimonoseki, Russia and China signed a defensive alliance—obviously against Japan—and to facilitate the movement of troops Russia was permitted to build railways through Manchuria to Korea and Vladivostock, a route considerably shorter than that via the Amur River and the coast. At the same time Russia and Japan agreed to equal rights in Korea. However, two years later China leased the ports of Dairen and Port Arthur to Russia for twenty-five years. By 1902 Russia had extended its railways to Port Arthur and could use it as a naval base. As Russia now had its warm-water port as well as a stranglehold on the economy of Manchuria, it could afford to permit Japan to increase its interests in Korea. To protect its railways during the Boxer Rebellion, Russia moved troops into Manchuria. This move was supported by France and Germany, but Britain and Japan, who feared that this was the first step towards permanent occupation, forced Russia to make an agreement with China promising to withdraw its troops. To mollify Britain, Russia also agreed not to build railways south of the China Sea, and Britain reciprocated by agreeing not to build them north of the sea.

During the last half of the nineteenth century Russia and Britain had been competing in the Balkans and south-west Asia, and they now were meeting on the Asiatic Pacific coast. Japan, resentful of Russia's actions after the Sino–Japanese War and its continuing expansion, was using the huge Boxer indemnity to build its war machine. In 1902, following Britain's isolation by the European nations after the South African War, an Anglo-Japanese Agreement was signed. The pact ended Britain's period of Splendid Isolation, permitted Britain to concentrate its naval power nearer home, and accepted Japan as an equal international power. It was obviously anti-Russian and had the objective of neutralizing the strong Russian Pacific fleet. A further agreement between Japan and Britain to guarantee the integrity of China and Korea not only checked further Russian expansion but also established a buffer state between Russia and Japan.

In three hundred years of contact with China (and less with Japan) Russia had never resorted to war to gain its ambitions. While other nations extended their control by force, Russia had remained aloof, gaining concessions through negotiations. Russia was not averse to making acquisitions through the militaristic efforts of other nations; often it shared in the profits from treaties or made "requests" in times of defeat, dissension, or chaos. At such times its claims were for sparsely occupied lands on the outskirts of the empire contiguous to Russia. Unlike other foreigners, Russia did not try to impose religious beliefs on China. During the Boxer Rebellions, Russia sent only a token force in the siege of Peking, but it received twenty-nine per cent of the indemnities. Its military occupation of Manchuria during the rebellion was for a short time, but by treaty it obtained economic concessions, railway rights, and a naval base.

THE SCRAMBLE FOR PORTS

At the end of the nineteenth century European nations commonly bartered colonies in return for concessions. Doctrines for "spheres of influence" were outlined at the Berlin Conference of 1884–85. For political reasons Germany encouraged France in Tunis (1881) and Italy in Tripoli (1911). Britain encouraged France in Morocco in return for its acceptance of British predominance in Egypt and Sudan (1898). Germany surrendered claims to Uganda and Zanzibar in return for Helgoland (1890). Britain and Russia agreed that Afghanistan should remain as an independent buffer state (1885). Asia became a new potential for colonial bargaining.

A race for Asiatic concessions by rival European nations followed the Treaty of Shimonoseki. Germany, France, and Russia had forced Japan to return Port Arthur to China. Port Arthur was then occupied by Russia. In the 1890's Britain, Germany, Belgium, France, and the United States eagerly sought rights to build railways in China as sources of investment as well as a means of controlling the neighbouring country.[12] Russia's extensions into Manchuria were typical of this pattern. In Korea, Europeans, Americans, and Japanese vied for trade and investment opportunities. The murder of two

German missionaries by bandits gave Germany an excuse for sending a naval force to China. Faced with this threat China was forced to grant Germany control of Kiaochow and the Shantung Peninsula. With these annexations Germany became an active participant in the intrigues of Far Eastern diplomacy. France took Kwangchow and expanded its control to Indochina, while in 1898, Britain obtained a ninety-nine-year lease in the New Territories.[13] By 1900 there were forty-six treaty ports in China where foreigners had special privileges, over one-half of which were British.[14] Western nations had concessions in thirteen of the eighteen provinces of China. Between 1900 and 1914 foreign investments doubled in China. Of these investments the British had thirty-seven per cent, Russia and Germany each had sixteen per cent, Japan had fourteen per cent, France had nine per cent, and the United States had three per cent.[15] There were also ceded areas such as Hong Kong, Weihaiwei, and Port Arthur.

By the treaty of 1895 Japan was to occupy the port of Weihaiwei on the north coast of the Shantung Peninsula until China's indemnity was paid. Britain, in return for guarantees that the Yangtze Valley would not be conceded to other powers, loaned China the money to pay the indemnity, and Japan therefore withdrew from the port. Port Arthur is only eighty miles from Weihaiwei, and to check further Russian expansion the Chinese leased Weihaiwei to Britain, the lease "to remain in effect as long as Port Arthur shall remain in the occupation of Russia," although Britain kept it after the Russo–Japanese War.[16] Britain had checked Germany's threat of moving into the Yangtze, had stopped its expansion on Shantung, and had parried Russia's occupation of Port Arthur. Japan had gained a friend and shortly the agreement of co-operation was signed with Britain.

THE UNITED STATES ENTERS ASIA

Within a year of its independence the United States had entered the China trade through Canton. In the ensuing years, often backed by capitalists from the American eastern ports, the Americans not only traded around the Cape of Good Hope but also became predominant in the maritime fur trade off the north-west coast. By the 1820's American whalers were scouring the Pacific, and American missionaries were established in Hawaii and other Pacific islands.

Involved with their own territorial expansion and dreams of Manifest Destiny, while at the same time condemning "imperialism" by others, the Americans did not seek to gain trading privileges by force. They believed that a better policy would be to encourage friendship with the Chinese, although they always protected their own rights and obtained privileges and extra-territorial rights comparable to the more aggressive Europeans. In the First

Opium War, the Americans in Canton, who were also selling opium, accepted the demands of the Chinese and, when the British withdrew, remained in the factory. The Americans acted as middlemen conveying goods between the British and Chinese merchants, a practice from which all profited. Shortly after the British forced China to accept the Treaty of Nanking, the United States signed the Treaty of Wanghai, by which they gained comparable privileges. Similarly, after the Treaty of Tientsin the United States made agreements protecting its rights of trade. However, whereas other nations were seeking territorial concessions, the United States concentrated on trading rights and the freedom of missionary activities.

While maintaining the facade of peaceful friendship with China, the United States was not averse to expanding into other strategic areas. Perry's visit to Japan carried a veiled threat which resulted in concessions by that country. Two years later Congress passed a law permitting the president to annex any island which was rich in the fertilizer guano, an important trading commodity. Thus in 1857 Baker Island was annexed, ten years later Midway, and in 1890, Wake. In 1878 a treaty with the ruler of Samoa gave the United States privileges including the right to establish a coaling station at Pago Pago. Here for the first time American interests in the Pacific clashed with the imperialistic plans of European nations; in this case both Germany and Britain protested. Negotiations and compromises extended over thirty years before the islands were divided between Germany and the United States. Thus, unobtrusively, the United States was extending its possessions in the Pacific by scattered holdings.

For over a decade after the Civil War the American navy was limited, but it began to grow rapidly as a result of the policies of President Garfield and the influential, persuasive writings of Captain Alfred Thayer Mahan. Mahan served in the United States navy for forty years, during which time he wrote twenty books seeking to arouse in Americans a recognition of their maritime responsibilities. His most famous book, *The Influence of Sea Power upon History* (*1660–1783*), was published in 1890. Translated into several languages, the book made a strong impression on the British and Germans, and has been credited with stimulating the increase in naval activities between 1900 and 1914. In analyzing the elements of sea power, Mahan claimed that the sea was the decisive factor in history and was related to military, national, territorial, and commercial developments. He stressed that military and commercial control of the sea was dependent on naval strength. As for the United States, Mahan noted that "except for Alaska, not a foot [of the United States] is inaccessible by land ... the weakest frontier, the Pacific, is far removed from the most dangerous possible enemies."[17] Within a decade of the book's publication, the United States was to control important, distant Pacific territories and Mahan was to serve in the Spanish–American War. Mahan was responsible for the foundations of American naval power, without which the influence of the United States in the Pacific would have been negligible at the turn of the century.

While the scramble for possessions was going on after the Sino–Japanese War, the United States became involved in the Spanish–American War over Cuba. This war gave it an excuse to invade the Philippines while at the same time annexing Hawaii, where it had established a coaling station at Pearl Harbor in 1887. An American fleet under Commodore Dewey captured Manila and with the help of anti-Spanish insurgents soon controlled the islands. When the insurgents realized that they were not to be independent but were exchanging Spanish rule for American, they rebelled against their "liberators" and were not suppressed for many years. By the Peace of Paris the United States paid $20 million for the Philippines and Guam.[18] The United States had become an overseas imperial power with the responsibility of protecting far-distant possessions. The Philippine invasion made little impression, on the Pacific coast states, especially Washington, which was more involved in the Klondike gold rush, although some recruits had been sent from western America.

At the same time the United States was alarmed by the increasing territorial concessions which threatened to close China to American interests. The United States differed from western Europe in that it had not been territorially aggressive in China. Secretary Hay sent a note proposing an "Open Door" policy to Britain, Germany, France, Italy, Russia, and Japan. This policy supported equality of opportunities for commercial interests and the guarantee of Chinese territorial integrity. With the exception of Russia, without definite commitment, the powers accepted this proposal in theory. Instead of territorial annexation they agreed to individual spheres of influence for economic control and exploitation. The answers were generally vague, but as there was no definite refusal the United States adopted the belief that the "Open Door" was an accepted policy. By 1900 the partition of the North Pacific seemed to be complete.

THE BOXER REBELLION

The increasing domination by Europeans roused a wave of anti-foreign demonstrations throughout China. The Boxer Rebellion was basically a protest against the foreign presence as well as against the weakness and corruption of the Manchu Dynasty, but the empress successfully diverted the uprising against only the foreigners. The eight western nations co-operated to crush the rebellions with a force of 18,000 (of whom 8,000 were Japanese and 2,500 were Americans) which relieved the siege of Peking. This was the first invasion of the Asiatic mainland by the United States. Once again large indemnities were levied against China.

Some years after the rebellion, Sun Yat-sen stated that even in 1900 the Chinese could not believe that western civilization was superior to that of the Chinese, and in order to demonstrate the greatness of Chinese civilization the Boxers insisted on using broadswords against rifles and cannons, with a resulting heavy death toll. He pointed out that the Boxer Rebellion did have two significant effects on Chinese relationships with foreigners. The Chinese finally recognized that, in some ways, the foreign civilization had advantages over the Chinese and a strong movement developed to accept and imitate foreign ideas. At the same time the rebellion revealed that the Chinese still had a "nationalistic spirit which could not be crushed."[19]

Even during the co-ordinated campaigns the international suspicions and rivalries were apparent. Russia used the war as an excuse to invade Manchuria —a move successfully checked by Britain and Japan. Other issues included the hesitation about using Japanese troops in international armies, Russia's fear of Japanese expansion, Wilhelm II's opposition to the "Yellow Peril," Britain's desire to gain the support of Germany against its traditional enemy Russia, and the mistrust by both Germany and Britain of the recent Franco–Russian Alliance. Even the final indemnity figures were not established for some time because of disagreements among the victorious nations.[20]

Events in Asia were one phase of the diplomatic manoeuverings through which European nations were attempting to increase their respective powers and prestige. The United States's desire to remain isolated from these intrigues was only partially successful. One outcome of the European power struggle was the showdown between Russia and Japan.

THE RUSSO–JAPANESE WAR

Manchuria, rich in agricultural and mineral resources, but part of China, attracted both Russia and Japan. Russia, by treaty, had gained special privileges in Manchuria. Japan hoped to come to an agreement with Russia which would limit these gains while at the same time obtaining recognition for its special rights in Korea. Russia vacillated, meanwhile building up its eastern army by means of the newly completed Trans-Siberian Railway. In 1904 Japan sent another request to Russia, outlining its demands for full authority in Korea and for a share in the economy of Manchuria. Russia did not answer.

In 1904, without warning, the Japanese navy destroyed the Russian fleet at Port Arthur, and at the same time Japanese troops invaded Manchuria from several points. The next day Japan declared war. The few remaining Russian naval vessels in the area were soon eliminated. A large fleet sent from the Baltic was not permitted by Britain to use the Suez Canal or any British ports and was forced to make the long journey around the Cape of Good Hope. In Tsushima Straits thirty-two of the thirty-five Russian ships were destroyed by the Japanese fleet. On land, bitter, indecisive fighting ensued as the Russians withdrew. Port Arthur was captured after a five-month siege, and Mukden fell after a battle which involved 750,000 men.

Both sides were now in trouble. Japan had not gained the swift decisive victory it had expected and Russian reinforcements were arriving at the front. Japan was financially strained and physically exhausted. Russia had lost several costly battles, its navy was destroyed, and it was faced with revolution at home. Neither side wanted an international peace conference—Russia remembered the Treaty of San Stefano and Japan remembered the Treaty of Shimonoseki. When President Theodore Roosevelt offered to mediate his proposal was accepted.

The peace agreement was signed at Portsmouth, New Hampshire, and was comparatively lenient. Russia recognized Japan's special interests in Korea (in 1910 it was annexed and given the Japanese name of Chosen), gave up the southern half of Sakhalin, surrendered its lease of the Liaotung Peninsula with Port Arthur, and surrendered parts of the South Manchurian Railway. Much against Japanese wishes, there was no indemnity, largely because of the influence of Roosevelt. Manchuria was to remain part of China, but an open door policy was proclaimed for all foreigners. In succeeding years Russia and Japan concluded a number of supplementary agreements by which north Manchuria was to remain under Russian influence and the south under Japanese. Communication and transportation were co-ordinated, and each country was to have the right to install guards to protect its railways. The Russian drive southward along the Pacific coast had passed its peak of expansion.

The moderate terms of the treaty were a disappointment to many Japanese, and riots had to be suppressed. Nevertheless, the war contributed another facet to Pacific history. For the first time a European power had been defeated by an Asiatic nation on both land and sea, and Japan had asserted its position among the great military powers. To the nationalistic movements in other Asiatic countries, the war was an encouragement in their efforts to regain independence. "Japan's rise has raised the standing of all Asiatic peoples."[21]

The war also illustrated the increased awareness of the United States in Far Eastern affairs. During the war the Taft–Katsura agreement of 1905 recognized Japanese control of Korea in return for Japanese assurances that it had no aggressive designs on the Philippines. In 1905, when the Korean king asked for assistance to stop Japanese control, Theodore Roosevelt refused and closed the American legation at Seoul.[22] Both the United States and Britain were pro-Japanese, the former concerned with maintaining the open door in the face of Russian expansion into Manchuria, the latter opposed to any Russian expansion. The Anglo–Japanese Alliance was broadened and strengthened in 1907 and again in 1911. A period of adjustment and apparent conciliation followed the war. With some relief from the Russian threat in the Pacific and faced with the increasing competition of Germany, Britain joined France and Russia in the Triple Entente in 1907. In the same year an agreement on the integrity of China was signed by Japan, Russia, and China, and a year later Japan and the United States agreed to uphold the *status quo.*

Eleven years after the Boxer Rebellion, a more successful rebellion overthrew the Manchus in less than one hundred days, and the Chinese Republic, the first republic in Asia, was established. The founder of the Chinese Republic was Dr. Sun Yat-sen, who upheld the three principles of "Nationalism, Democracy, Livelihood (Social Well-being)." Dr. Sun had been exiled in 1895 but in the following years directed from abroad at least fifteen uprisings before the 1911 success. After three months as president Dr. Sun yielded the office to the more aggressive Yüan Shih-kai.

The inefficient bureaucracy which had proven unable to adjust to western pressures ended, and, seemingly, an opportunity for changes and reforms had arrived. This was not to be, for the country, now deprived of its traditional leadership based on centuries of moral and political Confucian beliefs, was unable to substitute an adequate system offering transition from the established concepts to the new western ideas. As Dr. Sun stated later: "There has been no nation—our people have shown loyalty to family and clan but not to the nation."[23] China broke into fragments as "war lords," especially in the north, sought to gain control. Twenty years of fratricidal disorder were to delay unity and freedom from foreign control, even though Europe became involved in a disastrous war. When Dr. Sun Yat-sen died in Peking in 1925, there were some hopeful indications that the nation would be united by his party, the Kuomintang, under Chiang Kai-shek.

TRANSPACIFIC IMMIGRATION

The rapid expansion of improved railway and steamship lines brought to Asia the humanitarian, commercial, financial, and imperialistic interests of Europeans and Americans. The new transportation routes also offered means by which Asiatics could escape from their miserable living conditions. Thousands of Asiatics, searching for money, education, and status in distant places, left their homelands. Eventually they reached the Pacific coast of North America.

As in all of the United States, the peoples of the Pacific states were predominantly immigrants. The California gold rush had brought thousands from many parts of the world and this influx continued. The predominant stock was from the British isles, but there were French, Italians, Portuguese, Greeks, Germans, Swedes, and many others to overwhelm the native peoples and the early Spanish. As in other sections of the continent most of them assimilated, although in many cases groups would settle in specific localities where they would influence the economic, social, and cultural development.

Thus, the French and Italians expanded the wine industry of California, the Swedes turned to the forests, the Norwegians became fishermen.

British Columbia remained predominantly British. The early colony of Vancouver Island, controlled by the Hudson's Bay Company, received its traders, settlers, and miners from the company's ships. After the brief flurry of American miners to the gold rush, the colony of British Columbia, especially Vancouver Island, returned to its British traditions until the Canadian Pacific Railway was completed. Even after that, although a wide variety of settlers arrived by the railway, the Anglo-Saxon influence remained strong.

Some ethnic elements were unique to the Pacific coast. The native peoples were different from those of the east, economically and culturally. In California they had been strongly influenced by the early missions and remained as a decreasing insignificant people. The north-west Indians had at first traded as equals, but as the years passed they became dependent on the whites and their numbers were decimated by disease. The early history of the coast is interspersed with accounts of explorers, traders, and missionaries who were killed by dissatisfied natives. Sporadic uprisings occurred in Alaska, British Columbia, and Washington with short wars. All of these protests were suppressed, and the native peoples were forced to accept agreements or treaties which limited their territories or restricted their activities. Over a century of degradation was to pass before the question of Indian rights was to be revived and their claims to citizenship recognized.

In California during the Mexican régime, the missions had been stripped of their wealth and influence. The early Americans ignored the Spanish and Mexican heritage, and it faded into insignificance. Although historians revived an interest in the early Spanish backgrounds of the state and the missions became well-publicized tourist attractions, the people remained as a minority suppressed group. This attitude against "Mexicans" was intensified in the first half of the twentieth century when migratory labour was imported for harvesting and other unskilled, low-paying work.

THE CHINESE

Conspicuously different from the other immigrants to the west coast were those from the Orient, especially China, Japan, India, and, in the case of California, the Filipinos. At first these were to be found only on the west coast, and it was not until the twentieth century that significant numbers began to spread eastward.

The first recorded Chinese immigration occurred when John Meares attempted to establish a colony of Chinese labourers at Nootka, but these were taken to Mexico with Meares's captured crews and their fate is unknown. Over fifty years were to pass before other Chinese settlers arrived.

During the early years of the nineteenth century numerous Chinese began to migrate to neighbouring lands as labourers. The forcible removal of native peoples ("blackbirding") under conditions little better than slavery was comparable in the South Seas to the slave trade in Africa. "The so-called Pig Trade: from 1847 Chinese labourers were illegally and against the protests of the Imperial government, being shipped to mines, estates and plantations in the colonies in place of slave labour."[24] The common practice with Chinese was to take them as indentured workers under contract to various regions which required cheap labour. The contractors controlled the emigrants until they either accepted a "head tax" on delivery or until they had collected the advance fares, charges, and profit. The Chinese came from poor districts and were willing to accept these conditions with the expectation that they would earn capital with which they would return to their homeland and families. The first emigrants were taken to countries close to China, but they were soon taken to more distant places where foreign owned plantations needed cheap labour. In 1851 the first regular recruits by contract arrived in Hawaii, and ten years later there were 1,300, many of whom had come from California. Besides those working on the plantations there were many who opened stores or restaurants.

The first large influx to America came during the California gold rush (see Table 2).[25] Ostracized by the white miners and not as impatient for wealth, they worked the poorer abandoned placer mines. Most of the Chinese turned to menial labour or opened restaurants and laundries. The *London Times* in 1854 reported that immigration of Chinese to California was beginning to attract attention and to excite complaints, with the following description of their arrival: "During the fortnight from the 11th to 26th August the arrival of Chinese passenger ships amounted to ten in number, the passage varying from 43 to 300 days. One vessel reports 100 deaths, another 85, and so on to match; for the poor wretches are crowded between decks."[26] In 1849 twenty thousand Chinese emigrated to California, forming ten per cent of the population, a percentage which was to be maintained into the 1860's. To discourage immigrants who were not English-speaking, a foreign miner's tax of twenty dollars per month was imposed. This tax covered native Indians as well as Spanish-speaking Mexicans and Chinese. The tax was repealed in 1851, revived against the Chinese in the following year, and finally repealed in 1870.[27]

About the same time a few Chinese came to Vancouver Island, where they were accepted and opened businesses. With the British Columbia gold rush came a large influx, some from California. As in California, the influx of a large number of competitive alien people resulted in opposition and ostracism. Not welcomed by the white communities, the Chinese worked the poorer bars, gleaning what the whites left behind. Many became labourers while others opened small businesses or became gardeners (see Table 3).

TABLE 2: IMMIGRATION BY COUNTRY TO THE UNITED STATES, 1854–1970

	China	India	Japan	Korea	Philippines	Canada
1854	13,100					6,891
1860	5,467	5				4,514
1870	15,740	24	48			40,414
1880	5,802	21	4			99,744
1890	1,716	43	691			183
1900	1,247	9	12,635			396
1910	1,968	1,696	2,720			56,555
1920	2,330	300	9,432			96,025
1930	1,589	110	837			66,254
1940	643	52	102			11,078
1950	1,280	121	100	24	729	21,885
1960	1,380	244	5,699	1,410	2,791	46,668
1965	1,611	467	3,468	2,139	2,963	50,035
1970	6,427	8,795	4,731	8,888	30,372	26,850

Source: Historical Tables of the United States, C89–119, U.S. Department of Commerce, Bureau of Statistics.

TABLE 3: ORIENTAL IMMIGRATION TO CANADA

	Chinese	Japanese	East Indians
1887	124	—	—
1892	3,282	—	—
1897	2,471	691	—
1902	3,587	165	—
1907	291	2,042	2,124
1912	6,581	765	3
1917	343	648	—
1922	1,746	471	13
1927	2	511	56
1932	1	119	61
1937	1	146	11
1942	—	—	3
1947	21	2	149
1952	2,320	7	172
1957	1,686	185	334
1962	876	154	850
1967	4,142	503	5,827
1972	6,372	718	6,342*
1976	11,558†	498	8,985*

Source: Canada Year Book, various years.
† includes 10,725 from Hong Kong; * includes India, Pakistan, Bangladesh.

The similarity between the first large influx of Chinese in British Columbia and California was to continue, and the attitudes of the white people in both places were comparable for a century. Toward the end of the nineteenth century Washington and Oregon were to establish the same patterns. With the fading of the gold rushes came periods of unemployment and depression and the first strong criticism of the Chinese. The building of railways created a demand for labour which was most easily obtained from China. "The Central Pacific brought in coolies at 15,000 a year contracted by the Six Companies, a Chinese organization in San Francisco."[28] Fifteen years later in British Columbia, Andrew Onderdonk was forced to import fifteen thousand Chinese to build the western section of the Canadian Pacific Railway. Following the completion of the railroads, unemployment rose again and opposition to the Chinese resurfaced.

The United States, maintaining its policies of friendship and neutrality towards China, signed the Burlingame Treaty in 1868.[29] The Chinese were to have full rights to emigrate to the United States where they could have the same rights as other foreigners to settle, travel, or attend school, but not the right of naturalization, in return for which Americans were to be free to travel in China. However, by this time, discrimination was already obvious in the United States with the special tax on Chinese miners and the ineligibility of Chinese for citizenship. In 1871 riots in Los Angeles resulted in the killing of 122 Chinese.

With the completion of the railways there was increasing opposition to the Chinese, fanned by rumours and propaganda. It was stated that Chinese could not be assimilated. Stories circulated regarding their morals, especially concerning opium smoking and prostitution. They were portrayed as being satisfied with poor living standards and living mainly on rice. They spent very little, since they either sent their money back to China or saved it so they could return with it to their homeland. Numerous occupations were closed to them. In British Columbia, many municipal contracts forbade the use of Chinese labour, while in California in 1870 laws were passed prohibiting corporations from employing Chinese. Unaccepted in white communities, and often for protection, the Chinese tended to gather together and form crowded "Chinatowns." As the years passed some became successful businessmen opening trading companies, restaurants, laundries, and other enterprises. Others took the poorer paying labouring jobs which were open to them, such as working in the fields or coal mines. They were not permitted to fish, but they could work in canneries. Many entered domestic service, and most well-to-do families had their Chinese "boy" or cook.

In 1866 Mark Train had forecast that Americans would be forced to use Chinese labour because of its low cost.[30] American labour unions recognized this threat and by the 1870's were supporting the slogan "Chinese must go." Their influence spread to British Columbia, where opposition was becoming rabid. In 1877 during a strike at the Nanaimo coal mines on Vancouver Island the fact that Chinese continued to work led to violence, and ten years later a mob destroyed Vancouver's Chinatown. Anti-Chinese feelings in San Francisco reached a climax in the Sandlot riots. In 1885 demonstrations in several Washington communities resulted in some Chinese being killed, and for a short time, to prevent riots, Seattle was under martial law. At this time free passage was arranged from Seattle and over two hundred Chinese were shipped out to other places. Those left behind were attacked by a mob which was dispersed after one Chinese was killed. In the same year at Rock Springs in the Territory of Wyoming, one hundred and fifty white miners killed twenty-eight Chinese who refused to stop working during a strike. The enmity spread to Alaska where, in 1866, anti-Chinese riots occurred in Juneau. A house where Chinese were living was blown up and one hundred Chinese miners were taken from the Treadwell mine and were put on two small sailing vessels in which they reached Wrangell. After this Chinese in Alaska were not employed in mines and most worked in fish canneries.[31]

Public opinion, supported by strong pressures from the labour unions, forced state and provincial governments to take action, and presures were brought upon the federal governments of the United States and Canada. In 1882 the United States Congress suspended the immigration of Chinese labourers. The Chinese Exclusion Act was supposed to be for ten years, but it was renewed and amended in 1892, so that it actually lasted until 1943. The American action resulted in a bitter reaction in China where, for example, in 1905, the Chinese started a large-scale boycott of American goods to protest the treatment of Chinese in the United States.[37]

In 1883 the miners of British Columbia demanded that Orientals be excluded. Numerous provincial acts were disallowed by the federal government, which was anxious to maintain friendship with China in order to develop the trans-Pacific shipping and trade which were expected to follow the completion of the Canadian Pacific railway in 1885. Nevertheless, in that year a Dominion Franchise Act excluded Chinese (any person of the Chinese race) from voting and levied a head tax of $50 on every Chinese immigrant. This was raised to $100 in 1900 and $500 in 1905. The head tax resulted in some restriction, but as wages were rising and, more significantly, as contractors were willing to loan the increased levies against future wages, immigration increased. In the peak year of 1914 there were 7,078 Chinese immigrants.[33] Finally, in 1915, by order-in-council, skilled and unskilled labourers were forbidden to land in British Columbia ports. Thus Chinese immigration to both the United States and Canada had been discouraged.

THE JAPANESE

As the Chinese empire had no official representatives in foreign countries, the contracted Chinese labourers who left their homelands had no government support. On the other hand, the Japanese government was very interested in the well-being of its emigrant labourers. An example of this was shown in 1868 when the first contracted Japanese labourers were carried to work on the sugar plantations in Hawaii by a British ship without permission from the Japanese government. They were poorly treated, and when conditions did not improve following the protests of the Japanese government, the latter stopped emigration to Hawaii for twenty years.

The need of labourers in Hawaii (see Table 4) led to a convention in 1884 by which immigration was renewed on the understanding that the workers would be under the protection and supervision of the Japanese consuls. The immigrants were brought under a three-year contract, after which they were free. Some returned home, but most stayed to remain as plantation workers, to enter other employment, or to establish their own businesses. They established communities and a home life. Within a decade two-thirds of the plantation labour force was Japanese (see Table 5). In spite of the convention and the presence of consuls, they were poorly paid and often exploited. The sudden influx alarmed the resident islanders, but in 1897 when restrictions were imposed on immigration, Japan reaffirmed its concern by sending a number of naval vessels to "show the flag." This visit, with its implication of possible Japanese annexation, undoubtedly had an influence on the decision by the United States to annex the islands in the following year.

TABLE 4: IMMIGRATION TO HAWAII

	Chinese	Japanese	Portuguese	Filipinos
1852	293	—	—	—
1862	43	—	—	—
1868	51	148[1]	—	—
1872	61	—	—	—
1882	1,367	—	2,356[2]	—
1885	2,924	1,946	278	—
1892	—	3,129	—	—
1902	280	10,900	—	—
1912	491	3,465	860[3]	3,038[4]
1921	555	3,674	46	3,294

Source: "Memorandum on Introduction of Foreign Laborers into Hawaiian Islands," manuscript in Archives of Hawaii, 1931.
(1) no others until 1885; (2) 1882–84 total 7,700; (3) steady influx began 1911; (4) began about 1905.

With the Meiji or Restoration period in Japan came a rapid increase in population. Emigration was encouraged to Japanese possessions such as the northern island of Hokkaido. The *samurai* and the peasants suffered as Japanese industry expanded. An ambitious peasant could improve his conditions only by seeking industrial work or by emigrating. Thus, as with the early Chinese, there were men from the poorer districts, usually the south of Japan, who sought to make a stake which would establish them and improve their status in their home villages. During the early Meiji years several hundred Japanese students visited the United States and many stayed.

TABLE 5: ETHNIC STOCK, STATE OF HAWAII

	1853	1900	1940	1970	(%) 1970
Hawaiian	70,036	29,797	14,375	71,274[1]	9.3
Caucasian	1,687	26,819	112,087	301,429	39.2
Chinese	364	25,767	28,774	52,375	6.8
Filipino	5	—	52,569	95,354	12.4
Japanese	—	61,111	157,905	217,669	28.3
Total population	73,137	154,001	423,530	768,559	

Source: Data Book, State of Hawaii Department of Planning and Economic Development, Honolulu, 1976.
(1) includes part Hawaiian.

The great influx came within a few years after the Japanese emperor removed the general prohibition against emigration in the 1880's. Immigrants began to arrive on the west coast of Canada and the United States from both Hawaii and Japan. "Chinese Exclusion" now became "Oriental Exclusion." An example of the stereotyped attitudes of the time is shown by the following quotation:

> Unlike the Chinese these new settlers were not submissive and they threatened to take root in the country; these were strong men ... and they had the personal confidence which national greatness often gives and the assertion of which, to some extent, might have been excusable in such a new-born people; they were in contact with Canadians also more or less aggressive in character; they were in competition with some American labour interests which combined the characteristics of the continent with a certain in-born hatred of coloured races; very often they outworked the white men ... they had control to a considerable extent of the fishing interests of the Pacific coast; they created alarm in the matter of defence amongst people whose sympathies were American rather than Japanese and amongst people whose feelings favoured a United States alliance rather than that of Britain and Japan; they aroused racial fear amongst many ... as to how far the immigration might result in a Japanese rather than a white Province.[34]

Besides the fact that the Japanese government supported its immigrants there was the extra complication caused for Canada by the Anglo–Japanese Alliance. Canada was still a dependency of Britain, and Canadian (British Columbian) opposition to immigration was circumscribed by British foreign policies.

Canadians were divided on the problem. The Victoria Board of Trade passed a resolution "that the head tax on Chinese be reduced," while the Trades and Labour Congress "reaffirmed the principle of the present poll-tax of $500 on Chinese."[35] A petition from Vancouver women asked for the removal of the head tax in order to give them a chance to obtain domestic servants.[36]

Oriental Exclusion became a potent political factor on the west coast and led to acrimonious disputes between the province/states and federal governments. In the United States, where states have greater powers than Canadian provinces, state legislation was often successful, but numerous legal cases resulted from the problems of divided federal and state responsibility. In 1911 twenty anti-Japanese bills were proposed in the California legislature.[37]

When the San Francisco Board of Education segregated Japanese students in 1905, a wave of anti-American demonstrations spread throughout Japan, where the action was publicized in the press. President Roosevelt learned of the San Francisco decision through complaints from the government of Japan. After a long battle in the courts, the San Francisco Board agreed to rescind the legislation. At the same time President Roosevelt and the Mikado were attempting to restore friendly relations, and when the world-circling American "White Fleet" (showing the American flag) visited Japan, it received a warm welcome.

From these incidents resulted the "Gentlemen's Agreement" of 1907, by which the United States would permit Japanese children to attend public schools and Japan would refuse passports to skilled and unskilled labourers, thus drastically limiting emigration. The "Gentlemen's Agreement" was to last fifteen years. In the same year President Roosevelt forbade Japanese immigrants to enter the United States indirectly through Mexico and Canada. Meanwhile, following the Anglo–Japanese Alliance, Canada and Japan also signed a "Gentlemen's Agreement" limiting immigration in 1907. An American federal act of 1911 extended the scope of the act of 1882 which had prohibited Chinese from becoming citizens. Now citizenship would not be granted to others than whites or Africans.[38]

THE EAST INDIANS

A third Asiatic group which appeared about this time were the East Indians. About 1840, with the decline of slavery, indentured Indians were shipped to regions where workers were needed—south-east Asia, Indonesia,

Africa, the Fiji Islands, and the Caribbean countries. Others, who were merchants and traders, settled independently in distant places. From Mexico, the Caribbean, and Fiji the East Indians filtered into the United States. The immigration began about 1860, but the numbers were small and, as they were scattered throughout the United States, their presence was ignored. About 1900, East Indians began to arrive in larger numbers in the Pacific states and British Columbia. The reasons for this influx are uncertain. It may have been that Sikh soldiers, returning through Canada after participating in Queen Victoria's jubilee, carried home glowing reports of the opportunities in western North America. Undoubtedly, within a short time, steamship companies were spreading propaganda throughout India. The number of immigrants increased annually. In 1907 Canada officially recorded 2,124, while the United States recorded 1,072, but many others were entering illegally.

With their distinctive dress, the East Indians were obviously different. Now Oriental Exclusion was expanded to include the East Indians and, increasingly, demands were made that they be denied citizenship, that they not be employed, that immigration be stopped, and even that they be deported.[39]

In the United States, East Indians were to be found in all major centres of the Pacific coast. The American immigration authorities, influenced by the anti-Asiatic groups, applied rigid regulations, especially using health, in refusing admission. In 1908 a test case stated that an East Indian could never become a citizen of the United States. In Canada, once again, the British connection was a factor in regulations, for these people were members of the British Empire, and had the same British citizenship as Canadians. To handicap these immigrants, the Canadian government in 1908 passed the "continuous passage" legislation, which demanded that all immigrants come directly from their native country. (This also served to check those Japanese who were circumventing the Gentlemen's Agreement by infiltrating into Canada through Hawaii.)[40]

An attempt to challenge this legislation failed in what is known as the *Komagata Maru* incident. The *Komagata Maru* was a Japanese vessel chartered by an Indian businessman, Gurdit Singh, through a German shipping agent. The plan was to convey Indians from India directly to Canada. Unable to obtain a vessel in India, Gurdit had obtained the *Komagata Maru* in Hong Kong and in it he carried 376 passengers picked up in Hong Kong, Singapore, and Yokohama. The voyage had worldwide repercussions and revolutionaries in India used it for anti-British propaganda. British Columbians feared that it would be the first of many future shiploads of unwanted immigrants, the Canadian government saw it as a challenge to federal immigration laws, the British government was torn between its interests in India and Canada, the crew was Japanese, and there were also reports that Germany was encouraging the voyage in order to embarrass Britain and to increase its problems in India.

The vessel arrived in Victoria on 21 May 1914 after a voyage of eighteen days from Yokohama. After a brief stop for inspection it proceeded to Vancouver two days later, where its passengers (with a few individual exceptions) were forbidden to disembark. Here it remained for two months while angry citizens patrolled the waterfront and the case was fought in the courts. The legal decision upheld the illegality of this method of immigration and the *Komagata Maru* was ordered to leave. To enforce this order the cruiser *Rainbow* was brought to Vancouver and on 23 July it conducted the immigrant ship to the open ocean. Two months later the passengers were unloaded at Calcutta.

The East Indian problem of British Columbia had similarities to the Filipino question which was to rise in California in the 1920's. At that time the limitation of Orientals had caused a shortage of cheap labour, and this shortage was being relieved by Filipinos. As the Philippine Islands were American territory, exclusion was difficult to justify. The Filipinos themselves are an ethnic group, but to Californians they came from Asia and were classified with Chinese and Japanese, subject to the same discrimination.

In the prewar years demand for oriental exclusion increased. In 1907 a mob swept through Vancouver's oriental section destroying Chinese property, but it was repelled by the aggressive determination of the Japanese.[41] It was after these riots that Prime Minister Laurier appointed W. L. Mackenzie King to head a royal commission to assess and pay for losses sustained by Japanese and Chinese residents. Mackenzie King was deputy-minister in the Department of Labour. He had made several trips to the United States, where he had discussed the oriental immigration question with President Roosevelt. Roosevelt was apparently anxious that Britain and the United States should adopt common policies towards Asiatic immigration, and, later, when King visited Britain, he carried Roosevelt's ideas to the British government. King's interest in the opium question had been aroused when two opium factories in Vancouver claimed damages as a result of the riots, and in 1908 he attended the Shanghai opium conference. At this time, when few Canadians had any knowledge of the Far East, Mackenzie King was considered to be an authority.[42] However, in spite of his personal contacts with Roosevelt, both he and Laurier were suspicious of Roosevelt, who, they believed, was trying to involve Canada in his quarrel with Japan: "I thought the President and a large number of American citizens were only too glad to develop the opinion that the interests of the Canadian and American West were identical, and that the United States was the proper protector of the peoples of that shore... nothing would suit the purpose of the Americans better at this moment than that some such trouble should break out in Vancouver at the time the American fleet visited San Francisco."[43]

In 1913 another riot broke out in Nanaimo when Chinese were used as strike-breakers in the coal mines. In the same year a California law prevented the acquisitions by aliens of real property for the purpose of agriculture. The anti-oriental movement had repercussions in other parts of Canada; in 1912 Saskatchewan legislation forbade white women from working in places of business "managed by Oriental persons."[44] By 1914 the exclusion acts in the United States, the head tax in Canada, the quota on Japanese by the gentlemen's agreements, and Canada's "continuous journey" legislation had drastically limited oriental immigration and the percentage of population was declining.

THE ALASKA BOUNDARY

The Klondike gold rush of 1897–98 once again brought a flood of miners to the North Pacific. Between 54,000 and 64,000 miners reached the gold fields by various routes, but most arrived from ship from southern ports.[45] Arriving at Skagway, they faced an arduous hike through the American panhandle to the Klondike River in Canada's Yukon Territory. This boom, like that of California and British Columbia, lasted but a short time before it petered out.

The influx of miners revived an interest in the Alaska–British Columbia boundary. Negotiations on this question had been going on sporadically since 1884 with little success, largely because of Canada's unwillingness to compromise. The Klondike gold rush, the accession of Theodore Roosevelt to the presidency, and the desire of Britain for American friendship combined to force a decision. The boundary had been stated in the treaty of 1825 between Russia and Great Britain as "follow[ing] the summit of the mountains situated parallel to the coast...whenever the summit of the mountains... shall be more than ten marine leagues from the ocean the boundary line of British possessions shall be formed by a line parallel to the windings of the coast which shall never exceed the distance of ten marine leagues." The interpretation of this phrase was disputed—did this means ten leagues from the general coastline (as claimed by Canada) or did it mean from the heads of the long inlets?

Faced by the jingoistic Theodore Roosevelt, the British agreed to a commission of three "impartial judges" from each side. Three Americans, two Canadians, and one British representative were appointed. The Americans were known to be biased, and the British delegate was anxious to improve friendly relations with the United States. The resulting award was considered by many Canadians to be a British betrayal for its own interests. This dispute over a narrow strip of undeveloped wilderness, with few known resources, possibly allayed some British-American tension at the expense of increasing Canadian desires for greater autonomy, while at the same time reviving fears of American expansionism. With the decision, the complete land boundary between the United States and Canada was finally established.

RÉSUMÉ

Between 1870 and 1914 European imperialism passed its peak and began to decline. In China, where the Manchus had been displaced by republican China, Europeans still controlled the economy through concessions and treaties, but there was growing opposition to foreign control, frustrated by the uncertainties of unstable Chinese governments. The United States had entered the imperialistic race by annexing the Philippines and Hawaii but was still insisting on an open door policy for China. Russia had expanded to its most southerly Pacific point but had been forced to retreat from Port Arthur, southern Manchuria, and Korea by the military strength of Japan. Japan had shown that imperialism was not a European monopoly and that European armies were not invincible, but it had still to be accepted as an equal by the great powers.

Japan's position strengthened as the Anglo–French–Russian interests turned away from the Far East to the more imminent European threat of Germany. From this relaxation of aggressive involvement in the Far East the western European nations never recovered.

The uncertainty of the Asiatic Pacific coast was a contrast to the North American coast, where Canada and the United States had settled their boundary disputes and had entered a period of co-operation and friendship. Ties across the Pacific had been strengthened with the opening of transcontinental railways, trans-Pacific steamship lines, the laying of cables, the increase in trade, and the annexation by the United States of Pacific islands.

8

The Withdrawal of Europe
(1914–36)

If you look at a map of the world you will see that America has her back turned to us. (Count Aoki, Japanese Minister of Foreign Affairs, 1893).

I believe that our future history will be more determined by our position on the Pacific facing China, than our position on the Atlantic facing Europe. (President Theodore Roosevelt, 1905)

The First World War was fundamentally a European war, and the major decisions resulted from the war in Europe, although there were numerous minor campaigns scattered throughout the world. British Columbia and, later, the western states directed their war efforts towards helping the Allies against the Central Powers on the European front. On the Asiatic Pacific shores the stalemate in Europe offered an opportunity for Japan to expand its Asiatic interests.

JAPAN AND THE WAR

By this time Japan had visions of an East Asiatic community comprising Japan, China, and Manchuria, in which Japan would be the dominant partner. Therefore, using the Anglo–Japanese pact as an excuse, within three weeks of Britain's entry into the war Japan declared war on Germany. The British hoped to restrict the Japanese operations to the destruction of the German North Pacific fleet, without giving Japan an opportunity to injure British trade, but Japan's aims were broader than a limited patrol of the ocean. With Allied consent and active British support at Tsingtao, Japan proceeded to seize and occupy the German-controlled Shantung Peninsula as well as the Marianas, Caroline, and Marshall Islands. Protests from Australia resulted in Japan limiting itself to those German islands north of the equator, while Australia and New Zealand seized those to the south. Within a short time all German influence had been eliminated from the Pacific, and Japan was able to send four warships to the Mediterranean in 1917, the first Asiatic naval force to enter European waters.

With the Germans ousted from the Pacific, the European nations involved in a fratricidal war, and the Chinese Republic in disorder, the Japanese moved towards domination of China. In 1915 it presented China with Twenty-One Demands which would have resulted in control of the country. In spite of their commitments in Europe, the Allies, supported strongly by the United States, opposed these demands and forced their modification. The United States, not as yet an active participant in the war, feared that the Japanese move threatened the open door. Japan, nevertheless, retained a number of its demands and thus gained some expansion of its influence and authority. During the discussions in 1915 William Jennings Bryan, the secretary of state, said: "The United States frankly recognizes that territorial integrity creates special relations between Japan and Shantung and Manchuria." As a result of negotiations in 1917, by the Lansing-Ishii agreement the United States obtained an agreement on the territorial integrity of China in return for which it reaffirmed Japan's "special interests" in China "in view of territorial propinquity." The phrase "special interests" was to be exploited by the Japanese in the following years to the embarrassment of the United States and Britain.[1] In return for the American concession, Japan re-accepted the open door policy. No matter how conciliatory the language, the fact remains that the apparently innocuous phrases "special interests" and "open door" were interpreted differently by both countries, for, at their cores, they are contrary to each other.

THE SIBERIAN FIASCO

At the beginning of the war Russia had few naval vessels in the Pacific, and one of their two cruisers was sunk by the German raider *Emden*. When the German raiders had been eliminated from the Pacific, the remaining Russian ships were sent to the Mediterranean. Russia suffered during the war from its inability to obtain Allied supplies, the only routes being via Murmansk, which had no rail connections, or by the 6,000-mile Trans-Siberian Railway, and both were unsuitable for large shipments of supplies. "Russia completed new destroyers and submarines: some of the latter ... had been built in pieces in Canada, sent across the Pacific and then by Trans-Siberian railway, in packing cases to the Baltic and Black Seas."[2]

Shortly after the outbreak of the war, Czechoslovaks in Russia formed a separate brigade attached to the Russian army, in hopes of establishing an independent Czechoslovakia. During the revolution the Czechs remained as a unit and continued to support the tsar and Allied war cause. In March 1918 the Soviet government gave approval for the Czech brigade to leave

Russia by crossing Siberia. However, shortly after the Czechs had crossed the Urals, the Soviet leader Trotsky ordered them stopped, fearing that they might join the white armies in Siberia. The disciplined, well-armed Czechs seized part of the Trans-Siberian Railway and continued to move eastward against the opposition.

When the Russian Revolution broke out, large quantities of war materials had been accumulated in Vladivostock, and the Allies feared that these might fall into the hands of the Bolsheviks or Central Powers. The Allies also wished to encourage the beleaguered Czechs, with the hope that they would join the white army and continue the war against Germany. Ostensibly to help the Czechs, Britain sent a cruiser to protect the Vladivostock supplies. With most of its troops occupied in Europe, Britain asked Canada to supplement the "British" contingent. As most of the force was Canadian, the British force was under a Canadian commander, Major-General J. H. Elmsley, who was to work with the British war office but with the approval of the Canadian government. On 11 October the first Canadian troops, who included conscripts, sailed from Vancouver. Eventually 3,800 Canadians were in Vladivostock.

The British forces were soon joined by other Allied contingents. The Japanese were anxious to forestall any British or American influence in the nearby base of Vladivostock and the Amur River region, but they also recognized an opportunity to spread their own spheres of control. A heated discussion was held in the Japanese Diet on cabinet plans to send a large expedition to occupy independently sections of Siberia, but the major parties were opposed, so Japan decided to co-operate with the other expedition.

The United States also admitted its responsibility to help the Czechs, but it was more concerned that Britain and Japan might obtain special privileges, and, perhaps more significantly, it was opposed to the spread of Bolshevism. Thus the United States, whose only previous invasion of Asia had been during the Boxer Rebellion, reluctantly joined the British, Canadians, French, and Japanese in an invasion of eastern Russia. The United States and Japan had agreed to send 7,000 troops each, but the Japanese forces were almost ten times that number. While the others remained near the coast or close to the Trans-Siberian Railway, the Japanese moved inland and seized northern Sakhalin. Originally the invasion had two purposes—to revive Russia's participation in the war and to rescue the Czechs. When the armistice was signed in November, shortly after the arrival of the Canadian troops, there was some confusion among the allies as to their objectives in maintaining troops in Siberia, for obviously they were no longer fighting Germany.[3] They had become supporters of the vanishing white army. The Americans were still suspicious of the Japanese. The enterprise was not popular and was not supported by the peoples of Japan, Britain, Canada, or the United

States, wearied by years of war. Within three days of the Armistice, agitation was beginning in Canada for the return of its troops, but not until 5 June 1919 did the last one leave. Other troops, except the Japanese, were withdrawn within two years. The Japanese remained until 1922 and continued to occupy Sakhalin for an additional two years. The Czechs had escaped, many returning to their homeland through Canada. The Siberian expedition was dull, monotonous, and unpopular. Aside from addition to the mistrust of the communists for the Japanese, it had accomplished nothing.

ORIENTAL EXCLUSION

During the First World War Canada depended on the Japanese navy for protection of its west coast until the United States became an ally. Both Canada and the United States, although they were allies to Japan, were sympathetic to China in its opposition to the Twenty-One Demands. At home, with the demand for labour, oriental exclusion was put aside, and Chinese and Japanese immigrants contributed to the war effort at home and at the front.[4]

With the end of the war and the return of unemployed veterans, anti-oriental agitation revived. In the 1920's and 1930's the Chinese immigrants spread through the continent. Oregon and Washington were second to California in the number of Orientals, but whereas in California the great majority were in agriculture or fishing, in the other western states they became urbanized, establishing ghetto-like sections of cities and towns. In 1922 both California and Washington passed laws forbidding Japanese to own or lease agricultural land, and the following year several other states enacted similar legislation.[5] At this time Canada and the United States were both pressing for the termination of the Anglo–Japanese Alliance, and when they were successful the Gentlemen's Agreements ended.

In 1923 the Canadian Chinese Immigration Act (Chinese Exclusion Act), which was tightened in 1930, almost completely excluded Chinese, Japanese, and East Indian immigrants from Canada. The waves of European immigrants during the nineteenth century had filled most of the vast open spaces of the United States and satisfied the demands for labour, so steps were taken by the introduction of the quota system in 1912 to reduce the number of immigrants. Special restrictions were made against "unassimilable" Asiatics. The United States Immigration Act of 1924 (Exclusion Act) excluded the Japanese as "aliens ineligible for citizenship" and prohibited Filipinos from becoming citizens. A decade later the Philippine Independence Act of 1934 provided for an annual quota of fifty immigrants to the Hawaiian Islands and exclusion from the continental United States until the independence of the Philippines became complete. These acts, combined with growing resentment in Japan against the attitude of the League of Nations and the Washington Treaties, were followed by a period of anti-American riots and boycotts in Japan.

Thus, Asiatic immigration was apparently ended to the west coast. Canadian labour unions in the late 1920's decided that the solution for competition from cheap oriental labourers was to permit their membership in the unions, thus guaranteeing union wages for all. But the distrust continued and the Canadian- and American-Orientals, even to the third and fourth generation, remained "second class citizens."

THE PEACE TREATIES

In the Peace Conferences at Versailles, Japan was recognized as one of the "Big Five" powers, but as most of the proceedings were concerned with the adjustment of European problems, its contributions were minor. More significant to Pacific relationships than the treaties was the adoption of the League of Nations Covenant. As a permanent member of the League Council, Japan increased its prestige and had the power of veto. China as an allied power also attended the conferences, but its efforts towards greater autonomy and a relaxation of foreign controls met with little success.

The victorious powers were faced with the problem of rewarding the victors without seeming to destroy the spirit of Chinese integrity. This had been a "war to end wars," not just another example of imperialistic aggression for territorial gain. By earlier secret agreements, Japan was to gain Germany's interests in Shantung. The United States had not signed these treaties and Woodrow Wilson was opposed to the Japanese demands. Japan threatened not to sign the peace treaties. As the League of Nations Covenant was included in the treaties, such action would have seriously weakened, if not destroyed, the organization, which was a major objective of Wilson. Thus it was impossible to prevent Japan's occupation of Shantung, but in deference to the protests of China, there was a clause stating that it would be returned to that country in time. By adopting the mandate system the League was able to make territorial adjustments without obvious annexation, and thus Japan gained control of the former German islands north of the equator. However, Japan failed in its attempt to insert a clause in the covenant guaranteeing racial equality. The western states, British Columbia, and Australia all feared that this would lead to uncontrolled immigration of Japanese. Britain supported the members of the empire rather than its ally Japan. With this single exception Japan gained all of its objectives at comparatively little cost.

THE WASHINGTON CONFERENCE (1921–22)

The peace treaties had left many Pacific problems unsolved. In the United

States the Harding administration, noting the Twenty-One Demands and Japan's war gains, as well as Japan's abortive attempt towards racial equality in the League, not only feared an increase in Japanese immigration but also was suspicious that Japanese ambitions might upset American interests in China. Britain and the United States, vying at enormous cost for naval power, feared the increasing naval competition of Japan and furthermore recognized that Japan's alliance with either of the other two could destroy the existing balance. The United States was therefore disturbed by the Anglo–Japanese alliance, which implied a possible Anglo–Japanese naval agreement. Western Canada also opposed the alliance because the Gentlemen's Agreement between Britain and Japan establishing an "acceptable" quota system for immigration strangled any Canadian control of its oriental immigration policies.

The question of the "integrity of China" as well as the open door was in jeopardy since Japan still held the Shantung Peninsula. Finally China, almost ignored in the peace treaties, was insisting on a relaxation of foreign concessions. To lessen these problems, nine powers were invited to Washington and a series of treaties and agreements were completed.[6]

Although Australia and New Zealand supported the Anglo–Japanese Alliance since it diverted possible Japanese expansion from them, the Canadians, led by Prime Minister Arthur Meighen, who recognized the importance of good relations with the United States and their common immigration interests, supported the United States, and the alliance was terminated. The end of the alliance permitted the Canadian government to establish its own immigration policies and relieved the United States from the immediate threat of a two-nation naval pact. In an effort to limit the arms race and to reduce the enormous costs, a ratio of capital ships 5:5:3 was established between Britain, the United States, and Japan, although Japan had asked for 10:10:7. This agreement lasted until it was ended by Japan in 1935. The ratios were reasonable because the British fleet had worldwide commitments and the United States had two oceans to protect, whereas Japan was only Pacific oriented. The conference agreed to accept the *status quo* in the Pacific and to demilitarize naval bases in that area except for Japan's home islands, Hong Kong, Singapore, Hawaii, and Alaska. A decade later it became apparent that this agreement, along with control of its Pacific mandates, had not only given Japan naval supremacy on the Asiatic coast but also, because of the long supply lines required by its two naval competitors, had given Japan security from attack. Japanese aggression could be checked from the sea only by a combined effort of Britain and the United States, collaboration which proved to be impossible until Pearl Harbor.

The Twenty-One Demands were cancelled entirely as a result of the conference's agreement on the integrity of China, and Japan withdrew from Shantung, returning it to China. Agreement was made to hold later discussions on customs autonomy (which were completed in 1929). Attempts by China to modify other foreign concessions failed at the time, but in the following decade extraterritorial rights were rescinded and concessions of the treaty ports, except for the international settlements at Shanghai and Tientsin, were returned to China.

The Washington conference had ended the Anglo–Japanese Alliance, had brought relief from the tensions and costs of naval rivalry, had reduced the threat of Pacific conflict by limiting fortified bases, and had seen Britain accept the equality of another nation in naval power. China had accomplished its first diplomatic successes with foreign powers, but it had not achieved all of its expectations. The United States had gained almost all of its objectives, while Japan had gained little except for its recognition as a Pacific naval power, although it was not yet accepted in the first rank of the great powers. Almost twenty years later a Japanese writer was to state that the Washington conference was a complete triumph for American diplomacy over that of Japan.[7]

The United States and Japan were now the major Pacific naval forces, the former patrolling most of the ocean and the latter concentrating on adjacent waters. It is significant that the American policy of withdrawal and isolation from Europe after the First World War, as indicated by its withdrawal from the League and its refusal to enter into any European-based agreements, was not a fact in the Pacific area. The Harding administration apparently wished to counterbalance American withdrawal from Europe by an extension of American influence in east Asia. The Washington conference was a definite international commitment to uphold the *status quo* in the Far East and was the first American agreement on Pacific policies. However, the conference did ease the threat of a naval race and, coinciding with American isolationist policies, led to a policy of retrenchment. By accepting a reduction of its Pacific naval force the United States lessened its influence in the area as that of Japan increased. The attitude of the Americans against exterior commitments was reflected in the promise of 1934 to grant independence to the Philippines within twelve years, a step which would have further reduced naval responsibilities. The United States policy of friendship and the open door with China remained as investments and trade increased and student exchanges were encouraged. At the same time, although trade continued and diplomatic exchanges were formally correct, the underlying mistrust of Japan continued with the threat of possible immigration along with the growing economic competition not only in Asia but throughout the world.

THE 1920's

The success of the Russian communists undoubtedly had its influence throughout Asia. The communists had proclaimed the equality and sovereign rights of all the peoples as opposed to the colonization, extraterritorial rights, and imperialism imposed by other nations. These doctrines of independence had a strong appeal in China and Asiatic colonies and dependencies. "A great hope was born in the heart of mankind."[8] In 1921 Russian agents were active in establishing a Chinese communist party which co-operated with the nationalistic Kuomintang until 1927. As a further indication of good will, by the Russia–China Treaty of 1924, Soviet Russia renounced all unequal privileges and gave up its extraterritorial and former treaty ports rights. The Soviet policy of publishing and abrogating earlier tsarist "imperialistic" treaties and agreements was partially a sincere belief in their policies of anti-imperialism, but it was also an important propaganda message intended to gain support for communism. In Asia there soon appeared to be limitations to the Russian proclamations of freedom. The nominally independent Mongolian People's Republic was in fact economically dominated by Russia, and the Russians also maintained their railroad rights in Manchuria, so that their withdrawal from China was not as complete as had been implied. Whereas in Europe between the wars Russia adopted a defensive policy and made no commitments, it continued to be active in central Asia, and its interests in the Far East were indicated in 1932 when it began to double-track the Trans-Siberian Railway. At the same time Russia began to establish industrial centres in central Asia, which were far from both eastern and western enemies, but which could more easily supply required materials to the Far East.

The Battle of Tsushima during the Russo–Japanese War had shown the problems of moving a fleet through unfriendly waters to the east coast, and it was recognized that the Trans-Siberian Railway was a vulnerable route for supplies. The only alternative protected route was the north-east passage. Although Nordenskiold in the *Vega* had completed the journey in 1878–79, it was not until the 1930's that a determined effort was made to establish a practical passage. In 1932 the first east to west voyage in one year was made, and two years later the Canadian-built ice-breaker *Litke* left Vladivostock in June and arrived in Murmansk in September.[9] Within a few years cargo ships were using the passage.

Besides holding Mongolia, Russia retrieved two islands in the postwar years. In 1921 Britain had occupied Wrangell Island, but when Russia claimed it three years later the island was returned. In 1924 Japan withdrew from North Sakhalin, which it had occupied since the Siberian campaign, in return for oil development rights and special fishing rights along its coasts. The continuing Japanese economic interests were to be a growing source of friction.

Japan had profited from the war. Freed, for the time being, from European competition, it had expanded its sphere of influence well into the South Pacific islands. Industries, especially shipbuilding, had boomed. Gold reserves had made Japan a creditor nation. Democracy spread throughout the postwar years with moderate politicians in control. However, communism was strongly opposed, and two attempts to organize a communist party in the decade following 1922 were both crushed. Japan, a non-white, victorious, wealthy nation, emerged as a powerful force in Pacific affairs.

The wrangling over leadership weakened the Chinese position in the post-war conferences. Gradually the country was united, and the warlords were suppressed by Chiang Kai-shek's Kuomintang with the early assistance of the communists. The Kuomintang spread its influence southward and, by 1928, northward towards the regions being exploited by Japanese interests. By 1930 China had regained its tariff autonomy and numerous international agreements had returned to China increased portions of the Boxer indemnity, had surrendered the administration of residential concessions in some cities, and had restored sovereignty over the former British leasehold at Weihaiwei.[10] New treaties with some countries conceded China a status of equality, and old treaties with Belgium, Spain, Portugal, Denmark, and Italy were terminated unilaterally.

TOWARDS CANADIAN AUTONOMY

By the opening of the twentieth century Britain faced serious industrial competition and economic rivalry as well as the threat of a rising German militaristic empire. Britain was forced to abandon its policy of isolation and to seek allies: France 1904, Japan 1905, and Russia 1907. At the same time Britain faced increasing unrest in its advanced colonies, which were seeking self-government and which believed that often their interests were being sacrificed to the policies of Britain. Canadians had seen three examples of this in the boundary settlements of the west coast—the Oregon boundary, the San Juan Islands, and the Alaska boundary—as well as the problems of Japanese immigration. "Dominion" status was granted to Canada, Australia, New Zealand, and South Africa, while other colonies such as India had assemblies with limited power. The dominions continued to press for more autonomy—the right of veto, the control of their own military, and the responsibility for concluding their own foreign arrangements.

When the Dominion of Canada was formed in 1867 it was still a British colony, and these three powers remained in British hands. In the face of continued demands and also to save money, the British withdrew their armed forces from Canada and in 1905 turned over the naval bases at Halifax and Esquimalt.

By the Naval Service Act of 1910 Canada organized its own navy and purchased two outdated British cruisers, designating one for each coast. Thus when war broke out in 1914 Canada's naval defences on the west coast consisted of the single, obsolete cruiser *Rainbow*. On the eve of the war the

British Columbia premier, Richard McBride, heard that two submarines had been built in Seattle for Chile, but as that country had not paid for them they were for sale. McBride purchased them with provincial funds, and for three days, until the dominion government repaid the province, British Columbia was the only province to have its own navy.

At the beginning of the war, Germany had a considerable naval force in the Pacific, including two armoured cruisers, the *Scharnhorst* and *Gneisenau*, as well as two light cruisers, the *Emden* and *Nurmberg*. Information indicated that they were to be joined off the west coast of America by the *Dresden*, from the Caribbean. Off the coast of Chile they destroyed a smaller British fleet, but later, except for the *Dresden*, the German fleet was destroyed at the battle of the Falkland Islands.

British Columbians had heard that the *Leipzig* had called at San Francisco for supplies. There was speculation that it might raid northward to British Columbia, and the *Rainbow* sailed forth to intercept it but fortunately the *Leipzig* sailed westward. The visit of the Japanese cruiser *Izuma* with companion vessels a short time later, relieved the fears and apprehensions of Vancouver and Victoria, whose citizens probably appreciated for the only time the Anglo–Japanese Alliance. Five days later the British cruiser *Newcastle* reached Vancouver Island. The presence of the Japanese navy possibly kept the German ships in southern waters. Until the entry of the United States into the war, Canada's west coast was nominally protected by the Japanese navy, although all German threats in that region were eliminated early in the war.

During the war the dominions rallied behind Britain and willingly contributed large quantities of men, money, and materials. After the war their demands resulted in recognition in the peace treaties and in the League of Nations. Arthur Meighen successfully opposed the renewal of the Anglo–Japanese Alliance.

For almost two decades Canada isolated itself from involvement in international affairs. "From the time he first became Prime Minister, Mackenzie King had consistently opposed commitments to the League of Nations, to the United Kingdom, to the British Empire or Commonwealth, or to any other national or international authority which might involve Canada automatically in war."[11]

The Statute of Westminster, 1931, climaxed the struggle for independence by the dominions and established the (British) Commonwealth of Nations. The members continued allegiance to the Crown but otherwise they were autonomous nations united by sentimental and historical ties. Nevertheless, they still depended nominally on the British navy for protection, although Canada's west coast in reality relied on that of the United States. Paralleling these gains by the more advanced nations were more limited steps towards independence in other colonies. The growing demands for self-government in colonies throughout the world were concrete examples of the steady decline in European domination of world politics.

Canada was not a participant in the power struggle of Asia, but it was affected both by its British connections and its own expanding interests. From the completion of the Canadian Pacific Railway and the trans-Pacific steamship routes it had developed regular travel and commercial services to the Orient. Trade commissions were established in China and Japan in the early 1900's. Businessmen from both sides of the ocean had their agencies, and although trade was comparatively small it was important. Wood products and minerals were the main exports. The most glamorous import was silk, and for a short time, silk trains across the continent to New York en route to Europe had priority over all other traffic. Other imports included tea, spices, oranges, textiles, and novelties.

Probably Canada's greatest influence in the Orient was through her missionaries. The first of these had been sent in the mid-1800's, and in the 1900's several hundred missionaries were scattered through China, Japan, and Korea, approximately three-quarters being Protestant. With their endeavours they brought a glimpse of the outside world as well as educational and medical services. Unfortunately, they were "white" and were faced with the anti-imperialistic nationalistic forces, which were increasing among the native peoples.

THE MANCHURIAN "INCIDENT"

Nominally part of China, Manchuria had come under the control of the warlord Marshal Chang Tso-lin who, for his own interests, permitted increasing Japanese control of the economy. Overcrowded at home, many Chinese had immigrated to this northern country and they resented the position of Japanese businessmen and soldiers in the country.[12]

As Chiang Kai-shek's armies expanded their control northward, the pro-Chinese spirit in Manchuria increased. Chiang Kai-shek insisted on his suzerainty over Manchuria, and this control was acknowledged by the pro-Kuomintang Tso-lin with the support of his people. Tso-lin was killed in 1929 when his railway car was bombed, presumably by a Japanese fanatic who acted independently and without authority. Tso-lin's son, Chang Hsueh-liang, succeeded him, and not only did he continue to support the Kuomintang, but he also permitted the Chinese government to build railways which competed with those of Japan and threatened its economic domination.

Japan, with its dependence on world trade, was hard hit by the depression of the early 1930's. Its population had been increasing rapidly, and it was no longer self-sufficient in food. Unemployment increased, wages fell, farm prices declined. The government was forced to establish controls on the price of rice and also on sericulture. The latter was hard hit by low prices caused by the depression as well as the development of rayon. Instead of a favourable balance of trade there was a deficit. The resulting discontent was reflected in growing opposition to the moderate government parties, and the military factions again occupied key positions in the government. The armed forces continued to expand, and this increasing militarism was reflected by the unsuccessful attempt of Japan to achieve naval parity with the United States and Britain during the London Naval Conference of 1930. The loss of control over the food and natural resources of Manchuria threatened to disrupt Japanese life. For many years Japan had watched the expansion of Chiang Kai-shek's influence northward and now claimed that the "turbulent situation" in Manchuria was a result of his actions. Under the influence of the military leaders many Japanese believed that the solution of their problems was the occupation, by force if necessary, of Manchuria and even parts of China.

By 1931 anti-Japanese riots were occurring in both Korea and Manchuria, while the anti-Japanese boycott in China was revived. Claiming that the South Manchurian Railway had been damaged by bandits, Japanese troops moved in to protect their interests. In spite of international protests the army soon occupied key cities. When Japanese troops landed at Shanghai, on the pretext of protecting their nationals, the Chinese resisted vigorously before retiring. The invasion was condemned by the other powers and this opposition combined with the success of their armies intensified the anti-foreign nationalistic mood of the Japanese and further strengthened the influence of the military.

Within a year Manchuria was under Japanese control, and soon their influence spread into Jehol in northern China. Manchuria was proclaimed the independent country of Manchukuo under the rule of the puppet Pu Yi, the last Manchu emperor, who had been deposed in the 1912 rebellions. Manchukuo thus formed a buffer state between Japan, Russia, and China. Japan began a large-scale development of agriculture, iron and coal mining, and railway expansion to complement its own industrial and militaristic expansion.

INTERNATIONAL REACTION

China appealed to the League of Nations and the Council unanimously condemned Japan and called for the immediate withdrawal of Japanese troops, a demand which was ignored. In 1933, after the Lytton Commission's report, the League censured Japan's actions in Manchuria and recommended a policy of non-recognition for Manchukuo. Japan's response was to withdraw from the League and the World Disarmament Conference as well as the Washington agreements, which had set the naval quotas and restricted fortifications in the Pacific islands. With these Japanese actions the various efforts which had been made to establish a peace-keeping framework, at least in the Far East, had collapsed. Tension between Japan and China continued to mount.

The ineptitude of the League of Nations stemmed from the non-membership of the United States and the failure of the two dominant powers, Britain and France, to give positive leadership. Both of these had their own internal economic and political problems during the depression years, and both, especially France, were vitally concerned with the rise of the militaristic dictators, Mussolini and Hitler. France had few interests in the Far East north of Indochina. Britain was the only power which still had significant interests in China, and now found itself in a predicament. It did not wish to alienate Japan, which might turn to Germany or Russia. On the other hand, Britain had expectations of increasing its financial and economic investments in China, but Japan might resent any further expansion. The British cabinet split on the issue. Some members favoured friendship with Japan to ensure protection of their Far Eastern interests and to prevent Japan turning to Russia. Others wished to support China, hoping to enlarge British interests in northern China, which was threatened by the Japanese. Australia, New Zealand, and Canada were opposed to closer Anglo–Japanese co-operation. For a short time the British considered offering financial assistance to China if it would recognize the independence of Manchukuo and thus lessen the tension and accommodate both British objectives. Finally there was the question of relationships with the United States.

The United States had watched the manoeuvering of the League of Nations without actively supporting it. Britain was approached to see if it would agree to a joint Anglo–American statement not to recognize any agreements or changes brought about contrary to the obligations of the Pact of Paris. When Britain, wavering between its interests in Japan and China, hedged, the Americans, in 1932, sent a letter to both the Chinese and Japanese governments, stating that the American government would not recognize any treaty or agreement between them which might impair the rights of the United States, and, furthermore, it would not recognize any agreement brought about contrary to the Pact of Paris, 1928, which opposed changes brought about by force. This unilateral "Stimson Doctrine" was obviously anti-Japanese. Otherwise the United States took no firm position. Britain and the United States followed their individual interests and this lack of collaboration strengthened the Japanese. Nevertheless, the United States along with Britain was largely instrumental in organizing pressures by the powers to have Japanese troops withdrawn from Shanghai in 1932. They could not foresee that five years later Japanese troops would return to hold a victory parade in that city.

The United States had consistently refused to recognize the Soviet régime in Russia with its communist philosophy and anti-religious policies. Informal contacts continued, as in 1923-33 when American relief efforts had saved thousands of Russian lives, and in succeeding years when trade continued between the two countries along with the exchange of scientists, engineers, and scholars. The year 1933 caused a change in attitudes. The depression was at its peak and any markets, even Russian, were desirable. International negotiations verged on disaster—the World Economic Conference and the World Disarmament Conference had failed. The rise of the bellicose National Socialist party in Germany was a new disturbing force. Japan had successfully challenged the League of Nations before walking out of it. The desire of the United States to restore a balance in the Pacific against the aggressive Japanese was one reason for the United States granting recognition to Russia. In the following year, Russia filled the seat in the League of Nations which Japan had vacated.[13]

Actually, of all the European nations, only Russia, with its long border, was closely involved with the Manchurian question, and the inactivity of the others marks the end of effective European diplomacy in the Pacific. Europe was too immersed in its own internal crises. The North Pacific was now a separate theatre with its own actors.

Although the British navy continued to be a force in the Pacific, it no longer offered the widespread "umbrella of protection" since it was overshadowed by the navies of the United States and Japan. The United States now covered the American coast from Alaska to Cape Horn and extended westward to Hawaii and the Philippines. The Japanese held naval superiority on the Asiatic Pacific coast. The increasing challenge of the Japanese navy was but one phase in the anti-Japanese attitude of the Americans. Japanese trade competition had become serious, and now Japanese controls threatened to reduce American exports to Manchuria and China. This antipathy was especially true in the western states and British Columbia with their long histories of anti-orientalism stemming from immigration and economic competition.

Exclusion acts had practically eliminated Chinese immigration in the early 1920's; by agreement in 1928 Japanese immigration was limited to 150 annually; East Indian immigration was negligible because of the difficulties of transportation and distance. By excluding Orientals from the franchise in municipal and provincial elections, British Columbia had eliminated them from the federal vote, which in turn prevented many civil rights and limited the fields of employment. The Japanese, although restricted, continued to come to the Americas in small numbers. Whereas a passive China would permit discriminating laws against Chinese, aggressive Japan was sensitive to such laws. For example, the American 1924 immigration law resulted not only in bitter anti-American sentiment in Japan but also caused Japan to question the collective system of diplomacy, already mistrusted since the League of Nations racial equality attitudes. The American actions resulted in the revival of a vigorous campaign of "Asia for the Asiatics." Regulations against Japanese were met with protests from a protective Japanese government which forced both Canada and the United States to modify anti-Japanese regulations.

The "whites" of the west coast resented the infiltration of the Japanese into numerous economic fields such as agriculture, dry-cleaning establishments, and the "corner groceries." Most of all they detested the fishermen, who, working in well-organized groups, efficiently exploited the salmon and herring resources. With Japanese expansion into Manchuria and China the latent resentment against the local Japanese was reflected in the opposition to Japan combined with a sympathy for China. Japanese goods in stores were boycotted and demonstrations were held to protest the shipments of copper and scrap iron to Japan. The industrial and commercial interests were opposed to the boycotts and continued to export. From 1933 to 1938 the value of scrap iron exported to Japan from Canada increased from $122,000 to $643,000; of copper from $20,000 to $1,300,000; of nickel from $92,000 to $5,439,000.

Since the end of the First World War the Canadian government had withdrawn from active intervention in world affairs. Its policies were similar to the peaceful appeasement ones of Britain. Like Britain it did not wish to lose either the Japanese or Chinese trade. There was also the precarious position of Canadian missionaries in Japan and the territories occupied by Japan. To the growing anti-Japanese protests in the country the government simply stated that its policies were to support those of the League of Nations, an ambiguous position which permitted it to adopt no positive action. Canada was more interested in gaining autonomy from Britain while at the same time struggling to withstand pressures from the United States. With Britain wavering between Japan and China, the United States anti-Japanese and opposing Anglo–Japanese entente, Canada was in a difficult position. Fortunately, neither of the other two was prepared to take positive action and Canada was able to remain an unobtrusive observer without making any commitments. Faced with this passive attitude by the Canadian government, the protests and boycotts gradually faded, but within the people of the west coast remained a dormant force which was to result in excessive emotional reactions during the coming war years.

RÉSUMÉ

In the late 1930's some European nations still maintained a precarious hold of their international settlements and concessions in China, but as another war approached in Europe events in the Pacific became of secondary significance. Japan was free to exploit Manchukuo and to begin the invasion of China as a prelude to the "Co-Prosperity Sphere" of Asia, centred in Japan, and excluding all Europeans. Britain, the only remaining foreign power in China, was forced to retreat. When Europe became involved in war the only challenge to Japanese control of the western Pacific was the United States, but it was not prepared to counter the Japanese threat with military commitments. As the Europeans were forced to withdraw, Japan moved to fill the power vacuum left in eastern Asia.

9

The End of the European Era
(1930–53)

The Power that rules the Pacific is the Power that rules the world. (U.S. Senator J. Beveridge, 1900)

If we became preoccupied in Asia, Russia would gain a free hand in Europe. If we settled with the Communists the fact would be used against us in the most devastating manner through Asia. (President Harry S. Truman, 1956)

During the decade following the peace treaties and the Washington agreements political and power patterns in the North Pacific had changed from prewar times. Britain's navy was not as prominent, but Britain was still a major nation anxious to expand its influence and trade into both inland and coastal China. China had become united under Chiang Kai-shek, who had visions of consolidating the centralized nation to the borders of Russia. By 1930 he had obtained the cancellation of most foreign concessions. Russia, rebuilding after the Soviet Revolution, supported the nationalistic and anti-imperialistic Kuomintang as well as the outlawed Communist party. Although Russia had agreed to cancel the concessions forced on China by the tsarist governments, this action did not deter it from proclaiming Mongolia an independent Soviet state, from retaining its interests in the Manchurian railways, nor from holding the east coast of Manchuria as far south as Korea.

The United States, with numerous holdings, especially those of the Philippines and Hawaii, considered these to be jumping-off places for the expected expansion into Asiatic, especially Chinese, trade as well as naval bases for the protection of trade routes and for the support of the "Open Door."

These three nations—Britain, Russia, and the United States—continued their diplomatic rivalry, which had been common in the Far East for a century, vying for trade and watching each other's manoeuvres. In the middle, Chiang Kai-shek, following earlier Chinese practices, played one against the other while seeking to end all foreign controls. To all four the greatest threat to the uneasy balance was Japan, and, of the four, the United States was the most concerned.

THE RISE AND FALL OF JAPAN

The mutual distrust of Japan and the United States existed from the time of Perry's visit, but through diplomacy they were able to present a facade of friendship, especially around the turn of the century. Tension increased during the First World War as the Japanese navy foraged far into the Pacific and as her demands threatened to expand Japan's influence in China, even though circumstances forced the two nations to become allies against Germany. In 1917, following the Twenty-One Demands and after long discussions, a compromise known as the Lansing-Isheii Agreement included the statement that "Japan has special interests in China, particularly in that part to which her possessions are contiguous."

As the dominant naval power after the war, the United States was determined to restrict the threat of Japan. The United States recognized that the Philippines and Hawaii were vulnerable if Japan were to fortify the islands mandated to it by the League. In the Covenant of the League the United States had opposed attempts by Japan to establish "racial equality." By the Washington treaties the Americans had achieved almost all of their objectives: the Anglo–Japanese Alliance was terminated, the navies were limited so that the United States had a 5:3 ratio with Japan, new fortifications and military bases were largely prohibited throughout the region, and Shantung was returned to China. A temporary check had been made on Japanese expansion, and for a decade the United States was able to limit its naval presence in the Pacific. Anti-American sentiment in Japan steadily increased. However, for several years moderate governments controlled Japan and no drastic international incidents occurred.

In the 1930's, under the influence of military factions, Japanese ambitions revived. Manchuria was invaded and the United States by the Stimson Doctrine refused to recognize the Japanese-controlled puppet state of Manchukuo. In 1934, in spite of British and American protests, Japan proclaimed its ultimate objectives in the Amau statement: "Japan is solely responsible for the maintenance of peace and order in south-east Asia." Furthermore, it objected to the creation of "spheres of influence" or any international control in China.

Russia, unprepared for war when Japan invaded Manchuria, adopted a policy of strict neutrality. It refused, for example, to participate in the Lytton Commission. An attempt to negotiate a non-aggression pact with Japan was refused and Russia, which since the revolution had assumed that its main threat was from the west, was now forced to recognize that an immediate threat lay from the east. In 1934 Russia joined the League of Nations. In an attempt to gain time, Russia adopted a policy of appeasement and therefore sold its interests in the Chinese Eastern Railway to Manchukuo. Nevertheless, Japan's expansion brought it to the borders of Russia north of Manchukuo and Mongolia and the result was that between 1936 and 1939 numerous border clashes occurred. Combined with its isolation after the condemnation of the League, as well as the Anglo–American opposition to its policies, the tension with Russia was another reason for Japan joining the Anti-Comintern Pact with Germany in 1936 and three years later extending its agreement to include Italy. In 1937 Russia refused to renew the Russo–Japanese fisheries agreement established in the Portsmouth Treaty and it began to interfere with Japanese mining companies in Sakhalin. As Russian–Japanese relations deteriorated, Russia and China increased their co-operation. They signed a non-aggression pact, following which Russia supplied arms and munitions overland to China until 1941 when Russia was forced to stop its supplies to China because of the German invasion. Until almost the end of the war Russia was the only neutral power in the North Pacific theatre.

For a decade the Japanese had distrusted Chiang Kai-shek, first for his co-operation with the communists, later for his revival of nationalism in China and his opposition to Japanese interests in northern China and Manchuria. Since the time of the Boxer Rebellion foreign garrisons had been established in China. In July 1937, when a Japanese force was attacked near Peking, the Japanese government determined to take positive steps, claiming that its actions were in self-defence against the challenge of China. Japan refused to deal with the government of Chiang Kai-shek and stated that it looked forward to the establishment of a new Chinese régime. Thus began the "Chinese incident," which was to last for eight years.

With the invasion of China, Japan maintained continued pressure to force out British and American interests while at the same time maintaining the Manchukuo northern frontier and its drive through Jehol towards Mongolia as a check to Russia. Russia countered by encouraging the Chinese in their war against Japan with aid and at the same time encouraging the Chinese Communists to co-operate with the Kuomintang in resisting the Japanese. Russo–Japanese rivalry was eased in 1941 with the Neutrality Pact signing, subject to withdrawal on a year's notice. This agreement freed Russia from the threat of a two-front war in case of attack by Germany, which, unknown to the Japanese, was to come two weeks later, and enabled Japan to increase its activities against the United States by removing the threat of Russia. Russia's only sources of Allied supplies were through precarious Murmansk, the Persian Gulf, or via the Pacific, and about half were obtained by the Persian Gulf and the Pacific, which the Russo–Japanese agreement opened for some time.[1] The pact, however, foreordained that the coming Japanese drive would be basically south oriented rather than to the north.

Meanwhile, as the Japanese pressed their invasion of China, they repeatedly clashed with British and American interests. In 1937 Japanese artillery shelled the British gunboat *Ladybird*, but the British government, at that time supporting Neville Chamberlain's appeasement policy in Europe, took no action. When Japanese aircraft sank the U.S.S. *Panay* in the Yangtze River, the vigorous protests of the American government resulted in a Japanese apology and the payment of an indemnity. The Japanese also challenged France and Britain successfully by blockading the concession at Tientsin and occupying Hainan Island.

Anti-Japanese feeling, especially on the west coast, increased with the successes of Japan, and boycotts of Japanese goods as well as picketing of ships carrying scrap iron to Japan also increased. The latent anti-orientalism in both the western United States and Canada was kindled again as unfounded rumours spread, such as the one that Japanese fishermen were in reality spies connected with the Japanese military. In spite of the fact that in 1935 the Veterans Citizenship Act gave citizenship to any Japanese who had served with the American Army in the First World War, in the same year California forbade the employment of Japanese in any government position.

The United States and Britain had discussed the future security of China, but as neither country was willing to take a firm stand no action was taken. The United States unilaterally showed its opposition to Japanese activities by denouncing the "New Order" in 1938 and lent China $25 million towards the building of the Burma Road. The following year it informed Japan that it intended to abrogate the commercial treaty. From this time co-operation between the United States and Britain increased and gradually policies were adopted which were to be significant in the coming war with Germany.

In 1939 war began again in Europe, and the Japanese increased their pressure on the involved Europeans. In the following year Japan proclaimed the Greater East Asia Co-Prosperity Sphere, an economic union which was to include Manchukuo and China as "independent" states. Britain was forced to close the Burma Road supplying Chiang Kai-shek's forces and to withdraw its troops from Shanghai. The United States was asked to stop sending aid to China, which it refused to do. Fortifications in the mandated islands, which had been built up surreptitiously since 1935, were increased. When France collapsed in 1940, the Vichy government was unable to stop the Japanese from occupying Indochina. Russia, invaded in 1941, was unable to send further supplies to the Chinese. Thus, with China isolated, Russia neutralized by war and treaty, France and Holland defeated and occupied, and Britain struggling to survive, the Japanese were ready to remove their last obstacle in the domination of eastern Asia—the United States.

Japan's success against European interests alarmed the United States, and strong demands were made in that country and Canada by various organizations for a cessation of trade with Japan. Not until 1940 did the United States ban the export of strategic materials such as scrap iron, steel, and oil. With the occupation of Indochina the United States froze all Japanese assets and stopped all trading until Japan would agree to withdraw all troops from south-east Asia and China. Negotiations dragged on until 7 December 1941 when the Japanese, without warning, bombed Pearl Harbor, essentially destroying the American Pacific fleet and involving the United States in the war.

Numerous accounts have been written of the Pacific War (called by Japan the Great East Asian War), and only a few highlights need to be summarized here. Having eliminated the American fleet and captured the American outpost bases in the Philippines and Guam, the Japanese advanced rapidly. British and Canadian troops at Hong Kong were overrun. With the sinking of the battleship *Prince of Wales* and the battle cruiser *Repulse*, British naval support was destroyed. For some reason, possibly because it was neutral, Portugal was permitted to retain Timor and Macao, but the Netherlands East Indies were overrun. By mid-1942 the Japanese conquests extended from Attu and Kiska in the Aleutians to Guadalcanal, north-east of Australia.

The Japanese had underestimated the ability of the United States to recuperate. From the beginning Britain accepted American control of the Pacific War, and the United States naval effort was the main thrust against Japan. The India–Burma front of Americans, British, and Chinese as well as the China front of Americans and Chinese were basically holding campaigns designed to contain the Japanese, and force them to deploy their forces. Meanwhile the major allied offensive was to be by sea. Even though they accepted the Allied policies of an all-out attempt to defeat Germany first, the Americans were able to check the Japanese and to protect Australia. Beginning in May 1942 the Japanese advance was contained by the battles of the Coral Sea, Guadalcanal, and Midway. From that time they were inexorably pushed back towards their homeland. After the collapse of Germany in April 1945, plans were underway to consolidate the combined Allied efforts against Japan. At Yalta, Stalin had agreed to enter the war against Japan three months after the defeat of Germany in return for specified territorial gains including Sakhalin and the Kuriles. In April, Stalin notified Japan that he would not be renewing the neutrality pact. On 8 August Russia declared war on Japan and the Russians invaded Manchuria, the Kuriles, Sakhalin, and North Korea.

At the Yalta Conference in February 1945, Churchill, Roosevelt, and Stalin not only ensured the Russian entry into the Pacific War with its rewards, but also outlined the postwar Pacific. Spheres of influence were accepted: Britain in south-east Asia, Russia in the north, and the United States to control the Pacific Ocean as a zone of defence. The integrity of China under Chiang Kai-shek was recognized. Although China was not represented at the conference, President Roosevelt insisted on its unity and agreed to persuade Chiang Kai-shek to permit a Sino–Soviet agreement on the management of the Manchurian railways as a concession for the Russian guarantee of Chinese independence. These agreements, along with a demand for the unconditional surrender of Japan, were reaffirmed five months later at Potsdam.

The expected long campaign against Japan was drastically shortened by the dropping of the atomic bombs on Hiroshima and Nagasaki. On 15 August the Japanese government unconditionally surrendered and on 2 September 1945 signed the Instrument of Surrender on the U.S.S. *Missouri* in Tokyo Bay.

WAR ON THE WEST COAST

Canada entered the war a week after Britain in 1939. Priority in its war efforts, from the west coast to the east, was directed towards supplying men and materials to the war in Europe. Nevertheless, existing coastal defences were strengthened on both coasts and new defence positions were established. On the Pacific coast most defences were concentrated in the Strait of Juan de Fuca region, the Lower Mainland, and the Prince Rupert area.

Protected by the wide Atlantic, Canada believed itself to be safe from invasion, as did the United States. This smugness was disturbed when France collapsed in 1940 and Germany threatened to invade Britain. Rumours had it that if Britain were invaded the British government might move to Canada. It was not improbable that the collapse of Britain would be followed by German raids against Canada. Canadians were somewhat reassured from F. D. Roosevelt's promise in 1938 that Americans would not "stand idly by if domination of Canadian soil is threatened." If it was difficult to visualize invasion in the east, any such threat to western Canada and the Pacific coast was inconceivable, although in 1940 Germany sent an auxiliary cruiser, *Komet*, by the north-east passage (Russia still being neutral) from Bergen to the Bering Sea and into the Pacific to raid the trans-Pacific shipping routes from Vancouver.[2] The bombing of Pearl Harbor destroyed this complacency both in the United States and Canada.

As the Japanese extended their influence in Asia, Mackenzie King, faced with the growing anti-Japanese sentiment, especially on the west coast, feared retaliation from Japan against Canadian missionaries and traders. Early in 1941, to meet the west coast demands and to show his displeasure with the pro-German attitude of Japan, he had agreed to stop the shipments of wheat and timber, although the Americans were still shipping them.[3] He felt that "registration of all persons of the Japanese race in Canada over 16 years of age" was necessary to control any possible subversive activities. In January he refused a British government request that Canada remove contraband from

Japanese ships in the Pacific, as it would "focus all Japanese displeasures upon Canada." A similar request to stop some Russian vessels with vegetable oils which might be sent to Japan could create an incident either with the United States or Russia. "I felt very strongly that if war was to come between Japan and Britain... we must be careful to see that Canada is not made a scapegoat for Britain or the United States in a war with Japan."[4] By 1941 he feared a British–Japanese war in which the United States was not involved.[5]

Even within a few weeks of Pearl Harbor, the British (and Canadians) did not believe war was imminent with Japan, but nevertheless, to act as a deterrent, and probably to encourage Chiang Kai-shek, Britain decided to strengthen the garrison at Hong Kong. Canada willingly agreed to supply two Canadian battalions and, as these were presumably just for garrison duty, many of the soldiers were only partially trained. Some confusion existed in the embarkation of the troops in Vancouver and some equipment, sent on a freighter, was still en route when the Japanese attacked Hong Kong. After seventeen days of bitter fighting the city surrendered on 25 December 1941. 290 Canadians had been killed and another 264 were to die in captivity. Of the 1,975 Canadians involved, only 1,418 returned.

On 6 June 1942 Japanese forces landed on Attu and Kiska, two of the westernmost of the Aleutian Islands, and bombed Dutch Harbor, the American base on Unalaska Island. The Japanese apparently sought to hinder American attacks from the north, while Canadians and Americans feared attacks further south from these two North American islands. The Royal Canadian Air Force co-operated with Americans in bombing and surveillance of the two islands. On 11 May 1943 an American assault on Attu killed almost all of the Japanese garrison of over 2,300 and regained the island. Kiska had a larger garrison and elaborate plans were made for the invasion. Canada requested that it be included in the project. The assault force of 34,000, including 5,300 Canadians, landed on Kiska on 13 August, only to find the island deserted. Although the Kiska attack has been termed a fiasco, it marks two interesting developments in Canadian military history. For the first time a Canadian force served under American command and for the first time an expedition left Canadian shores prepared for immediate offensive action.

Canadian personnel, in limited numbers, served in various Pacific theatres as observers or technicians. H.M.C.S. *Uganda* worked with the United States Pacific fleet in the advance towards Japan in 1945. With the collapse of Germany plans were made for a Canadian Army Pacific Force to join the invasion of Japan, with the proviso that this force would be used in the North Pacific. Before the force was fully prepared, Japan collapsed and the projected campaign was cancelled. The Canadian force was disbanded. Canada did not participate in the occupation of Japan.

Vancouver Island had experienced threats from the Pacific before. During the Crimean War there was fear of the Russian fleet; during the First World War there were rumours that the German cruiser *Leipzig* was approaching from the south. Now there was the threat of Japan, especially after the occupation of Attu and Kiska. The western states had never before faced this situation. There were fears of naval raids, of enemy submarines, of air attacks on military or industrial objectives, of sabotage, especially of the Panama Canal, which was essential to the American fleet. The cities of the entire west coast prepared for air raids—air raid sirens were installed, school children were drilled on procedures, black-out curtains covered windows, wardens patrolled the streets.

Rumours kept the coast in a state of tension. The whereabouts of the Japanese fleet after Pearl Harbor was unknown (actually it had returned to Japan). On 11 December 1941 the headquarters of the Pacific fleet was informed that a Japanese fleet was west of San Francisco and heading northeast, presumably for British Columbia or the United States naval base at Bremerton. In February 1942 coastal defences picked up an unidentified flying object (later believed to be a weather balloon) near Los Angeles, and when the anti-aircraft guns began firing wildly the citizens were near panic. A major attack never came, but isolated Japanese submarines did maintain the pressure. Hawaii especially felt threatened, and it was shelled once.

The submarines cruised anywhere from California northward, usually in pairs. In December 1941 two tankers (one bound for Vancouver) and a lumber carrier were torpedoed off the California coast, the first two being sunk. In February 1942 a submarine shelled the oil fields at Elwood, California, with little damage, and in June two submarines shelled Ft. Stevens at the mouth of the Columbia River, again doing little damage. These two incidents marked the first attack by a foreign power on the United States since the War of 1812. The submarines *I 25* and *I 26* sank a vessel off Cape Flattery, following which, on 19 June, the *I 25* torpedoed the British freighter *Ft. Camosun*, fourteen hours out of Victoria in the Strait of Juan de Fuca. The *Ft. Camosun* was salvaged by a combined effort of Canadian corvettes and Canadian and United States tugs. The next day the same submarine lobbed twenty shells at Estevan Point lighthouse on Vancouver Island, again with little damage. This was the first and only attack on Canadian soil by a foreign power since 1867. Similar sporadic attacks were made later in 1942, and the Japanese claimed that the submarines dropped incendiary bombs in Oregon, with little damage, and reconnoitered the Seattle harbor to determine whether there was a fleet concentration there. In summary, five ships were sunk, two damaged, thirteen crewmen were lost, but little shore damage was accomplished.

Paper balloons, some as large as thirty-three feet in diameter, carrying incendiary bombs were floated from Japan in 1944 and 1945. They were reported from Mexico to Alaska and as far east as Michigan. They were probably intended for their psychological effect rather than their practical value, for they had little success in starting forest fires.[6]

EVACUATION

Pearl Harbor kindled anew the simmering anti-Japanese feelings on the Pacific coast and resulted in drastic measures. Hawaii, with its large Japanese population, presented a special problem. Immediately, large numbers of leading Japanese, including teachers and Buddhist and Shinto priests, were arrested. Japanese radios and newspapers were banned, and schools and temples were closed. But Japanese were essential for the labour force, and most were permitted to stay with special identification cards and restricted activities. Over a thousand were shipped to the mainland.

Both Canada and the United States quickly arranged to move coastal Japanese inland to relocation centres or camps. In February 1942 the United States established West Coast Security zones from where any citizens (Japanese or American) could be excluded or evacuated. Many Japanese moved voluntarily. In May the government began mass evacuation. After being gathered together in assembly centres, all people of Japanese ancestry were moved into inland evacuation centres, some of which were as far east as Arkansas. Mexico evacuated a sixty-two-mile zone along the coast. In Canada thirty-eight Japanese were arrested immediately after Pearl Harbor, Japanese fishing boats were impounded, language schools and Japanese vernacular newspapers were closed.[7] Mackenzie King was hesitant at first since he feared retaliation against the Canadians captured at Hong Kong, but the fear of Japanese raids and possible disorders on the west coast forced him to accept evacuation.[8] In February 1942 mass evacuation was announced, and Japanese were assembled in centres and distributed to inland camps, some as far east as Ontario.

Families were broken up, and Japanese assets such as fishing vessels, businesses, and automobiles were seized and sold at minimal prices. No differential was made between the recent arrivals and those who had lived in the country for many years and become naturalized. Those born in both American countries were not exempt, and three-quarters of the Canadian internees and two-thirds of the Americans were in this classification. In Canada 23,000 were moved, in the United States 110,000. The speed of evacuation caught both the Japanese and the authorities unprepared. Makeshift accommodations of the first few months resulted in suffering and degradation before steps were taken to alleviate conditions by federal aid. The Canadians proved to be the more vindictive, and it is estimated that Canada spent only one-third per capita as the United States did on making life bearable for the transshipped Japanese.

Thirty years later John G. Diefenbaker condemned the Canadian treatment of the Canadian Japanese, pointing out that there had not been one case of sedition proven against any person of Japanese extraction.[9] This belief in the unnecessary harsh actions of the Canadian government is commonly accepted today, but Diefenbaker could not appreciate the deep-seated historical animosity to Orientals of the west coast, not being a west coast man himself. He adds, correctly, "overheated popular feelings are a poor basis on which to determine the course of government." Undoubtedly, Canadians and Americans overreacted.

After the first initial shock subsided, the co-operation of some Nisei was sought. A few had joined the Canadian forces before Pearl Harbor and had fought in Europe, but west coast opinion was opposed to their enlistment. Premier Pattullo of British Columbia feared that if the Nisei were recruited they would demand the franchise.[10] However, early in 1945 Nisei volunteers were accepted to a quota total of 150. In the United States, after military personnel had visited some relocation centres, in 1942, 4,500 men formed the all-Nisei 442nd Infantry Combat Team Battalion, which was a separate unit from the already existing 100th Infantry Battalion of Americans of Japanese extraction.[11] The Nisei of both countries fought in Europe and became important as interpreters and translators, broadcasting propaganda, translating pamphlets, interrogating prisoners, and assisting in the occupation of Japan. Whereas the American battalions shared in combat and received recognition for their fighting qualities, little recognition was given to the Canadians.[12]

As the war progressed, both the United States and Canada offered to repatriate the Japanese to their homeland, and, under duress, many accepted the offer.[13] Most, however, remained to start a new life after the war, largely in centres far from the west coast, where their return was still strongly opposed. These people, led by the Nisei, organized to recover their losses of the war years and to demand citizenship. Whereas Canada had liquidated all Japanese property, often by auction, the United States authority took over the protection of the property and acted as intermediaries only for those internees who wished to sell their goods. In both cases, at the end of the war, attempts were made to repay some of the losses. The United States awarded 26,500 claims a total of $38 million.[14] In both countries the compensation paid was far below actual losses.

The war years scattered the Japanese population across the continent. California has only one per cent of the population (although they outnumber the Chinese and Filipinos), and New York has more Japanese than Oregon.[15] Out of a total of 37,260 Japanese in Canada only 13,585 are in British Columbia, while Ontario has 15,600.[16]

In 1947 the Canadian Chinese Immigration Act of 1923 was repealed, and some restrictions were lifted. In the same year East Indians were given the franchise, and two years later the vote was extended to Chinese and Japanese citizens. Other modifications followed until 1967, when a new immigration act removed all discrimination based on colour, nationality, or ethnic group. In Canada the "continuous journey" regulation which handicapped the East Indian immigration was revoked. The McCarren–Walter Act of 1952 in the United States ended both the policies of denial of citizenship to Japanese residents and racial discrimination against immigrants. In 1965 this was supplemented by an immigration law which eliminated discriminatory national quota provisions. In 1946 the granting of independence to the Philippines removed early restrictions in the United States against Filipinos.

TABLE 6: POPULATION BY ETHNIC GROUP BY PROVINCES, 1971

	Chinese	East Indian	Japanese
Newfoundland	610	460	20
Prince Edward Island	25	135	15
Nova Scotia	935	1,345	85
New Brunswick	575	465	40
Quebec	11,905	6,510	1,745
Ontario	39,325	30,920	15,600
Manitoba	3,430	3,205	1,335
Saskatchewan	4,605	1,625	315
Alberta	12,905	4,400	4,460
British Columbia	44,315	18,795	13,785
Yukon & NWT	200	70	55
Totals	118,815	67,925	37,260

Source: Statistics Canada, Census 1971: Population. Reproduced by permission of Information Canada.

Over a century of oriental discrimination in Canada and the United States has passed, but now Chinese, Japanese, Filipinos, and East Indian ethnic groups can claim to be first class citizens (see Table 6). Nevertheless, some bias still simmers on the west coast. Only time will tell whether the animosity, hatred, and persecution of former years can be eliminated and forgotten.

JOINT DEFENCE

Although Canada was embroiled in the war two years before the United States, two necessities brought the countries closer together: the increasing Allied demand for supplies and the growing American awareness of the need to strengthen its defences. In August 1940 the Ogdensburg Agreement provided for the establishment of a Permanent Joint Board of Defence to ensure co-ordination of North American defences. With the entry of the United States into the war co-operation was essential.

In 1944 Franklin D. Roosevelt pointed out that the Great Circle route for sea and air navigation from Puget Sound to Siberia and China passes very close to the Alaskan coast and stated: "From the point of view of our national defense it is essential that our control over this route shall be undisputed."[17]

Air bases on the Aleutian Islands, Alaska, and British Columbia were used by both air commands. Alaska was recognized as a vital region which was susceptible to invasion, could be used as a base for Japanese planes to raid North America, was necessary for the protection of shipping routes, and might be used for an offensive against Japan.

The ocean route along the west coast to Alaska was susceptible to Japanese submarines, and therefore inland routes must be developed. Edmonton became the headquarters for the north-west staging route of planes en route to Alaska from central Canada and the United States. To clear the route to Russia and the Pacific the Canadians joined the American forces in August 1943 on the expedition against Kiska. The announcement of this incident was used to show that Canadians were co-operating with Americans on the west coast and also served to show a balance to the Australian–American efforts in the south.[18] Prince Rupert boomed as it became a base for American troops for Alaska and the North Pacific.[19]

The idea of an overland route from the United States through Canada to Alaska was not new. About 1935 President Roosevelt and Prime Minister Mackenzie King had discussed highways, air routes, and even a railroad, through British Columbia and the Yukon.[20]

During the prewar years Premier Pattullo had been an enthusiastic supporter for a road through British Columbia to Alaska and after visiting President F. D. Roosevelt in 1938 he told Mackenzie King that Roosevelt was prepared to lend up to $15 million for a highway. King was dubious about permitting American financial penetration into Canada and also feared that the United States might use the road if it became involved in a war with Japan while Canada was neutral.[21]

A United States–Canadian commission was appointed in 1938 to explore the financial and political problems of such a road, but its unenthusiastic progress was slow. It took the war to bring quick action. With the occupation of the two Aleutian islands by the Japanese a highway became a necessity and work was begun in August 1942 to build a passable road as quickly as possible. In just over a year a rough road over 1,600 miles long was completed at a cost of $13.8 million, and was upgraded the following year.[22] The Alcan route not only served Alaska but was of strategic importance to Russia. As Russia and Japan were not at war, Russian ships ferried goods from Seward to meet the Russian railway system. Supplies were also being sent by air via Edmonton and Fairbanks. In 1943 one-third of all American shipping was sent in Soviet vessels from the west coast ports to the Soviet far east.[23]

At the end of the war maintenance of Alcan was transferred to Canada, which in 1962 turned it over to the British Columbia Department of Highways. Maintenance is expensive and negotiations have continued, with little success, to have the United States contribute to the cost of upgrading the only land link between that country and the state of Alaska. Another common defence project of the war was the oil pipe line (Canol), "the costly scheme for piping oil from Norman Wells to Whitehorse," which was abandoned after the war.[24]

In the postwar years joint defence remained, and in 1958 the North American Air Defence Command (NORAD) was established. This agreement permitted the joint establishment of defence posts in Canada's north and has been periodically renewed. In recent years criticism has arisen in Canada which disapproves of the presence of American forces in Canada, questions the value of the defence lines, and emphasizes the desirability of Canada controlling its own air space.

EUROPE LEAVES THE PACIFIC

For over a century the British navy had opened the Pacific to trade and maintained order. The British objective was basically commercial expansion rather than territorial annexation. In using its military strength Britain often employed ruthless and unnecessary violence, which became a pattern for other European expansionists. Today, these policies of earlier years have left an underlying mistrust of westerners.

During the Pacific War, the British navy had been unable to protect the Pacific possessions, especially after the loss of the *Prince of Wales* and *Repulse*. The defences of Hong Kong and Singapore had proven to be untenable. It was the American navy which saved Australia and pushed back the Japanese. The British were more active in saving India and recovering Burma and seemed to be more interested in restoring the East Indies to Holland and Indochina to France than in freeing China. Toward the end of the war, when Germany was defeated, some assistance was sent from Britain and Canada, but the brunt of the advance towards Japan was carried by the United States.

The postwar years saw the virtual disappearance of two former colonial powers from the Pacific. In 1949 The Netherlands granted independence to Indonesia, which was led by Dr. Sukarno. By 1954, France, after years of bitter fighting, had been forced out of Vietnam, and retained only a few scattered islands in the South Pacific. Portugal's only remaining colony in 1975 was Macao.

The British Empire was shattered as its parts became independent, although many maintained fragile ties through the Commonwealth. Britain and the United States, as allies of Chiang Kai-shek, had promised in 1943 to surrender all their extraterritorial rights and concessions to China. After the war all that remained visible of Britain's former power in the North Pacific was Hong Kong, a precarious foothold dependent after 1949 on the whim of the Communist People's Republic of China, and the west coast of Canada, an independent country which maintained its historical British heritage and remained a loyal member of the Commonwealth. Even the thousand optimistic missionaries who had returned to China after 1945 began to withdraw within four years, and by 1953 all had left the country.[25] Britain recognized the communist government in China in 1950, hoping to regain some of its prewar commercial interests. In 1971, following a policy made by the Labour government in 1968, Britain began the withdrawal of its military personnel "east of Suez."

POSTWAR JAPAN

Postwar Japan was put under the control of a thirteen-nation Far Eastern Commission with headquarters in Washington and a four-power Council in Tokyo.[26] The Supreme Commander of the Allied Powers was the American General Douglas MacArthur. His strong leadership overcame the bickering among the council members and resulted in the demilitarization and reorganization of the country. It was MacArthur's responsibility to limit Japanese territory to the four main islands along with the minor adjacent ones, to eliminate militarism, and to exact reparations. Trials of twenty-eight war criminals resulted in seven being condemned to death, while others were given varying prison terms.

The council worked with the Japanese government to draw up a new, more democratic constitution. Some of the terms of the revised constitution are significant. The emperor became a constitutional monarch, no longer deified, but subject to the people. The cabinet was to consist of civilians, responsible to the Diet. The Japanese people renounced war and disbanded all military forces—army, navy, and air force. The suffrage was extended to all men and women twenty years of age and over.

Other reforms included the recognition of trade unions, a reform of land-holding, legislation against monopolies, compulsory education for nine years, and encouragement of individual thought.

During the occupation years two Asian events resulted in closer ties between the United States and Japan. By 1949 China, including Manchuria, had been taken over by the communist Chinese and the Kuomintang had fled to Taiwan. The Korean War (1950–53) made Japan strategically important to the American and other United Nations forces. In line with a policy of revitalizing Japan, some of the earlier regulations were revised. Large industrial complexes were encouraged to rebuild. The police reserve forces were reorganized as the self-defence forces and increased on land, sea, and air. The success of the commission's work combined with events in China and Korea encouraged the completion of a Japanese peace treaty.

In 1951 representatives of fifty-two countries met at San Francisco. By the ensuing treaty Japan was reduced to its boundaries of 1895; it lost Korea, Manchuria, Taiwan (Formosa), the Pescadores, the Kuriles, and South Sakhalin. The United States, revising its decision after the First World War not to take mandates, agreed to take over the Japanese mandates as trust territories and thus gained the Ryukyus and the Bonin Islands with special interests in Okinawa. Occupation troops were to be withdrawn unless they were requested to remain by the Japanese. Reparations were to be negotiated with individual nations. Burma, India, and Jugoslavia did not accept invitations to attend the conference. Russia wanted to invite Communist China, while the United States supported Nationalist China, so neither China was invited. Besides the China problem Russia disapproved of the close links being forged between the United States and Japan and therefore refused to sign the treaty. Five years later Japan and Russia signed a separate peace agreement, but not a treaty, which included clauses on fishing rights.

Thus, in fifty years Japan had expanded its area to encompass almost the entire western coastline of Pacific Asia except for that held by Russia and had lost all its gains in a few disastrous years. Two of its cities have been the only victims of nuclear warfare. From these experiences has emerged a nation whose constitution forbidding war is supported by a people who have experienced the most devastating effects of modern warfare. Today they are unique in that without becoming a military power they are one of the world's most influential nations whose prestige is not limited to the Pacific Rim.

THE UNITED STATES AND CHINA

During the 1920's two groups, the Kuomintang and the Communists, gained control of China from the warlords. The Chinese Communist party was formed in 1922 and, encouraged by Russia, co-operated with Chiang Kai-shek's Kuomintang to unite the country. The Chinese communists were never subordinate to the Russian Communist party and their leader, Mao Tse-tung, never trusted the Russians, nor did he believe that the theories upheld by Russian communists were applicable to China. In 1927 Chiang Kai-shek turned against the communists, massacring a large number in Canton, and beginning a period of persecution. While the Japanese were occupying Manchuria and spreading into adjacent Chinese territory, fighting increased between the two Chinese groups, with the communists being driven back. Eventually, in 1934–35, they were forced to flee into the inland mountains of Szechwan and from there took the "Long March" northward until they established themselves inland near Yenan, south of the Great Wall.

As Chiang Kai-shek held the richer, more densely populated areas near the coast, he was recognized and assisted as the leader of China by the foreign powers for, to them, he represented the only hope for a stable government. When Japan invaded China, he was powerless to stop its advance, partially because of his struggle to destroy Mao Tse-tung's communists. Chiang Kai-shek withdrew far inland to Chungking, where he continued to receive supplies by the Burma Road and overland from Russia. With the successes of Germany in Europe these routes were closed.

When the United States entered the war against Japan, it became the ally of Chiang Kai-shek. In 1943, as an indication of its acceptance of China as co-belligerent, the United States abrogated all of its earlier "unequal" treaties with China, including a promise to restore the administration of the International Settlements at Shanghai and Amoy, and persuaded Britain to do the same. With Britain occupied in Europe, India, and Burma, it was left for the United States to assist China. Unable to commit large quantities of war materials, the Americans supplied technical and military advice. The following four years were some of the most frustrating in American diplomatic history. They continued to put their hopes in a strong Chinese offensive under Chiang Kai-shek. "President Roosevelt's directives were... Keep the Chinese armies in the war."[27] The Americans realized that a coalition of the Kuomintang and Communists was essential: "During the war the immediate goal of the United States in China was to promote a military union of the several factions in order to bring their combined power to bear upon our common enemy, Japan... Our long range goal was the development of a strong, united and democratic China."[28] Chiang Kai-shek refused an alliance unless he was in complete control, a situation which a distrustful Mao would never accept. Thus American expectations of a major land offensive to divert the Japanese were destroyed by internal intrigues and the personality clashes of the Chinese leaders. Much of the military equipment being sent by the United States to help against the Japanese was being held back by Chiang or actively used against the communists.

Winston Churchill insisted that China be considered one of the powers in the Pacific War and looked upon Chiang Kai-shek as the leader of China. Britain, and to some extent the United States, underestimated the strength of the communists and, moreover, believed that they were under Russian influence. In fact, they were basically nationalistic, and it was only after the war ended that they received appreciable support from Russia. During the war, Stalin accepted Chiang as the Chinese leader and had hopes of co-operating with him.

In 1945, by a Sino–Russian agreement, Russia agreed to respect China's rights to Manchuria on condition that Dairen be internationalized, Port Arthur become a joint Sino–Russian naval base, the Chinese–Eastern and South Manchurian railways be under joint ownership, and China accept the responsibility for protecting Soviet rights. Immediately after declaring war on Japan, Russia invaded Manchuria. Its troops advanced rapidly and inflicted heavy losses on the Japanese, although Russia was only in the war six days before it ended. The Russians agreed to withdraw from Chinese territory within a month.

In their advance the Russians seized large amounts of machinery. The Japanese surrender terms stated that the Japanese forces were to surrender to Chinese (Nationalist) troops, but when the Chinese delayed in sending troops to Manchuria, the Russians continued to destroy the factories and to remove immense amounts of machinery and tools and did not prevent the Chinese communists from seizing large stocks of Japanese war materials.

> It was impossible for Chiang to occupy Northeast China and South Central China with the Communists in between the rail lines. It was perfectly clear to us that if we told the Japanese to lay down their arms immediately... the entire country would be taken over by the Communists. We therefore had to take the step of using the enemy as a garrison until we could airlift Chinese Nationalist troops to China and send marines to guard the seaports.[29]

Although the Americans airlifted Chinese troops to accept Japanese surrender in key cities, Chiang Kai-shek was diverting some of his airborne forces against the communists and was thus slow to move into Manchuria. Into the vacuum left by the withdrawal of the Russians and the non-arrival of the nationalists moved the Chinese communists. Officially Russia was still collaborating with Chiang Kai-shek, and it maintained embassies in Nationalist China until its collapse.

The Americans were determined to establish a single China under Chiang Kai-shek and hoped that the communists would co-operate. With the war drawing to a close President Truman sent George C. Marshall to unite the two Chinese forces with offers of aid to both groups if they would consolidate, but, largely because of the uncompromising attitude of Chiang Kai-shek, his attempts at mediation failed.[30] As the American attempts at forming a coalition faded, the communists turned towards a more sympathetic Russia. The latter still nominally supported Chiang in accordance with the Yalta agreements, but with the ending of the war the former United States–Soviet alliance faded to be replaced by the era of the "iron curtain" and the "cold war." The American plans for a centralized, strongly governed China threatened to be broken by the formation of a separate communist state in the north. This determination to maintain a single China and to prevent another communist takeover caused the United States to pour men and munitions into China in support of Chiang Kai-shek. The effort was in vain. In 1949 the nation of the Kuomintang was reduced to the island of Formosa (Taiwan). Mainland China was united under Mao Tse-tung and the communists.

Russia and China now had a common dislike of the United States, and in 1950 they signed a thirty-year treaty of friendship and mutual assistance, an agreement aimed obviously at the United States or a possibly resurgent Japan. Russian troops were withdrawn from Port Arthur in 1954, an independent Mongolian People's Republic was recognized, and Russia made a loan to China and agreed to provide it with supplies, materials which China used in the Korean War. Chinese–Russian friendship was to survive for only five years.

The United States had anticipated that there would be three great powers in the north Pacific, but in 1949, as in most of the world, the balance was between it and Soviet Russia. Twenty years were to pass before the Americans accepted the fact that there was indeed a third Pacific power—the People's Republic of China.

POSTWAR UNITED STATES

Before the end of the war the victorious nations were planning to re-establish a world organization which would be more effective than the defunct League of Nations had been in preserving peace. The United Nations Charter was adopted in 1945 at the Pacific coast city of San Francisco. Of the five permanent powers on the Security Council, Russia, China, Britain, and the United States had possessions on the North Pacific coast and France had interests in Indochina.

In contrast with its abandonment of the League and the subsequent period of isolation, the United States not only joined the new world organization but became a leader in international affairs. Even as the delegates met it was obvious that a wall was being raised between the communist and "free" worlds. The United States became the leader in the defence against communism and as such joined the North Atlantic Treaty Organization (NATO) as well as a later parallel organization, the South-East Asia Treaty Organization (SEATO). As members of NATO both Canada and the United States continued co-operation and as one step established NORAD. NORAD was planned basically as a defence against attack from the north since, with the advent of jet planes and missiles, attack from Russia could be expected not from ships on the Pacific but from the air.

Defence against aggression in the Pacific became almost entirely the responsibility of the United States. It could expect limited support from Canada, from Australia and New Zealand, with whom it co-operated through ANZUS, and from some members of the United Nations. Basically the burden of containing communism and maintaining the *status quo* depended upon its leadership and policies.

With the experience of Pearl Harbor the United States was determined to establish a ring of outer defences as a buffer against another threat from

Asia. A long line of defensive positions was established by agreement or possession from Alaska through Guam, the trust territories, and the Philippines to Australia. Demilitarized Japan was tied to the United States by an alliance which permitted American bases. For many years Taiwan was protected by the American Seventh Fleet, and for a few years there was an idealistic hope that eventually Chiang Kai-shek with a strong force would recover the mainland.

Thus the United States had established a protective zone and was prepared to contain communism in the Pacific as well as in other parts of the world. The Russians seemed to be satisfied with a united and independent China as envisaged at Yalta and were at first more sympathetic to the communist régime than they would have been to that of Chiang Kai-shek. At first the Russians gave the new rulers encouragement and advice, but as they became more firmly established, the Chinese insisted on autonomy and the development of their own concepts of government, and relations between the two deteriorated and eventually became antagonistic. This rivalry lessened the pressures on the United States. The Americans were forced unofficially to recognize the existence of Communist China but they were determined to prevent further communist expansion in the Pacific region and acted quickly when Korea was threatened.

THE KOREAN WAR

At Potsdam it was agreed that the United States would occupy Korea from the south and Russia from the north as a temporary measure until a united Korean government was established. The two forces met at approximately the 38th parallel. In 1947 the UN appointed the United Nations Temporary Commission on Korea (UNTCOK) from seven nations to assist in unification. Both the United States and Canada, which had been nominated by the United States, served on the commission. Its actions were neutralized when the Soviets would not permit it to function in the north. Against the wishes of Australia and Canada, the United States arranged elections for the formation of the Republic of Korea on 15 August 1948. In the following month, under Soviet guidance, this move was countered by the formation of the Democratic People's Republic of Korea in the north and Russian troops were withdrawn.

On 25 June 1950 North Korean troops invaded the southern republic. Resolved not to repeat the weak appeasement policies of the League of Nations, the UN Security Council two days later called upon its members "to repel the armed attack and restore international peace and security in the area." Seventeen nations responded and actively participated in the ensuing war. A force of fifty-five major warships, including sixteen from the Commonwealth, encircled North Korea and permitted amphibious landings behind the North Korean lines. The commander of the UN forces designated by President Truman was General Douglas MacArthur. Russia, which was boycotting the UN at the time, did not use its veto to stop the resolution, but although it remained officially neutral, it did provide military personnel and materials to the North Koreans.[31]

Successes in this bitter war alternated from one side to the other. The UN forces were handicapped by the fact that not only were Chinese volunteers actively assisting the North Koreans but that they also had an invulnerable source of supply depots in China. President Truman stated: "We had reached a point where grave decisions had to be made. If we chose to extend the war to China, we had to expect retaliation. Peiping and Moscow were allies.... If we began to attack Communist China we had to anticipate Russian intervention."[32] When General MacArthur wished to bomb the supply depots in China, Truman replaced him with General Matthew B. Ridgeway rather than risk a full-scale war with China.

Armistice talks began in July 1951, and negotiations dragged on for two years before agreement was reached. Joint UN–Communist teams patrolled a demilitarized zone. The UN appointed a supervisory commission of members from Poland, Czechoslovakia, Sweden, and Switzerland, but within two years the UN claimed that the first two were biased and that North Korea was not co-operating, so it abolished the commission. In the hope that eventually the two Koreas will unite the UN established the Commission for the Unification and Rehabilitation of Korea (UNCURK), whose mandate is renewed periodically. The two Koreas remain divided by the truce agreement, and although lip service is given by both to unification, the two are far apart. North Korea maintains good relations with both China and Russia. A force of American troops remained to bolster the south.

Canada, with a minimal professional army, was dubious about involvement in the war. It had few interests in Korea, but after some discussion the government agreed to support its commitment to the UN with the definite understanding that it was not declaring war against any state but was acting in a collective police action. Three Canadian destroyers were immediately placed at the disposal of the United Nations and steps were taken to recruit and train the Canadian Army Special Force. In Korea the troops became part of the First Commonwealth Division. Canadians co-operated in all phases of the war—on land, sea, and air.

Altogether the UN forces consisted of 272,000 South Koreans and 266,000 troops from other nations, as well as the many thousands employed along lines of communication and in other supporting roles. A total of over four million Americans served in the war, of whom 1,153,000 were active. Casualties numbered 157,000, of whom 33,000 were killed.[33] Canada had 29,000 active participants, with 1,557 casualties including 312 dead. It was Canada's last involvement as a military combatant, but it established the precedent that Canada would co-operate with the UN in international crises.

The Korean War revived American activities in Pacific affairs. The year before this war the People's Republic of China had been proclaimed and recognized by a number of nations. When the Korean War broke out, the American Seventh Fleet was sent to patrol the straits off Taiwan. Negotiations were speeded up to conclude a peace treaty with Japan followed by the US–Japanese defence treaty and the China (Taiwan)–Japanese peace treaty. SEATO was organized (1954) to check the further advance of communism into south-east Asia. Although there was at one time the threat of a Chinese–UN (United States) military confrontation during the war, Soviet Russia remained out of the conflict, and during the 1950's "peaceful co-existence" resulted in a lessening of the cold war tensions and gave promise of future understandings between the two atomic "super-powers." However, the United States has hesitated to abandon South Korea. Such a step would injure American prestige in Asia generally, but, more important, it would destroy Japan's faith in its support. Japan would be forced to strengthen its ties with China and Russia.

VIETNAM

The United States was to be involved in one more disastrous war in Asia— in Vietnam. Canada, as a member of the International Control Commission (ICC) for Laos, Cambodia, and Vietnam proclaimed that its responsibilities in this body demanded that it remain neutral, although it continued to sell billions of dollars worth of war equipment to the United States. At the end of the war Canada was an unwilling member of the new International Commission of Control and Supervision in Vietnam (ICCS), but after a year of frustration withdrew.

The United States entered Vietnam by providing advisers for the French, whose attempts to regain control after 1945 had been bitterly opposed, especially by the communist forces in North Vietnam. When the French withdrew after decisive defeats in 1954, the Americans remained, increasing the number of their military advisers and personnel until by 1964 they were engaged in active combat. Thus began the longest war in American history, the last troops being withdrawn in 1973. Over eight million troops had been involved and 40,000 were killed.

The early policies of the United States in the Far East had been peaceful; there had been no attempts to support traders or seize concessions by military force. Commodore Perry's visit to Japan had the implications of a threat, but its objectives had been gained without military action. After this the United States had not hesitated to "show the flag." President T. Roosevelt had sent a fleet to visit Japan and American naval vessels appeared in the ports of Asia. American troops had been used to protect its citizens; they had participated during the Boxer Rebellion in the 1900 relief of Peking and had protected Shanghai in 1927. The American policy was to assist its missionaries and to maintain the open door for trade.

With the weakening of European influence and the resulting responsibilities thrust upon it, the United States has taken a more active military role and has become involved in numerous actions, all of which, with the exception of the defeat of Japan, have been disastrous. These began with the annexation of the Philippines, which was followed by many years of subjugation of an unwilling population, who were finally granted their independence in 1946. During the Pacific War and the immediate years after, the United States supported Chiang Kai-shek, who was eventually driven off the mainland. In Korea the result was a stalemate, and in Vietnam the final victory was for the north. It is doubtful if American public opinion will again, at least in the near future, support any military intervention in Pacific affairs.

POSTWAR CANADA

Between 1940 and 1953 Canada was involved in two Pacific wars. During the late 1930's, while tension between Japan and the United States increased, Canada strengthened its west coast defences, but in 1939 with the advent of war in Europe priority in defence returned to the Atlantic. When Japanese expansion threatened European Asiatic possessions late in 1941, the Canadian government agreed to send two battalions to support the British garrison in Hong Kong. This was the only major Pacific action in which Canadians participated, although some troops were with the Americans who invaded abandoned Kiska.

Canada's military contribution on the Pacific was limited to co-ordinating the defences of the west coast with those of the United States. Defensive fortifications were built, and sea and air patrols were established. Transport routes by land and air were developed from the United States through western Canada to Alaska. Canadian warships also joined the American forces in the final drive towards Japan. When the war in Europe ended, arrangements were made for Canadian troops to participate in the invasion of Japan, but with the sudden ending of the war these troops were not required. Actually the Pacific War had little direct effect on Canadian life during the European war years except for the controversial expulsion of the Japanese from the west coast. Canada became a member of the Far Eastern Commission but not of the Tokyo-based Four Power Council established for the reorganization of Japan.

In the postwar years Canada became a signatory of the UN Charter at San Francisco and actively supported its specialized agencies. Canada's most significant contribution to the United Nations has been its participation in the numerous commissions and peacekeeping forces serving in disputed areas of the world. Thus, in the Pacific, Canada served on commissions in Korea and Vietnam. It was as a member of the UN that Canada contributed army, naval, and air force personnel to the Korean War.

After the fall of Japan, Canada continued to co-ordinate its defences with those of the United States, refused to recognize the newly established communist states, signed the Peace Treaty with Japan, entered the Korean War, and joined UNCURK after the Korean armistice. Canada, however, was determined to maintain its independence in foreign affairs. It had no ambitions to expand its political influence and was primarily interested in the restoration of stability for the expansion of commerce and the maintenance of peace. Although the Korean War brought a temporary boom period, it was accepted as an irksome duty and did not arouse any national fervour. Most Canadians were interested in domestic adjustments and reforms. Among these internal policies the relaxation of immigration regulations again permitted the entry of Asiatics into the country, thus resolving almost a century of vacillation, emotional distrust, and persecution. Involved in their own affairs, most Canadians were little interested in the power struggle for the North Pacific.

RÉSUMÉ

The Second World War was the first major war to be fought in the Pacific and encompassed the entire area. The combatants on both sides employed the most advanced war machines then available, with resulting heavy losses in material goods and human lives.

The immediate result of the war was the defeat, but not the destruction, of Japan and its empire. The North Pacific was dominated by a new combination of powers. The postwar years brought rapid changes and new problems in international relationships as the world emerged from the shambles of destruction. Colonial peoples demanded autonomy and from this insistence on independence came two further costly Pacific wars in Korea and Vietnam. The war had introduced more deadly methods of warfare: battleships were replaced by aircraft carriers and long-range submarines, airplanes were supplemented with jet-propelled missiles, bombs were the carriers of nuclear warheads. To maintain international peace and security, and to achieve international co-operation, the United Nations was formed with the objectives of solving economic, social, cultural, and humanitarian problems. Along with this organization rose a demand for human rights and for human freedoms without discrimination of race, sex, language, or religion.

The war made the North Pacific a region of vital importance in world affairs. Facing each other across the ocean were the nations with efficient destructive capacities which could destroy the world.

10

An Era of Equilibrium
(1953–   )

The Canadian Government's view is that the extension of our more traditional
horizons, particularly the United States and Europe, towards the "New West"
would prove to be of immense mutual benefit. (Prime Minister Pierre Elliott
Trudeau, 1973)

Our policy is to learn from the strong points of all nations and all countries,
learn all that is genuinely good in the political, economic, scientific, and technological fields, and in literature and art. (Mao Tse-tung, 1956)

Dare we hope that the approaching century will be an era when all the diverse
nations and peoples of the Pacific will discover and learn to build upon their
mutual independence? (Prime Minister Takeo Miki, 1976)

With the establishment of an unresolved truce in Korea followed by the
unsuccessful intervention of the United States in Vietnam, the nations of
the North Pacific adopted a policy of co-existence approximating the patterns
outlined at Yalta. The Pacific Ocean was patrolled by the United States navy,
the north-east of Asia with its offshore islands was controlled by Soviet
Russia, Japan was limited to its major islands, and mainland China was
united and independent. The United States, Soviet Russia, and the People's
Republic of China, each with nuclear weapons, had the world's most powerful
military forces.

The other nations of the North Pacific, although not militarily significant,
were nevertheless important in international affairs. With determined energy
the Japanese had rebuilt their nation to the status of leadership in industry,
commerce, and finance. Canada, with its long Pacific coastline, wealth of
resources, and extensive trade, held a strategic position. Korea, although
divided, was in a critical position with three influential, powerful neighbours.
Both Koreas have expanded the development of their resources and trade.
Thus, the partition of the North Pacific as envisaged at Yalta existed thirty
years later. The only unforeseen developments were the communist régime

in China, the unresolved division of Korea, and the rapid recovery of Japan. None of these changed the projected control of specified geographical regions.

In a changing and advancing world new international disputes and crises are certain to arise, and in the North Pacific, although there seems little serious threat at present to the *status quo*, differences have arisen and disputes need solutions. Problems are evident in the categories of territory, the conservation of resources, and trade rivalry. It is to be hoped that these will be counterbalanced by bilateral and multinational discussions and agreements which will stabilize the rival claims as well as by cultural exchanges which will result in better understanding among the peoples.

THE PROBLEM OF TAIWAN

The most serious territorial dilemma of the North Pacific is that of the two Chinas. In October 1972, after many years of debate, Communist China was accepted for membership in the United Nations with a permanent seat on the Security Council, but it agreed to membership on the condition that there be only one recognized China. Taiwan therefore lost its membership and with it the original permanent seat on the council which Chiang Kai-shek had received.

This action by the UN had worldwide repercussions. Canada recognized the People's Republic of China after negotiations in Stockholm in 1970 and ended its diplomatic relationships with Taiwan but continued to trade extensively with that country.[1] Other countries have adopted similar attitudes. In the United States the UN recognition resulted in mixed reactions. Although Mao Tse-tung could not forget that the Americans had supported Chiang Kai-shek in the civil war, after 1949, with the communists successful, there were signs that friendly relationships might be established between the United States and the communists. Unfortunately, the Chinese aid to North Korea, the dispatch of the Seventh Fleet to Taiwan coinciding with the increasing tensions of the cold war in Europe, and an era of hysteric anti-communism in the United States, followed by Chinese support to North Vietnam all combined to destroy possibilities of an agreement. The United States became committed to the support of an independent Taiwan, although by the 1950's it recognized that the reconquest of mainland China was improbable.

By 1970, while refusing to accept Communist China's claim to Taiwan, the United States was forced to face the fact that mainland China was a major power, that its position on the Pacific was permanent, and that it offered potential trading opportunities. Steps towards better relationships began in 1971 when an American table tennis team (ping-pong diplomacy) was invited to visit the People's Republic. The following year President Nixon visited China, and with Premier Chou En-lai he issued a joint communiqué expressing hope that the two governments would restore normal relations.

This meeting was followed by increasing signs of cordiality, including conferences between government officials, visits by tourists, the opening of liaison offices in each other's capitals in 1973, and a reopening of trade, highlighted by a large grain purchase from the United States in the same year. Problems remained. The United States could not, as yet, disown Taiwan and thus reveal itself as an unreliable ally to other friendly states. It continued to supply over $200 million worth of arms to Taiwan annually in the hope that the island would become "self-sufficient in defence" and thus free the United States from any involvement in future disputes.[2]

The 1976 Olympiad in Montreal revealed the continuing issue of the two Chinas. Mainland China refused to participate as long as Taiwan was recognized as a separate entity. The Canadian government, which recognized mainland China but not Taiwan, refused to allow the latter to participate as the Republic of China but agreed to accept its competitors as visitors from Taiwan. When the Taiwanese delegates refused to march under any other flag or name than that of the Republic of China, with their national anthem, they were forbidden entry into the country. The United States threatened to withdraw from competition when this action was taken but reconsidered and participated.

The death of 87-year-old Chiang Kai-shek in 1975 followed by those of 77-year-old Chou En-lai and 82-year-old Mao Tse-tung in the following year marked the end of an era in Chinese history. However, soon after the deaths of the older leaders the new leaders, Taiwan Premier Chiang Ching-kuo and China's Chairman Hua Kuo-feng, both stated that they could not imagine any reunification of the two Chinas except by force. These statements may have been propaganda by which they sought to establish themselves during the interregnum period.[3] Communist China has been less aggressive in its attitudes in recent years, and once they are entrenched, the new leaders may continue conciliatory attitudes. China has a reputation for patience, and it may be that the leaders of the mainland believe that, in time, the island will be quietly absorbed.

AN UNCERTAIN CHINA

For several years China, with its strong defensive army, has shown no inclination to expand its mainland frontiers, but there is no guarantee of similar future policies from a country whose centuries-old history has many periods of expansion. The conquest of Tibet and the forcible establishment in 1962 of a new border, with the seizure of twelve thousand square miles of territory from India, a country which had been the first to recognize the communist government, has shown that China intends to hold its own.[4]

However, the tension with Russia continues. Intermittent clashes along the four-thousand-mile border, along which massive forces are deployed by both sides, resulted in the initiation of talks between the two countries in 1969, but these negotiations to lessen border incidents have remained stalled. The attitude towards *détente* was shown in 1978 when, after a small raiding party crossed the Ussuri River into China, the Russians quickly apologized. At one time China controlled Mongolia, Korea, and the Pacific coast north of the Amur River, territories now directly or indirectly under Russian influence. An irredentist movement in China could bring pressures to regain some or all of these Russian territories, especially with the rapid increase of China's population. Russia recognizes this danger and will oppose any such action even if it means war.

"The highest organ of state power" is the elected National People's Congress with 2,885 deputies elected for five-year terms. It meets at irregular intervals. The most powerful political body in the country, however, is the politburo of the Communist party, which consists of eight or nine members. Within the Communist party itself are numerous factions vying for power. These factions vary from extremists to moderates, their different policies usually relating to economic priorities. In August 1977 the Communist party's eleventh National Congress elected Hua Kuo-feng to succeed Mao Tse-tung as party premier. Hua apparently favoured a policy of vigorous industrial development but, while encouraging better relationships with the United States, he was adamant on Taiwan.

Because of its size China has a diversity of regional interests. In spite of the country having a strong central government, some regions will remain agricultural while others will become industrial, some will develop primary industries while others will establish secondary industries, and some will be sparsely populated while others will be densely populated. These diverse factors will lead to a variation in priorities along with a disparity in wealth.

China, therefore, still has internal issues of organization and there are dissensions on basic political theories, problems which will occupy the leaders for some time, but nevertheless the country remains a quandary to the West. Censorship is rigid and the Chinese are determined to be self-sufficient. This was demonstrated during the great earthquake of 1976, when not only were foreign observers unable to obtain official statistics on the losses and casualties but also offers of aid were refused. The only way in which the outside world can establish the power structure of the government is by the publication of pictures, by identifying leaders on podiums at parades and ceremonies, or by public announcements of ranking chieftains. In the 1970's increasing numbers of businessmen, government officials, and tourists visited China, but tourism is still subject to restrictive regulations and screening, exemplifying China's continuing doubts about the outside world.

Foreign observers of China are handicapped by the lack of published statistics. The last census was taken in 1953 and therefore present population figures quoted by outside sources are estimates derived from a variety of methods. The calculated figures in 1976 varied from 842 million to 964 million. Similarly, production figures are also estimates, although some indications of trade statistics can be obtained by co-ordinating reports from other nations.

China apparently has no immediate plans for territorial wars, but nevertheless it refused to sign the non-proliferation treaty. It exploded its first nuclear device in 1964, its first hydrogen bomb in 1967, and launched its first earth satellite in 1970. Its nuclear test programme continued and it continued to explode hydrogen bombs "for peaceful purposes." It was reported to be developing intercontinental ballistic missiles with a range of 8,100 miles (which could reach all parts of the Soviet Union) and to have ICBMs with a range of 3,500 miles.[5] On the positive side, China actively supported the developing nations of both Asia and Africa and offered them economic and military arms assistance along with communist ideological and political theories. Thus, although there was no threat by military conquest, the influence of Chinese propaganda was widespread. As mentioned above, the deaths of Chou En-lai and Mao Tse-tung in 1976 and a purge of dissidents which followed add to the uncertainties of the future, and foreign policies may be drastically revised by leaders who emerge from the power struggle. Many times in the past, in numerous countries, the threat of selected foreign powers has been used by leaders to divert internal unrest and to achieve unity within the nation.

RUSSIA'S PACIFIC PROBLEMS

With the end of the Second World War Russia established a shield of pro-communist states on its European frontiers and was able to divert its interests to Asia, where it had gained considerable territory in accord with the agreements at Yalta. Outer Mongolia was recognized as autonomous, and Russia gained the Kuriles and South Sakhalin, with special interests in the Manchurian Railway system and Port Arthur. With a friendly Communist China as well as a government it had established itself in North Korea, Russia seemed to have achieved all of its objectives.

These bright prospects soon clouded over. The distrust between the western nations and Russian communism had been simmering since 1917 and, although it was temporarily suspended during the critical war years, it revived soon after 1945, bringing the strain of the cold war. In this situation Soviet Russia could not but be gratified by the expulsion of the American-supported Kuomintang from China. However, as the tension increased, the Russians became more aware of the proximity of American troops in the Pacific Islands and Japan. The Soviets boycotted the UN when it refused to seat Communist China, and it was during this period, with the Russian veto absent, that the UN entered war against North Korea. However, it was the Chinese, not the Russians, who actively supported North Korea and came face to face with American-led UN troops. When the United States arranged for the 1951 peace treaty with Japan, Russia would not participate, partially because Communist China was not invited, but also because it opposed the ensuing United States–Japan Security Pact.

Russia cannot relax in the belief that its borders are firmly established. Repeated clashes with China along the Sinkiang and Manchurian frontiers, sometimes resulting in heavy casualties, demand large troop concentrations in Siberia, a vulnerable region depending on the Trans-Siberian Railway for supplies. The continuous vituperation of Russia by Chinese leaders includes an implication that China may seek to extend its frontiers northward. Russia would oppose any threat against the communist government of North Korea. There are still unsettled problems with Japan.

For centuries Russia was landlocked, primarily interested in securing its expanding frontiers. Now its interests are worldwide. Heretofore the navy was mainly defensive, but now its vessels are to be seen in all oceans, filling the vacancies left with the withdrawal of the British "East of Suez." Second to the United States it has concentrated its strength undersea, presenting both defensive and offensive capabilities.[6] In the North Pacific the Russian navy is the only challenge to the United States.

A RELUCTANT UNITED STATES

The war's end saw the United States supreme in the Pacific, with numerous former Japanese islands as trust territories, the American military controlling Japan, a friendly China, and occupation troops in South Korea. The following years brought the withdrawal of the Kuomintang to Taiwan, the cold war with Russia, and a period of anti-communist hysteria in the United States. There is no natural geographic defence line in the Pacific. The Americans recognized that occupation of Japan would be for a limited time, but they were resolved to secure themselves from future Pacific threats and also to check the spread of communism in all parts of the world. Thus they became involved in the defence of Taiwan, South Korea, South Vietnam, and Cambodia.

The United States realized that a friendly, revitalized Japan would be an asset to American defence and arranged the peace treaty followed by a binding mutual security treaty, which allowed American troops to remain in Japan for a number of years. At the same time the United States retained its trust islands and defences on Okinawa and the Bonin Islands.

By the 1970's three decades had passed since the war years, and new generations were demanding revisions of the postwar settlements. The American people, concerned with growing concern over domestic problems, disillusioned in Vietnam and Africa, and paying ever increasing taxes, questioned the necessity of maintaining global military forces. Only three powers, the United States, Soviet Russia, and China, could defend themselves from a major attack, and Americans recognized that they lacked the capabilities of protecting all nations from either of the other two powers. Americans believed that, as other nations regained their strength, industrial potential, and confidence, they should also accept the responsibilities of defence. Peace could be maintained only through patient co-operation by the great powers and by the establishment of mutual agreements in economic and social problems.

Japan had become a great commercial and industrial power and had a stable government, and many Japanese opposed the American ties while supporting a revival of interests in Asia. The United States responded by returning some islands to Japan and reducing its forces in Japan and Korea. Its policy has been a gradual withdrawal from Asia. Increasing problem areas to the United States are the isolated Pacific islands, as well as the trust territories where the American stewardship awarded by the UN in 1947 will expire in 1981. The various islands and groups, reflecting global attitudes, seek independent status as members of an American commonwealth, as self-governing states having free associations with the United States, or complete independence. Most wish to have self-government, defence and foreign relations remaining with the United States.[7] If the Americans do not establish some form of permanent association with them, they may come under the influence of other powers, possibly Japan, a development which could become an aggravation to other Pacific powers, especially China or Australia. In 1975 the Mariana Islands voted to join the United States as a commonwealth. Troops have been withdrawn from the Taiwanese islands of Quemoy and Matsu.

The United States, China, Soviet Russia, and Japan have recognized that there must be a clarification of their mutual rights and responsibilities if stability and peace are to be maintained. Thus, while Japan is increasing its economic and political contacts in east Asia, it depends on the American navy and nuclear power for protection. This situation, along with the presence of American troops in Japan, is resented by nationalistic Japanese. In 1960, when the Japanese–American Security Treaty was renewed, protests in Japan by almost six million opponents caused President Eisenhower to cancel his projected visit to that country, although he did visit Korea and Taiwan.

An increasing number of Americans resent the increasing Japanese economic competition at home and abroad. Faced with an enormous military budget, these people believe that Japan should pay for its own defences, even it this means revising the Japanese constitution and reinstalling military forces. As early as 1950 some Americans were supporting a policy of the withdrawal of troops from both Asia and Europe and a return to the earlier policies of "Fortress America."[8]

For twenty years, although the United States had no territorial concessions in China, no rivalry for trade, and no disputes over such irritants as fishing rights, antagonism between the two countries continued. During 1969 steps were taken to overcome these tensions with the removal of American naval patrols from Taiwan Straits. In the following year President Nixon stated: "Communist China should not remain isolated" and issued the "Nixon Doctrine," which stated that the United States would keep all of its treaty commitments, would provide a nuclear shield for any nation whose survival it considers vital to its security, and would furnish military and economic assistance in accordance with treaty commitments but would leave the primary responsibility of providing manpower to the threatened nations. This meant that there would be a reduction of the American presence in East Asia and that American involvement would be only indirect.[9]

It is questionable whether China favours complete American withdrawal from the Far East. A strong United States presence in the western Pacific counters Soviet influence in the area and contributes to a stable Japan. China must realize that the withdrawal of American residual forces from Taiwan would undermine the United States's credibility in the area; therefore some compromise may be achieved. In 1972, when President Nixon visited Chou En-lai in Peking, the unprecedented visit ended with the issuing of the joint "Shanghai Communiqué," which pledged the two powers would work towards a "normalization of relations." In 1977 President Carter reaffirmed that this communiqué would be the basis of further negotiations. Athletic, cultural, and educational exchanges, as well as an increase in trade were encouraged. However, the question of official recognition of Taiwan remained unresolved.

JAPAN

Following the signing of the peace treaty and the Mutual Defence Assistance Agreement (renewed 1960) Japan has steadily pressed for complete sovereignty, free of American influence, for international recognition, and for the restoration of legitimate territories. Thus, American troops and installations have been reduced and replaced for internal security by the Japanese Self-Defence Forces. In 1956 Japan was admitted to the United Nations and has served one term as a non-permanent member of the Security Council, but it has not, as yet, been appointed as a permanent member. Advances have been made to restore normal relations and trade with its neighbours: a joint Russo–Japanese communiqué (1956) improved relationships by establishing an agreement on fisheries, and a peace treaty was signed with the Republic of Korea (1965). Japanese–Chinese trade started as early as 1949 in spite of the two countries being technically at war, and trade increased markedly with renewed diplomatic relations and the severance of relations with Taiwan (1972). Japan, however, did maintain its economic contacts with Taiwan by establishing non-governmental organizations there. In furtherance of its non-military policies Japan signed the Limited Nuclear Test Ban Treaty (1963) and the Nuclear Non-Proliferation Treaty (1970). One of the problems facing future Japan, as new generations forget the horrors of the last war, is to decide whether it should rearm fully, probably even becoming a nuclear power. With Japan's advanced technology this step would not be difficult.

Japan has sought to encourage cultural exchanges. The 1964 Olympic games were held in Tokyo and the 1972 Winter Olympics in Sapporo. Athletic and artistic exchanges are common. Student interchanges are encouraged.

Japan has regained the Bonin Islands, the Ryukyu Islands, Marcus Island, and Okinawa from the United States. Only islands held by the Soviet Union are in dispute. Russia still occupies the four islands of Habomai. Shikotan, Kunashiri, and Etorofu, which it had seized during the war. As Russia had not signed the 1951 peace treaty, negotiations for a separate treaty began in 1955 and normalization of relations in trade, economic co-operation, and cultural exchanges started in the following year. However, because of the inability of the two countries to agree on the four occupied islands, a final agreement on the proposed peace treaty was never concluded. Until this is consummated, relations between the two countries will remain strained.[10] Russia's attitude is that there are no unsolved territorial problems between the two countries. In 1977, when both nations proclaimed 200-mile fishing zones, each included the four disputed islands within its own zone.

Although Japan has maintained a low profile in international affairs since the war, unless the issue was of direct significance to its security and national status, such an attitude is not true in the field of economic influence. World-wide trade and investments by revived immense corporations backed by a technically advanced dedicated people and an involved government have made Japan a leading force in the modern world.[11] With a minimum of defence expenditures to support, Japan has been able to divert a large percentage of its capital to industry. This capital, coupled with the new technology introduced from abroad on a large scale after the war, contributed to increasing production, which provided new investment opportunities and had the effect of further promoting capital accumulation. Japanese trade increased at a rate higher than that of world trade. As against the 41 per cent of world exports (1958–63), Japan recorded a 100 per cent increase, and its degree of dependence on imports during the period remained stable.

In the postwar period government officials entrusted with the framing of economic policies were leaders in guiding the country towards economic development. One of their most significant achievements was to have planned the sophistication of Japan's industrial structure.

With the worldwide technological innovation of the postwar period, the appearance of synthetic products reduced the importance of raw materials. The position of buyer was strengthened and the fact that Japan is a small island country now became an advantage, for with the increasing use of large vessels, maritime transportation has a clear advantage over land-based systems.[12]

Japan's phenomenal economic rise is illustrated by trade statistics (see Tables 7 and 8). It ranks third as an importer and exporter after the United States and the Federal Republic of Germany. Of its total $55,530 million exports in 1974, 28 per cent went to east and south Asia, 24 per cent to the United States, 15 per cent to Europe of which 11 per cent went to the E.E.C., 4 per cent to Australia, and 3 per cent to Canada.[13] Japanese worldwide investments make it an international economic force. It has large investments in Canada (see chart, Japan's Investment in Canada by Industry Sector)

TABLE 7: JAPAN'S MAJOR TRADING PARTNERS, 1976 ($ U.S. MILLION)

	Exports	Imports	Total
United States	15,669	11,802	27,471 (20.8%)
Saudi Arabia	1,884	7,821	9,706 (7.3%)
Australia	2,303	5,355	7,659 (5.7%)
Iran	1,703	4,446	6,150 (4.6%)
Indonesia	1,635	4,087	5,722 (4.3%)
Republic of Korea	2,820	1,912	4,733 (3.6%)
Canada	1,549	2,714	4,264 (3.2%)
Taiwan	2,277	1,188	3,466 (2.6%)
Fed. Rep. of Germany	2,236	1,227	3,463 (2.6%)
U.S.S.R.	2,247	1,165	3,413 (2.6%)
Total trade	67,120	64,745	131,865 (100%)

Source: "Japan's Imports and Exports," compiled by Minister of Finance, Japan.

TABLE 8: TRADE TABLES, JAPAN ($ U.S. MILLION)

Year	Exports	Imports	Year	Exports	Imports
1938	1,109	1,070	1968	12,972	12,987
1948	258	684	1970	19,318	18,881
1958	2,877	3,033	1972	28,591	23,470
1963	5,452	6,736	1974	55,536	62,110
1967	10,442	11,663	1976	67,120	64,745

Source: U.N. Statistical Yearbook, 1974; Canada's Trade with Pacific Countries, Department of Industry, Trade, and Commerce, Ottawa.

JAPAN'S INVESTMENT IN CANADA BY INDUSTRY SECTOR
(cumulative as of March 31, 1977)

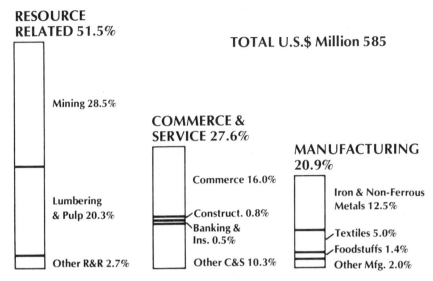

RESOURCE RELATED 51.5%

TOTAL U.S.$ Million 585

Mining 28.5%

COMMERCE & SERVICE 27.6%

MANUFACTURING 20.9%

Commerce 16.0%

Lumbering & Pulp 20.3%

Iron & Non-Ferrous Metals 12.5%

Construct. 0.8%

Banking & Ins. 0.5%

Textiles 5.0%

Foodstuffs 1.4%

Other R&R 2.7%

Other C&S 10.3%

Other Mfg. 2.0%

Source: Department of Industry, Trade, and Commerce, Ottawa

JAPAN'S IMPORTANCE AS A MARKET
FOR CANADIAN EXPORTS 1977
Japan is our leading market for:

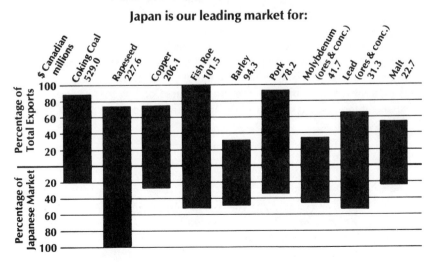

Source: Department of Industry, Trade, and Commerce, Ottawa

and in the near future may co-operate with Russia in the resource develop-ment of Siberia. Wherever sizable communities of Japanese–Americans exist, Japanese language education is flourishing. As a result of Japanese investments in Alaska, Sitka is the only community in all the Americas where the Japanese language is part of the regular curriculum in the elementary school.[14]

Another illustration of the economic power of Japan is the fast-growing power of the Japanese yen. As sterling, along with other monetary systems such as those of the American and Canadian dollars, have fluctuated and weakened, the yen has strengthened. Japan economists expect that before too long the yen will be joining those reserve currencies which now dominate foreign exchange transactions: the dollar, the West German mark, and the Swiss franc.[15] Such a development would reduce some of the Atlantic region's economic power by the establishing of more economic strength in the Pacific.

Japan with its trade unions is no longer a source of "cheap labour," and its capitalists are being forced to invest in secondary industries near sources of raw materials or to accept imports which are partially processed. Japan has a restricted supply of electric power, and the escalating costs and uncer-tainty of supplies of petroleum are serious problems. Increased aggressive competition plus the reaction against competitive imported goods in many countries are causing Japan's sensational trade growth to taper off, and the next few years will probably see a levelling. Measures are being taken to increase imports, especially from the United States, where industrial interests are lobbying against the competition of Japanese goods and opposing the imbalance of trade. Nevertheless, in 1977 its projected growth rate was 6.5 per cent annually as compared with Canada's projected 4.6 per cent and the E.E.C.'s 3.6 per cent. Along with its attempts to escape dependence on the United States, which has been so dominant since 1945, Japan may be expected to increase its trading efforts towards its immediate Asian neigh-bours, south-east Asia and the European Common Market. Because of its proximity by sea, Canada could become an important field for increased investments as well as being a continued source of raw materials and semi-processed goods (see chart, Japan's Importance as a Market for Canadian Exports, 1977).

THE UNEASY DETENTE

The future of the North Pacific depends on four powerful nations: the People's Republic of China, Soviet Russia, the United States, and Japan. At the Korean armistice their divided interests in the North Pacific were revealed as the Soviet Union and China supported North Korea while the United States, Japan, Taiwan, and Canada backed South Korea. Since that time these separate groupings have been dissolved by significant events: the

Sino-Soviet conflict beginning in the late 1950's, the recognition of China at the expense of Taiwan, North America's improved contacts with both mainland China and the Soviet Union, Japan's lessening dependence on the United States and its turning towards Asiatic neighbours, the decision of the United States to lessen its Asiatic commitments—if not to withdraw from some areas totally—and the decreasing influence of the major powers in the United Nations.

In 1953 the United States and South Korea signed a Mutual Security Treaty, and in 1965 Japan recognized the Republic of Korea as the "sole legitimate government of Korea." Following the report of the Nixon Doctrine, the United States withdrew a division of troops from Korea in 1970–71. In 1977, forty thousand American troops still remained when President Carter announced that all ground troops would be withdrawn by 1981. Token forces remaining would include intelligence, observation, air and naval forces, along with fighter bombers, as an indication of the American determination to maintain a firm commitment to its defence treaty. Japan and Korea are neighbours, with Japan controlling sixty-two per cent of the total investment in Korea. The American withdrawal will cause a readjustment of Japan's neutral attitudes and may result in further accommodations with the Soviets. Another Korean war would inevitably draw Japan into the conflict, either directly or indirectly, and would undoubtedly result in a revival of the Japan–United States military alliance.

Tensions have also been lessened by the numerous "summit" meetings of leaders which a few years ago were such rare events that they were hailed as major breakthroughs. Now, with modern aircraft, leaders can make spectacular headlines as hosts or visitors to foreign states and such excursions have become commonplace. The leader need be absent from his homeland for only a short time. Usually such meetings are followed by innocuous joint communiqués of good will and common efforts to better understanding, although they may lay a foundation for later positive actions.

The result of all these developments in the North Pacific has been termed a "balance of power," which Henry Kissinger defined as "to [the] extent that the term balance of power implies a belief that security requires a measure of equilibrium, it has a certain validity."[16] The questionable use of the word "balance" reflects the variations in the four great powers. A better phrase would probably be "multipolar balance." There is no historical, religious, or cultural bond between the North Pacific powers as in the European states. Except for Japan they all have immense military establishments and nuclear weapons although China has not yet achieved equality. China has a large massive defensive army, but, unlike the other two, it has no naval power. Japan has signed the non-proliferation agreement on nuclear weapons, but the impact of Japan's commercial and financial policies throughout the world necessitates recognition of its influence, even if not as a military power.

Even with the détente between the Soviet Union and the United States, uncertainty still prevails in the North Pacific, especially with the People's Republic of China becoming a third military force. As the United States maintains a military balance of co-existence with Russia and at the same time moves towards acceptance and better relations with China, Canada relaxes, and Pacific military defence becomes less pressing. The future cannot promise stability. Dissension between Russia and China continues, with its threat of war. The foreign policies of both countries have been affected by changes of government.

Not only in China and Russia do changes in leadership lead to uncertainty. Since Truman's decision to use the atomic bomb, Pacific policies have affected American presidential choices. The delays in terminating the Korean war were among the reasons for Eisenhower's decision to become the Republican candidate in 1952 and were generally recognized as the main reason for his success. The ending of the Korean War and Eisenhower's promise to support Chiang Kai-shek resulted in his re-election four years later. In 1960 Kennedy's attitude towards non-defence of Quemoy and Matsu almost lost him the presidency to Richard Nixon. In 1968 pressures of the Vietnam war resulted in the withdrawal of Lyndon B. Johnson from the presidential race. Richard Nixon originated the Nixon Doctrine supporting less American presence in Asia. In 1977 President Carter announced his intention of working for a better understanding with China by supporting this doctrine. Korea and Japan add to the uncertainty of the future. With unopposed governments in both Koreas, tension is high, and aggression by either could have dramatic repercussions, with ultimate confrontation of the three great powers. Even Japan's disavowal of nuclear weapons does not obliterate the distrust of Japan by its Asiatic neighbours with memories of its earlier ambitions. There is a revival of nationalism in Japan, with the story of Japan's earlier greatness being again taught in the schools. Japan's defence budget has risen from $3.9 billion in 1962–66 to a projected $27.7 billion for 1977–81, which will give it the second largest military force in the North Pacific, next to China. "Japan–United States cooperation is not enough for the protection of Japanese sea lanes and Japan should also act in concert with the navies of Australia and Canada. This is the minimum requirement and provides the basis for the future planning of national defence."[17]

The improved relationships between the United States and Soviet Russia and the United States and China (but not Soviet Russia and China) have made possible an unofficial recognition of each other's interests and an aversion by any to cause ripples of dissension. American–Soviet relationships will continue to be tense, changeable, and competitive, but mutual interests will demand some co-operation, especially through non-official levels. Definite attempts have been made by the United States and Soviet Russia to limit their nuclear race by SALT (signed 1970, and which, although subject to renewal in October 1977, was not renewed because of fundamental differences on individual weapons) and the Treaty on Underground Nuclear Explosions for Peaceful Purposes, which limits the size of blasts and outlines control features. These countries are also trying to limit the spread of nuclear weapons, but they are faced with the uncertain policies of China, which has refused to sign any treaties for nuclear control. This spread of nuclear power by other countries adds to uncertainty. The Stockholm International Peace Research Institute forecast in 1976: "About 35 countries will be able to make atomic weapons within nine years and nuclear war will become inevitable."[18]

The powers thus avoided confrontation which might lead to nuclear war even if it meant abandoning a smaller nation. The United States is withdrawing from Asia, which will lessen tensions. Co-existence implies that there would be no military interference in Taiwan or Korea, which would reactivate American action.

As the tensions have thawed, attention has been given to the possibility of peaceful international agreements. At present, except for co-operation in United Nations agencies and a few conservation agreements, all treaties and agreements are bilateral. A military or defence association such as NATO or the Warsaw Pact does not exist, but the extension of the United States–Japan treaty to include ANZUS is not inconceivable. There is no sense of a "North Pacific Community" as the term is understood in NATO and the Warsaw Pact, nor is there a unifying spirit as in the western nations. Russia has never accepted the United States–Japanese treaty, and both China and Soviet Russia wish for the end of SEATO in the South Pacific. The American defence agreement is now opposed by a large sector of the Japanese population. The end of this treaty would force Japan to maintain friendly relations with both China and the Soviet Union. In such a case the only bilateral military agreement remaining in the North Pacific would be NORAD, a defence measure which does not threaten the Asiatic coast.

Further economic agreements are more probable. There are already two regional councils concerned with the North Pacific. The Pacific Basin Economic Co-Operation Committee (PABEC), organized in 1968, includes leaders in business, industry, and finance. Original members were Japan, New Zealand, Australia, Canada, and the United States, but it now includes the eight-member Pacific Regional Committee with underdeveloped countries including the Republic of Korea. The Private Investment Corporation of Asia (PICA), formed in 1969, consists of members from twelve countries. Of the 112 shareholders a total of 95 are from Canada, the United States, Japan, and Australia. Its aim is to raise and facilitate private capital investments for developing countries in Asia. These do not include communist states and, by their present character, never would.[19]

Some international agreements concerning the North Pacific are necessary and are well on the way to completion.[20] These are agreements regarding the protection and conservation of the ocean resources, which are of vital concern to all countries in the region.

A DISINTERESTED CANADA

Of the six North Pacific nations Canada has the smallest population. With the second largest area in the world, it has millions of square miles of unoccupied land and has no territorial ambitions except to hold the land which it claims. Its people being "unmilitary," Canada's foreign policies, which are passive rather than aggressive, have been to support the United Nations and to co-operate in North American defence through NORAD. Through the UN it has been a member of all peacekeeping forces, a recognition by most nations of its non-territorial ambitions and a fact which Canadians regard with pride.[21] Commitments to the United Nations forced Canada to participate in the Korean War, but as a member of the ICC it excused itself from direct involvement in the Vietnam War. It agreed with the UN acceptance of the People's Republic of China and ended diplomatic relations with Taiwan, although it hedged on a definite statement by including in the agreement with mainland China the phrase that Canada "takes note" of Peking's claim to Taiwan.

Overshadowed by the population and military powers of Soviet Russia, China, and the United States as well as by the population and wealth of Japan, Canada has had little, if any, influence in establishing postwar territorial limits in the North Pacific. This is not a new position for Canada. Until the end of the First World War Canada followed the leadership of Great Britain but at the end of the war insisted on independent recognition in the peace treaties and the League of Nations. Once it was a member of the League, Canada sheltered behind that body and refused to make any commitments which might lead it into war. Traditional ties brought it voluntarily into the Second World War, but its influence on war policies was minimal. "Canada's exclusion from all influence on the conduct of the war astonished and outraged the officials of the Department of External Affairs." Mackenzie King stated: "The US and Britain would settle everything between themselves."[22] This attitude continued into the peace settlements, where Canadian influence was negligible.

Mackenzie King, Louis St. Laurent, and Lester Pearson were all more interested in the United States and Atlantic connections than in the Pacific. The Colombo Plan roused little enthusiasm, although Canada later became a leading contributor, and Canada did not join SEATO. Even its contributions to the Korean War were made from a sense of obligation to the United Nations, rather than from a desire to exert an influence on Pacific development.

With its limited population Canada supports a comparatively small military establishment, partly by necessity but primarily by choice, and thus it does not have the authority of the great powers. Confronted by the costs of developing a huge area with a small scattered population of diverse interests, Canadians do not favour spending large amounts on military forces which they do not need. Reflecting the attitudes of the people, governments are inclined to be low-keyed in foreign affairs and adopt a conciliatory position.

But although Canada may be ignored as a military power or threat to the existing *status quo*, it cannot be ignored in the North Pacific. The length of its coastline with its immense potential maritime resources demands respect. Its area, resources, highly advanced industry, scientific and technical knowledge, trading status, and foreign investments ensure its position in North Pacific developments. In a world where cultural, scientific, and educational exchanges are becoming more common, Canada is among the leaders. It is an important contributor to investments and aid to the Third World. With more land, coastline, and natural resources per capita than any country in the world, Canada cannot be detached from Pacific affairs.

CANADIAN SECURITY

The threat of attack from the sea is not unknown to Pacific Canada. During the nineteenth century fear of American expansionism as well as the threat of Russian invasions resulted in periodic alarms and a recognition of vulnerability to enemy raids from the sea. Protection depended on the British navy, and in the latter years of the nineteenth century as Britain became more involved in the North Pacific, increasing emphasis was placed on the Esquimalt naval base.

In the Second World War the military forces of the United States and Canada were involved in both the Atlantic and Pacific oceans. In the postwar period it became obvious that there were also dangers from across Canada's third ocean, the Arctic, as long-range bombers, missiles, and anti-missiles became more efficient. In spite of its desire to remain neutral, and much as it dislikes the fact, Canada was forced to co-operate with the United States on defence.

Canadians are fully aware of the pressures exerted by the United States. Living beside the wealthiest and most powerful nation in the world has both advantages and disadvantages. Canada's international glow is often lost in the shadow as the ·American presence sparkles. Royal commissions, associations, books, speeches, and demonstrations have all been concerned with the threat of American influence in commerce, investment, transportation, cultural growth, and the many other facets of an advanced, complex, and growing nation such as Canada. The relationships between the United States and Canada is not one of equals. A basic tenet of Canadian foreign policy is to develop harmony with the United States but at the same time to affirm an individual national personality.[23]

Problem areas have always existed in Canadian–American relations, but, while insisting on their right of independent action, Canadians have recognized their dependence on the United States, especially in the fields of industry and commerce. Along with this assumption of independence is a fear of reprisals against any action which Canada might take which is injurious to the United States. With seventy per cent of Canadian exports going to the United States, American regulations restricting trade could be disastrous to Canadian industry. These fears are accentuated by irresponsible statements such as that made by an American judge during the discussions of the Mackenzie gas pipeline route: "Even if it is assumed that a Canadian government would come to power predisposed to act unreasonably, such imprudence could be countered with equally unsavory activities on the part of the United States."[24] In spite of the desire for mutual co-operation in both countries national interests take precedence.

Canadians have adopted a policy of leaving the solution of international problems to others. Thus there would seem to be no Canadian policy for defence of the Pacific coast except through NORAD, which implies dependence on American intervention. NORAD negates Canadian sovereignty in its air defence and implies an intermingling of Canadian and American forces.[25] Fear of being embroiled in a war because of United States policies has been a worry for half a century.

Violent reactions followed the announcement in 1975 that the United States would establish a Trident submarine and nuclear base on Puget Sound within sixty miles of Vancouver and Victoria. A protest petition with some 10,500 citizens' names was presented to the House of Commons, the city of Vancouver proclaimed a "Trident Concern Week," and a demonstration was held at the site by placard-carrying Canadians—all to no effect.[26] Although the base could strengthen Canada's security, Canadians feared that it would be the object of a nuclear attack in the event of a Russo–American war.

Security of the west coast is low on Canadian defence priorities. Canadians are disturbed, nevertheless, by the fact that Soviet nuclear submarines with tactical nuclear weapons maintain an almost continuous patrol off the west coast of Canada and the United States. Therefore Canada co-operates with the United States in planting anti-submarine warning detection devices (ASW) off the coasts of North America. Canada is vitally interested in military uses of the seabed, and although it is not a partner in bilateral secret agreements between the United States and Soviet Russia on this aspect of the problem, it, along with ninety other states, signed and in 1972 ratified the Seabed Arms Control Treaty.[27] Canadians are also monitoring a Soviet

18. San Francisco in 1849. During the mid-nineteenth century San Francisco controlled trade from Alaska to Mexico and to the Hawaiian Islands.

19. American Camp on San Juan Island showing a group of artillerymen. Americans and British both maintained a force of one hundred men on the island from 1860 to 1873.

20. Chinese work crew on the Canadian Pacific Railway. Fifteen thousand Chinese were imported for construction work.

21. Canadian Pacific construction train entering Hell's Gate on the Fraser River. The old Cariboo Highway can be seen in the background.

22. Anti-Chinese riot in Denver, Colorado. *Canadian Illustrated News.* 20 November 1880.

23. The salmon fishing fleet at the mouth of the Fraser River c. 1900 during the period of sails and oars and before power-driven fish boats were used.

24. H.M.S. *Rainbow* accompanying the S.S. *Komagata Maru* out of Vancouver Harbour in July 1914.

25. The Canadian submarines "C C 1" and "C C 2" were purchased in Seattle on 4 August 1914 by Sir Richard McBride, premier of British Columbia, for $1,150,000. Three days later Canada refunded the money. The two warships shown with the submarines on Esquimalt Harbour are the British *Shearwater* and *Algerine*.

26. Japanese troops at Vladivostok, c. 1919. Japan sent the largest contingent of troops to Siberia and seized considerable territory.

27. Dr. Sun Yat-sen and Chiang Kai-shek photographed on a train in Canton, 1920.

28. Flight of Canadian missionaries following Japanese invasion of China in 1936.

29. Fishing boats seized from Japanese by the federal government and impounded at the Annieville Dike on the Fraser River, 1941. They were later auctioned.

30. American and Canadian Forces land on Kiska, Aleutian Islands, 13 August 1943, only to find that the Japanese had already deserted the island.

31. This picture of the N.K.K. Steel Company Ogishima Yard illustrates the vast quantities of coal imported into Japan. Coal ranks first in Canadian exports to Japan.

32. Sea otters transplanted from Alaska and released near Bunsby Island off the north end of Vancouver Island, 1972. Sea otters were extinct in British Columbia, but this experiment promises to reinstate the industry.

scientific crew floating on a drifting iceberg in the Arctic which is outside the 200-mile zone from Canadian land but is north of Canada. Doubts have arisen that this group of Russians is involved in purely scientific research.[28]

Canada's policy is to restrain from involvement in the power rivalries of the North Pacific but absolute impartiality is impossible with its close ties to the United States and its economic and political connections with the non-communist world. From the Asiatic viewpoint, Canada is a friend, if not an ally or satellite, of the United States. Absolute isolationism is impossible for Canada because of its commitments—and Canada does have international commitments. Basic to its foreign policy, which reveals its continuing interest in Europe, is NATO. Admittedly Canadians are often lukewarm, in fact doubtful, about their membership in this anti-communist bloc, but criticism by other NATO members after years of Canadian lassitude resulted in dramatic expenditures to modernize the air and tank forces. Besides an increase in the size of the armed forces, the defence budget was increased by $400 million in 1976. Between 1977 and 1993, defence planners expect to spend $16 billion for new weapons, repairs of existing equipment, maintenance, and research.[29]

The other fundamental base of Canada's foreign policy is the United Nations. Already, in Korea, Canada has been involved in war through its membership in the UN. As all nations of the North Pacific except Korea are members of the UN, that body offers an organ for the peaceful solution of disputes, although this has been weakened with the decreasing credibility of the UN in recent years. The Korean War was possible only because Russia was absent from the Security Council and did not use its veto. Some similar unforeseen action could again result in disastrous consequences.

Projections on the future of international affairs in the North Pacific must be modified by the fact that no one region is immune from events in others, whether they be in the Middle East, the Arab states, or Cuba. The presence of Russians and Chinese in the evolving states of Africa results in countermeasures from the non-communist world. The withdrawal of Britain and the United States from the Indian Ocean left a vacuum which is being filled by the Russian navy. The presence of these ships will have an influence on southeast Asia, India, and Pakistan, which in turn could result in indirect Russian pressures on China from the south.

Interaction among the nations of the North Pacific cannot be isolated from the broader field of worldwide international relationships. Because of its position, Canada cannot escape involvement in Pacific affairs.

CULTURAL EXCHANGE

Although common usage associated the word "culture" chiefly with the arts, the "cultural pattern" of a nation encompasses a wide spectrum of many adjusted parts which touch almost every aspect of the everyday life of a people.

Ignorance and misunderstanding lead to mistrust and antagonism. Communication between groups, either through the media or personal contacts, lessens misconceptions of different peoples and becomes a powerful factor in international tolerance and understanding. Modern mass media have broken the barriers of time and distance. An earthquake in Japan is reported around the world within minutes, and immediately plans are underway to ship needed supplies to the stricken area by jet aircraft. Newspapers, radio, television, and periodicals now have foreign correspondents assigned to most important capital cities, and rarely a day passes when radio or television newscasts do not carry the phrase "reporting from." As the world grows smaller the differences between peoples become blurred.

Today more books are translated than ever before, and the poetry of China, the writings of Mao Tse-tung and Stalin, as well as other writers, who a few years ago would be unknown or banned, share American and Canadian bookshelves with English (or French) writers. Supplementing these are the thousands of photographs carried home by camera-carrying tourists.

On a visit to Japan, Prime Minister Trudeau said: "The purpose of these visits is to invite the people of other countries to focus attention on the other, to gain by cameras and the pens of the journalists observing us a better understanding of another's homeland and policies. Each time we return we realize how very little we know of your country and of your customs."[30]

Tourism is a major contributor to the economy of many regions, and trans-Pacific travel is increasing annually. In 1976 Hawaii had almost three million visitors, of whom one-third were Americans, but 400,000 came from Japan and 210,000 from Canada. In the same year, 109,000 Japanese visited Canada, spending an estimated $80 million. Increasingly Canadians are travelling to Asia, the Pacific Islands, and Australia. The great mass of Canadian tourists visit the neighbouring states, but thousands travel annually to Europe. They are drawn across the Atlantic not only by historical or ethnic ties but also because of the low travel rates. Air fares from Vancouver to Asia are over double the fares to Europe. Trans-Pacific tourism is handicapped by the inconveniences and costs of transportation, but it also suffers from the uncertainties to be encountered in lands with strange languages and customs. If Canada is to increase the potentially rich Pacific tourist trade efforts must be made to improve transportation and to accommodate tourists who are arriving in a strange land.

International tours by artists are encouraged, and it would be impossible in a small space to enumerate the individuals or groups which cross the Pacific in a year. Such a list would include dancers, singers, ensembles, orchestras, painters, and many others. Representatives of most athletic and sporting events crisscross the ocean, pitting their abilities against comparable opponents and at the same time teaching and learning new skills. The Canadian Department of External Affairs lists one hundred and fifteen examples of bilateral exchanges between Canada and China during the years 1971-77, inclusive. In 1964 the Olympic games were held in Tokyo, twelve years later they were in Canada. In 1977 Canada participated in more than one hundred fairs and missions abroad.[31]

Scientists share their discoveries. In July 1975 the United States and Soviet Russia in a joint Apollo–Soyuz test space project arranged for astronauts to meet in space. Medical specialists, such as those from China with a knowledge of acupuncture, exchange visits.

One of the most important types of mutual exchange for the future is that of students. Throughout Canada and the United States exchange programmes are arranged, often with government financing, for university students. Tomagawa University of Japan opened its agricultural campus near Nanaimo, British Columbia, and for the opening ceremonies flew the University Choir from Japan. A number of Japanese universities have established Canadian studies courses, and universities across Canada have opened Asiatic studies faculties.

These many travellers for pleasure, education, or business are breaking down earlier barriers of misconceptions and distrust, not only between nations but also among the ethnic groups at home. In Canada and the United States this division was accentuated by the anti-oriental bias of earlier times. Today, this segregation is disappearing and citizens of all ethnic groups are being assimilated. At the same time recognition is being given to a multicultural society, and each group is being encouraged to preserve its traditions as contributions towards a broader, more interesting, and diverse national entity.

CANADA AND PACIFIC TRADE

Beginning with the demands for spices, luxury goods, and tea, the driving force which led Europeans to the Far East was the prospect of trade. By the nineteenth century the pattern changed as Asia promised new markets for the manufactured goods of the Industrial Revolution. Europeans were dazzled by the possibilities offered by the millions of people in China, an unrealistic vision, for the masses of Chinese could not afford, in fact they did not want, the goods produced in western factories. Thus the trade, although considerable, never achieved the expectations. This concept of a vast potential market still survives but has become more selective in the types of trading goods.

Since 1950 several factors have made the Pacific along with the European Common Market and the United States one of the three major trading regions (see Table 9).[32] Most obvious is the rise of Japan as a leading world exporter and importer with expanding worldwide investments. China has shown an interest in reopening trade with the world and holds regular trade fairs. Sales of wheat to China and Russia have become significant to the prosperity of North American Pacific ports. Trade in Taiwan and Korea has flourished.

Pacific trade is increasing and will undoubtedly continue to do so (see Table 10). The area includes the two greatest trading nations, the United States and Japan, while Canada ranks sixth in the non-communist world. These three countries, along with Soviet Russia, are among the most highly industrialized and technologically advanced. China is aiming to join them

TABLE 9: UNITED STATES TRADE WITH PACIFIC COUNTRIES, 1821–1931
($ U.S. MILLION)

	Exports				Imports			
	Total	Canada	Japan	China	Total	Canada	Japan	China
1821	55	2	—	4	55	—	—	3
1841	112	6	—	1	123	1	—	4
1861	220	23	—	7	289	23	—	11
1881	902	38	1	5	643	38	14	22
1891	884	38	5	9	845	39	41	19
1901	1,488	106	11	10	823	42	29	18
1911	2,049	270	37	19	1,527	101	79	34
1921	4,485	594	238	108	2,509	335	251	101
1931	2,424	396	135	56	2,091	266	206	67

Source: Historical Tables of the United States, U.S. Department of Commerce, Bureau of the Census.

TABLE 10: WORLD TRADE, 1976 ($ U.S. MILLION)

Country	Exports	Imports	Total	Balance
U.S.A.	(1) 114,997	(1) 129,565	(1) 244,562	−27,588
W. Germany	(2) 101,977	(2) 88,209	(2) 190,186	+13,767
Japan	(3) 67,167	(3) 64,748	(3) 131,915	+ 2,419
France	(4) 57,162	(4) 64,391	(4) 121,553	− 7,229
U.K.	(5) 46,264	(5) 55,978	(5) 102,242	− 9,714
The Netherlands	(7) 40,067	(7) 40,696	(6) 80,763	− 629
Canada	(6) 40,155	(8) 40,564	(7) 80,719	− 409
Italy	(8) 36,960	(6) 43,423	(8) 80,383	− 6,463
Belgium	(10) 32,781	(9) 34,992	(9) 67,773	− 2,211
Saudi Arabia	(9) 36,041	(10) 11,759	(10) 47,800	+33,996

Source: Canada's Trade With Pacific Countries, December 1977, Department of Industry, Trade, and Commerce, Ottawa, from International Financial Statistics, p. 27.

in these modern techniques. Aside from the Common Market no other region has as much wealth, international influence, and technological knowledge as that bordering the North Pacific. Trading is keenly competitive, and competition among these nations for available markets will increase. The resulting growth will seriously challenge, if not ultimately surpass, the influence of western Europe on the commerical world (see Table 11).

As a trading nation Canada is a force in the North Pacific (see Table 12). In 1975 Canada completed agreements to widen its contacts by the European

TABLE 11: GROSS NATIONAL PRODUCT AND AVERAGE MONTHLY EXPORTS, 1974 ($ U.S. MILLION)

	Gross National Product	Average Monthly Exports
United States	1,420,200	8,209
Japan	451,400	4,628
West Germany	385,700	7,430
France	274,000	3,825
United Kingdom	186,800	3,225
Italy	149,000	2,524
Canada	144,300	2,732

Source: London, Keesing's Limited, Vol. XXII, 1976, pp. 27, 501.

TABLE 12: CANADA'S TRADE WITH NORTH PACIFIC COUNTRIES, 1976 ($ CAN. MILLION)

	Exports		Imports	
	1975	1976	1975	1976
China	376.4	196	56.4	88
South Korea	79.0	116	169.2	303
Japan	2,115.3	2,386	1,232.8	1,523
North Korea	4.9		.1	

Source: Pacific Division, Department of Industry, Trade, and Commerce.

"contractual link" with the EEC. Canada's trading patterns are dominated by the United States; sixty-seven per cent of its exports go to that country compared with twelve per cent to the EEC and seven per cent to Japan (see Table 13). The United States supplies seventy per cent of its imports. On the other hand, United States exports are twenty-three per cent to the EEC, twenty per cent to Canada, and eleven per cent to Japan (see Table 14). In spite of the fact that it would be political suicide for a Canadian government to use the term, Canada and the United States are a *de facto* economic union, each country being dependent on the other for resources, markets, and investments.

TABLE 13: CANADA'S EXPORTS AND IMPORTS, SELECTED COUNTRIES, 1976
($ CAN. MILLION)

	Exports	Imports
Total	38,146	37,468
U.S.A.	25,795	25,736
United Kingdom	1,867	1,152
E.E.C. (excludes U.K.)	2,599	1,925
U.S.S.R.	535	n/a
Japan	2,389	1,525
P.R. of China	196	88

Source: Canadian Statistical Review, April 1977.

TABLE 14: UNITED STATES TRADE, SELECTED COUNTRIES, 1975
($ U.S. MILLION)

	Exports	Imports
E.E.C.	22,862	16,733
U.S.S.R.	1,835	254
Japan	9,563	11,425
Canada	21,743	22,170
Taiwan	1,659	1,946
Korea	1,761	1,442
Total Trade	107,591	96,940

Source: Statistical Abstract, U.S. Department of Commerce, Bureau of the Census.

Since San Francisco controlled the economic life of the Pacific coast in the mid-nineteenth century, coastal trade between British Columbia and the Pacific American ports has continued to be important both to provincial exports and the tourist trade. The north–south mountain ranges and valleys form natural transportation routes which are serious challenges to the man-made, difficult overland routes connecting the Pacific coast to the rest of Canada. These natural passageways tend to bind British Columbia to the competitive agricultural and manufacturing industries of California, which with a population of over twenty million approximates the total of the remainder of Canada.

The two isolated states of the United States, Alaska and Hawaii, have important trading connections with Japan and Canada. Japan has more investments in Alaska ($200 million in 1971) than in all the other states, most investments being in pulp, lumber, natural gas, and minerals. Alaska exports to Japan (1970) totalled over $100 million and to Canada over $10 million; imports from Japan totalled over $42 million and from Canada, over $25 million.

Japanese influence in Hawaii is also strong. From 1961 to 1972 the number of Japanese firms in Hawaii increased from twelve to ninety-four. In trade, Hawaiian imports from Japan (1974) totalled $108 million and exports to Japan totalled $61 million. Canada ranked fourth (after Japan, Taiwan, and Hong Kong) in imports with a total of $12 million and third in exports with $1.2 million. Hawaii's trade deficits are balanced by the tourist industry.

At the turn of the century Canada's major import from Japan was tea and the major exports were lumber and coal. In eighty years the trade pattern of imports has changed dramatically but that of exports has not. Today Japan is shipping manufactured goods, but Canada is still supplying Japan with raw materials. In ten years (1965–75) the two-way trade has grown seven times, with an average growth rate of more than twenty per cent per annum. In the five years between 1972 and 1977, Canada's exports to Japan rose from $962 million to a record $2.5 billion, of which thirty-five per cent were agricultural products (including grains). In imports, in 1977, Canada purchased $1.8 billion in producer goods, consumer durables, and non-durables, including trucks, motorcycles, and the ever present Japanese cars (see Tables 15, 16).

Japan and Canada, as industrial nations depending on world trade, are in some ways similar. As Pacific nations both have unique relationships with the United States, both have accepted non-proliferation of nuclear weapons, and both have international influence without significant military power. Yet in some ways the two countries are complementary: Japanese needs require an expansion in imports of Canadian products such as coal, rapeseed, copper and lead ores, forest products, herring roe, and wheat. Canadian requirements include many products of Japanese specialized manufacturing as well as investments.

Japan has moved ahead of the United Kingdom, ranking second to the United States as a trading partner. As an advanced technical nation, with surplus capital to invest and an increasing need for raw materials, Japan

TABLE 15: CANADA'S TRADE WITH JAPAN (VALUE, $ CAN. THOUSANDS)

Year	Exports	Imports	Balance
1950	20,443	12,076	+ 8,367
1962	214,573	125,354	+ 89,214
1972	961,696	1,071,331	–109,412
1973	1,793,457	1,018,262	+775,195
1974	2,219,722	1,426,943	+792,779
1975	2,115,093	1,204,706	+910,387
1976	2,386,190	1,523,727	+862,463
1977	2,503,005	1,802,475	+700,503

Source: Department of Industry, Trade, and Commerce Report, 1977, 1978.

TABLE 16: CANADA'S TRADE WITH JAPAN, 1977 (PRODUCTS, IN $ CAN. THOUSANDS)

Leading imports		Leading exports	
Sedans, new	269,183	Coal	529,225
Televisions, radios, phonographs	154,798	Rapeseed	227,622
Telecommunications and related equipment	158,027	Copper	206,061
Other motor vehicles	82,702	Wheat	174,399
Photographic goods	79,198	Wood pulp	145,725
Sheet and strip steel	59,122	Lumber, softwood	180,000
Other transportation equipment	54,795	Fish roe	101,502
Office machines and equipment	44,616		

Source: Department of Industry, Trade, and Commerce.

can be expected to affect Canada's historic trading patterns as its significance increases in the Canadian economy.

Excluding the United States, Japan accounts for sixty per cent of Canada's exports, and seventy-five per cent of Canada's exports pass through British Columbia ports. Over ninety-five per cent of Canada's exports are raw materials. Of the fifty-four principal commodities selling to Japan, forty-eight come from the western provinces. British Columbia, the Yukon, and the Northwest Territories combined to lead exports with a total amount of $1.8 billion in 1974, of which $462 million was copper and $309 million was forest products, these two commodities alone accounted for more than one-third of all Canadian export earnings to Japan.[33] On the other hand, western Canada receives only 26 per cent of Japanese imports while Ontario and Quebec take 67 per cent.[34] Japan also has considerable investment in Canada, concentrated primarily in the extractive resource industries. Most significant in 1977 were mining (28.5 per cent), lumbering and pulp (20.3 per cent), and iron and non-ferrous metal industries (12.5 per cent). The tendency is towards more diversification in investment and commerce accounts for sixteen per cent of Japanese investment in Canada. Already alarmed by American controls through investments, some Canadians are dubious about the entry of another foreign investor.

Although the increasing trade with Japan is important and profitable to Canada, it must be recognized that as Canada supplies only 5 per cent of Japan's total imports the trade is more important to Canada than to Japan. Furthermore, exports to Japan exceed imports from Japan; in 1977 imports were $1,802 million and exports $2,503 million. Canada is endeavouring to expand its Japanese trade, but there are problems. The fact that western Canada is diminishing its raw materials by exporting, often from industries in which Japanese capital is involved, has led to demands that these be partially processed in Canada, thus providing employment. "I took great pains to explain in Japan that we have no intention of parting with our raw materials unconditionally."[35] In central Canada competition to manufacturing industries such as in automobiles, television, radio, and textiles has resulted in pressures for protection.

Prime Minister Trudeau has travelled to Europe and Asia in the hope of increasing good relations and understanding, in efforts to increase Canadian trade, and in attempts to lessen Canada's economic dependence on the United States. In 1976, in Tokyo, an agreement of co-operation was signed with Prime Minister Takeo Miki. The Japanese were interested in ensuring a supply of raw materials and in protecting their fishing industry in view of Canada's unilateral proclamation of a 200-mile territorial zone. The Canadians were interested in attracting risk capital and in increasing the sale of goods other than purely raw materials. For example, it was suggested that Japan might be interested in the Canadian Short Take-Off and Landing Aircraft (STOL) or in atomic reactors (CANDU). Both countries wished to reduce any attitudes towards protection which might affect their exports. Japan and Canada have a continuing joint programme of economic co-operation and in 1977 the Canada–Japan Economic Committee began annual meetings to increase the sale of finished Canadian exports to Japan from three per cent to ten per cent of the total within five or ten years.[36] In one year Canada had eight missions with Japan.[37]

In the international trading environment, competition is challenging and often ruthless. In the free enterprise system of industrialized democracy, government leaders, in consultation and by bilateral agreements, can increase favourable attitudes and reduce restrictions. After governments have set the stage for co-operation, in the words of Prime Minister Trudeau: "It is up to the private sector in both countries now. There is a challenge to be picked up by the private sector of Canada."

Although overshadowed by Japan, other countries of the North Pacific (Taiwan, South Korea, and North Korea) have had remarkable trade expansion in the postwar years. Taiwan claimed to have increased its international trade by thirty-nine per cent in 1976, most exports going to the United States and most imports coming from Japan.[38] Its tourist industry increased in twenty years from $1 million to $452 million, over one-half of the visitors being Japanese. Canadian businessmen continue to maintain contacts, although Taiwan is not officially recognized by the Canadian government and, "at present we have no intention of opening a trade mission in Taiwan."[39] The Canadian textile industries have vigorously opposed the importation of cheap textiles from Asia, and in 1975 reserves were set for eleven countries, by which Taiwan agreed to a reserve of 205,125 dozen shirts as well as restraints on other clothing goods.[40]

The Republic of Korea has expanded dramatically since the Korean War.

The bulk of Korea's exports is concentrated in two major markets, the United States and Japan (see Table 17). In 1976, with total exports of $8.1 billion, the leading percentages were: United States thirty-three, Japan twenty-three, Germany five, Hong Kong four, and Canada four. Canada's relations with the Republic of Korea have been increasing steadily. A Korean embassy was established in Ottawa in 1964, and a Canadian embassy was opened in Seoul in 1973. Canadian–Korean trade has risen rapidly from a total of $33 million in 1970 to $245 million in 1975, with the balance approximately two to one in Korea's favour. Canada is the ninth largest supplier of goods to Korea, and Korea's fifth largest market. Textiles and garments constitute the largest category of Canada's imports. Surprisingly, seventy-two per cent of Canada's exports are fully manufactured or semi-fabricated materials.

TABLE 17: TRADE TABLES, REPUBLIC OF KOREA ($ U.S. MILLION)

Year	Exports	Imports
1958	17	378
1968	455	1,463
1974	4,460	6,844

Source: U.N. Statistical Yearbook, 1974.

Since 1969 Canada has been increasing its trade with North Korea. In 1975 exports totalled $4.924 million, of which $4.922 million were wheat. Imports, mainly calculating machines and clothing, totalled $.108 million.

One of the most controversial exports to the Republic of Korea has been the sale of a CANDU power reactor in January 1976, subject to the safeguard procedures outlined by the International Atomic Energy Committee. This sale, made to a government which is questionably democratic, aroused the fears of nuclear proliferation which were obvious in the criticisms of parliamentary opposition members, who questioned whether it is possible to have adequate guarantees and safeguards.[41]

Successive Canadian governments between 1949 and 1968 examined the possibility of entering into official relations with the new government of the People's Republic of China, but there were serious obstacles, especially the tensions caused by the Korean War and the problem of Taiwan. Canada was a strong supporter for the People's Republic's acceptance into the United Nations, and established diplomatic relations in 1970. Despite the lack of diplomatic relations, China had emerged as a major market for Canadian wheat after 1960. Since the establishment of relations, strenuous efforts have been made by numerous ministerial visits to improve communications. In 1973 a most-favoured nation trade agreement was negotiated (renewed 1976), and an annual Joint Trade Committee was established by the two countries. Scientific, cultural, and athletic exchanges have increased the feeling of a mutually beneficial relationship.

Although China is a large country in size and population, international trade plays only a minor role in its economic development, comprising less than one per cent of world trade, and totalling less than one-quarter of Canada's international trade figure (see Table 18). Recent policies indicate a more aggressive attitude. In 1970 China first started to use its own ships to carry cargo and by 1977 approximately fifty ships loaded at Vancouver. One of the problems of this development is the large trade surplus in favour of Canada, for the ships often arrive almost empty.

TABLE 18: CHINA'S MAJOR TRADING PARTNERS, 1975 ($ CAN. MILLION)

	Imports	Exports
U.S.S.R.*	143	139
Romania	220	220
Germany	523	224
France	362	166
Japan	2,211	1,501
Singapore	50	239
Australia	278	76
Canada	376	56
United States	304	171
Hong Kong	6	1,360
Total trade $ U.S. million	4,975	4,360

Source: Department of Industry, Trade, and Commerce, Ottawa, 1976.
* 1974

Canada's most important export to China historically has been wheat. Between 1965 and 1972, only once was the percentage of wheat exports less than ninety per cent of Canada's total exports to China. Since 1972 exports have become more diversified, but in 1975 wheat still comprised eighty-two per cent and in 1976 totalled seventy-three per cent. Besides wheat, China has become one of the largest markets for wood pulp and takes a variety of minerals as well as a few end products. Approximately three-quarters of Chinese imports into Canada are textiles. Exports to China in 1976 totalled $196 million, and imports totalled $88 million. The China grain trade has become of major importance to the economies of the farmers of the prairies and to the people of British Columbia who handle it (see Table 19).

Canada is hoping to broaden its China market with the sale of products such as chemical fertilizers, machines, and special metals. As yet China has been reluctant to open its doors wide to extensive foreign trade, especially with firms that have American interests, but it promises to be a potential market for Canadians. Until regulations are relaxed, the tourist industry will remain insignificant.

Only a small part of North American trade moves across the Pacific to the U.S.S.R. This trade, like China's, tends to be one-way, and is largely

TABLE 19: CANADA'S TRADE WITH CHINA ($ CAN. MILLION)

	Exports	Wheat/percent of exports	Imports
1965	105	104/99%	15
1970	142	122/86%	19
1971	204	191/94%	23
1972	261	234/90%	48
1973	273	187/69%	53
1974	438	334/76%	61
1975	376	307/82%	56
1976	196	143/73%	88

Source: Department of Industry, Trade, and Commerce. Preliminary figures for 1977 show export totals of $369 million, of which 84 per cent is wheat, and import totals of $82 million.

based on grains: from Canada, wheat, and from the United States, wheat and corn. In 1976 the Soviet Union agreed to a long-term agreement with the United States in which the Soviet Union is committed to buy annually a minimum of six million metric tons (approximately 228 million bushels) of wheat and corn combined, and in that year the Soviets purchased the minimum. In 1976, with its large grain sale, the United States sold $2.3 billion worth of products to Russia, while the Soviets sold only $221 million to the United States.[42] In 1972–73 the Soviet Union was Canada's largest market for Canadian wheat, buying 147.9 million bushels, which was thirty per cent of Canada's total wheat exports. This figure was slightly above the total exports to China, while Japan, which imported 50.6 million bushels, was Canada's third largest wheat market. In that year wheat comprised eighty-five per cent of Canadian exports to Soviet Russia. However, sales to the U.S.S.R. are uncertain because of the inconsistencies of Russian harvests. Russia had not been considered a major trading nation, but there are signs that it intends to become more competitive by increasing its merchant marine and by offering low rates for shipping.[43]

The U.S.S.R. has immense natural resources. It is self-sufficient in all major industrial minerals except bauxite, tin, and uranium, and intensive exploration and geological research are continuously increasing the known reserves. The Soviet Union is the highest producer of iron ore, with an estimated thirty-nine per cent of the world's total, and in 1974 its output was about three times that of second-ranking United States. In recent years the centre of energy production and raw materials has shifted to Siberia. Although the resources in this region are relatively cheap to exploit, there are serious difficulties. The biggest problem is the area's undeveloped transportation system. Highways are few, and the Trans-Siberian Railway, although now double-tracked and electrified, has a limited capacity and serves a restricted area. In 1974 a new railway was begun farther north through the wilderness and is targeted for completion by 1982 to specially constructed ports on the Pacific coast.

Canada and the U.S.S.R. have many common problems. Both are opening vast new resources which require special technology to work them in the cold north. Both are handicapped by the lack of transportation and are planning railways and roads into undeveloped, but potentially rich, areas. Both have difficulty in attracting the necessary labour force, despite the offer of high wages and other special benefits. Both lack the investment funds necessary for the development of their northern resources. Recognizing their common problems, the governments and private sectors of the U.S.S.R. and Canada have held a number of exchanges in order to co-operate in research. To date, these discussions have resulted in very little of a concrete nature.

Today competition in world trade is becoming more intense and ruthless. Canada must be prepared to be aggressive if its position as a leading industrial nation is to be maintained. Concerted efforts must be made to overcome the disadvantages stemming from high unit costs which result from Canada's small population and the resulting handicaps to the development of technical innovations.[44] Between 1968 and 1974 exports rose on an average annual rate of 5.7 per cent in Canada, 8.8 per cent in the U.S., 12.1 per cent in France, and 13.5 per cent in Japan.[45] Canada's merchandise trade balance moved from a peak surplus of $2.7 billion in 1973 to a deficit of $639 million in 1975. In 1976 Canada had an overall trade deficit of $5 billion, the U.S. anticipated a deficit of $3.5 billion, France of $2.75 billion, while Germany and Japan ran up surpluses.[46]

With the co-operation of government and business Canadians are endeavouring to increase their sales of manufactured goods, finished products, and technological expertise while improving their trading position. In many cases this means joint ventures or partnerships with foreign capital, which creates the unpleasant prospect of increased foreign influence unless these are under rigid controls. Canada is the most dependent of all industrial nations on foreign trade; for example, with only one-fifth of the population of Japan, Canada exports more than one-half of the Japanese total. Fifty per cent of everything produced in Canada is exported. Seventy per cent of the exports go to one market, the United States, which means that the United States absorbs thirty-five per cent of everything produced in Canada. Twenty-five per cent of all jobs in Canada are related to our export trade, as is some twenty-three per cent of the income of Canadians.[47] International trade is a matter of economic life or death for Canada.

The North Pacific offers opportunities for Canadian business. Success will depend on an aggressive approach, efficiency, low unit costs, availability of materials, dependable delivery, competitive prices, and an understanding of the structures and policies of the governments of prospective markets.

THE OCEAN RESOURCES

Common to all the North Pacific nations are industries dependent on the sea. From earliest times to the present the fishery resources have been an important food source, and fishing has been a major industry. From the sea the native people obtained skins, oil, whalebone, and a wide variety of shells. With the coming of the Europeans the exploitation of sea resources has become more intense and efficient.

The first important European industry in the North Pacific was the maritime fur trade in search of the sea otter. This animal had been almost exterminated by the early traders before 1830, but it was saved by the conservation policies of the Russians in Alaska. When Alaska was sold to the United States, the Americans revived the hunt. In 1911 commercial hunting by both the United States and Canada was banned. The sea otter had been exterminated in British Columbia, however; the last one was seen near Kyoquot in 1929. A few herds in the Aleutians survived, as well as some in California and scattered groups off north-eastern Siberia. The sea otters were also believed to be extinct in California, but in 1938 residents near Monterey discovered a herd of ninety-four. These have since increased to an estimated seven hundred.

Whereas by the early 1900's the sea otter population had probably been reduced to two thousand, under conservation the number is now estimated at fifty thousand survivors in the Aleutians and the offshore islands of north-eastern Siberia. In 1959 the Alaska Department of Fish and Game began transplanting sea otters from their concentrations near Amchitka (near the testing grounds of the Atomic Energy Commission) to various other sites. In 1969 thirty animals were sent to each of Washington State and British Columbia. Apparently none of the Washington animals survived and the success in British Columbia was uncertain. Further transplants were made in 1970 and 1972 to the Bunsby Islands off north-western Vancouver Island. In the latter project eighty-nine sea otters were released, and in 1977 surveys showed fifty-five otters still inhabiting the Bunsby Islands and fifteen at Nootka, leading to the supposition that others are scattered throughout this forty-mile stretch. The annual net increase for the next decade is expected to be ten per cent. In 1968 a limited number of Aleutian pelts were sold in Seattle, but harvesting was disallowed in 1972 with the introduction of the U.S. Marine Mammal Protection Act.[48]

The fur seal presents a similar story. These mammals have their breeding grounds in the American Pribiloff Islands in the Bering Sea. The Russian–American Company set a limit on the catch to preserve the animal, but it could not prevent pelagic sealing, the taking of seals in the open ocean during their annual migration. As in the case of the sea otter, with the purchase of Alaska the slaughter of seals revived. The United States closed its ports to sealers in 1879, but they moved to Victoria, which became the centre of the North Pacific industry. This port thrived on the pelagic sealing industry for almost fifty years until 1911. The 122 schooners directly employed almost three thousand people and the industry affected the entire commercial life of the city.[49]

The American regulation of 1879, combined with attempts to stop competition by the Alaska Commercial Company, which did its sealing on the Pribiloff Islands, resulted in strong American opposition to the continued presence of Canadian pelagic sealers. In 1886 the Americans seized three Canadian sealing schooners in the Bering Sea, and continued the practice in following years. At that time Canada's ocean rights were protected by the British navy and, furthermore, diplomatic negotiations for Canadian problems were carried out by Britain. Eventually Canadian pressures caused Britain to protest the seizures, but the discussions dragged on for several years. In 1892 Britain and the United States agreed to submit the problem to an arbitration committee of seven, two from Britain and the United States and one each from France, Italy, and the Kingdom of Norway and Sweden. The tribunal stated that the United States had no rights beyond the three-mile limit, but recommended that the United States should control a pelagic sealing zone of sixty miles around the Pribiloff Islands, a regulation which was accepted by Canadian sealers, although it was unsatisfactory. The tribunal also proclaimed that there should be no sealing between 1 May and 31 July in the Bering Sea or Pacific Ocean north of 35° latitude and east of 180° longitude. Five years later Britain and the United States agreed that the latter would pay Britain $473,151.26 in settlement of the damages. By this time Japan, uninhibited by the British–American agreements, had begun pelagic sealing on a large scale.[50]

Whereas it was estimated that in 1860 there were more than five million fur seals, by 1910 it was estimated that only 125,000 fur seals remained, and drastic action was necessary. The following year a treaty of conservation was signed by Japan, Russia, the United States, and Britain (for Canada) limiting the hunt and restricting pelagic sealing. This was the first international agreement on conservation signed by these four Pacific nations. In 1940 the Japanese abrogated the treaty when they claimed that the fur seals were injuring the fishing industry. In 1955 agreement was reached again when the original signatories accepted the North Pacific Fur Seal Convention.

The original Convention of 1911, by Article V, also includes the protection of the sea otter. Further protection was extended by a presidential proclamation of Woodrow Wilson on 31 May 1913 and an executive order signed by Calvin Coolidge on 14 January 1929. The 1955 Convention states that it covers the "waters of the Pacific Ocean north of the thirtieth parallel of North Latitude, and includes the Bering Sea, Okhotsk Sea and the Sea of Japan." Pelagic sealing, "the killing, taking or hunting in any manner whatever of the fur seals at sea," is forbidden. The agreement excludes Indians, Eskimos, Ainos, and Aleuts dwelling on coasts contiguous to the convention waters "in canoes and propelled entirely by oars, paddles or sails and manned by not more than five persons and without the use of firearms." If the number of seals on either the Kommander or Robben Islands falls below 50,000 head, killing on that island will be suspended. Canada and Japan each receive fifteen per cent of Russian and United States catches.[51]

The indiscriminate slaughter of whales has threatened them with extinction, and to conserve this resource the seventeen-member International Whaling Commission each year sets a quota on the number of each species of whale which may be killed.[52] This figure decreases annually, indicating the continued reduction of whale stocks. Traditional whaling nations such as Norway and Great Britain have long since withdrawn from commercial whaling, the United States catch is negligible, and Canada has not engaged in commercial whaling since 1972. With the exception of the small Minke whale, the largest quota for the North Atlantic for 1976/77 and 1977/78 was 685 for sperm whales. The decimation of the southern hemisphere is revealed by the fact that the quota for male sperm whales was reduced from 5,870 in 1976 to 3,894 in 1977, while the quota for female sperm whales was reduced from 4,870 to 897 in those years, although in 1978 figures were increased to 4,538 and 1,370 respectively. The June 1977 meeting of the IWC recommended that the total whale catch be reduced from 28,050 to 17,389, a reduction of thirty-six per cent. The only major whaling region remaining is the North Pacific. Quota figures for the North Pacific are as shown in Table 20.

TABLE 20: WHALING QUOTAS IN THE NORTH PACIFIC

Species	1976 Quota	1977 Quota	1978 Quota
Bryde's	1,363	1,000	524
Sperm male	5,200	4,320	6,444*
Sperm female	3,100	2,880	
Minke	none	541	400

Source: Environment Canada, News Release, 57/07/12/76. Vancouver Sun, 24 June 1976. The minke is a small species about nine metres long. Bryde's whales average sixteen metres. * The original figure was set at 763 but protests by Japan and the U.S.S.R. resulted in an increase in December 1978 with a vote of fourteen to one by the IWC.

A significant product from the whale hunt is whale oil. Whale oil production for 1973–74 totalled 137.7 thousand metric tons divided into 72 tons Antarctic, 36 North Pacific, and 11.5 Japan. In spite of protests, Japan and Russia, the two greatest whaling nations, continue to scour the seas, claiming that the need for food and other whale products makes this industry essential. Of the metric tons caught Russia had 73.9 and Japan 42.7 (see Table 21).

TABLE 21: NUMBER OF WHALES CAUGHT

	1966/67	1974/75
U.S.S.R.	20,918	15,083
Japan	20,124	10,083
U.S.A.	246	21
Canada	1,304	nil

Source: U.N. Statistical Tables, 1975.

Various groups, such as Project Jonah of Bolinas, California, and the Greenpeace Foundation of Vancouver, British Columbia, have been formed to stop whaling.[53] The Canadian group by 1977 had established several international branches, especially in the United States. It had already gained publicity for its irritating interference with French nuclear tests in the South Pacific and the seal hunt in the North Atlantic, before it began to campaign vigorously against the Japanese and Russian whalers. In 1976 and 1977, the vessel *Greenpeace III*, although unable to contact the Japanese whalers, followed the Russian fleet and claimed not only to have disrupted its schedule but also to have saved a number of whales by interposing itself between the whalers and their quarry. After the 1976 expedition it was unofficially reported that Russia would limit its whaling after two years.

Following the Alaska boundary dispute, Canada and the United States adopted a policy of co-operation and negotiation for settling disputes. In 1909 the permanent International Joint Commission was established to settle boundary disputes and to supervise the rise, diversion, or obstruction of boundary waters which might affect the levels of purity of waters common to both countries. Conservation of common resources was planned.

The fishing industry of the north-west coast is important to both countries (see Table 22). In 1923 they signed the Halibut Conservation Treaty for the control of halibut fisheries especially along the northern coast.[54] This was the first international treaty signed by Canada without a British signature

TABLE 22: FISH CATCHES, 1973 (METRIC TONS, 000)

Japan	10,709
Republic of Korea	1,654
Canada	1,151
China	7,574
U.S.S.R.	8,619
U.S.A.	2,670

Source: U.N. Statistical Yearbook, 1974.

and indicates Canada's growing independence in international relations. Three years later Canada sent its first representative to the United States, the beginning of diplomatic representation in foreign countries. It is significant that within three years the next two embassies were to France and Japan.

Salmon is the most important fish resource of both the United States and Canada. Common fishing in the Strait of Juan de Fuca led to overfishing and the threat of extermination of the species. Fishing is a renewable food source, but just as intensive agricultural practices without soil conservation can impoverish the land, so intensive fishing can decimate the ocean. Aquaculture means the scientific harvesting which is necessary to perpetuate the living resources of the sea. With this concept of perpetual yield, research in aquaculture becomes increasingly important.

At the turn of the century fish boats were still unable to venture into the open ocean, and most fishing was done near the shores and river mouths. Improvements in canning methods increased the number of canneries and the markets for fish products. In 1901 there were seventy-three canneries in Puget Sound and on the Fraser River depending on the Fraser River run.[55] The result was overfishing and a serious threat to the stocks, and both Canada and the United States began to make efforts to control them. In 1905 a joint commission studied the problem, but the two countries were unable to agree on procedures. After twenty-five years of bickering the International Pacific Salmon Fisheries Commission was formed in 1930, with three members from each country. "Inasmuch as the purpose of this Convention is to establish for the High Contracting Parties, by their joint effort and expense, a fishing that is now largely non-existent...that they should share equally in the fishing...an equal portion of fish may be caught each year by the fishermen of each Party."[56] The commission was not only to divide the harvest but was also to rebuild the salmon runs. The Pacific Salmon Fisheries Convention Act of 1937 was concerned with only sockeye salmon, but in 1957 it was extended to include pink (chum) salmon. The Reciprocal Fisheries Agreement of 1973, renewable in 1977, included regulations for coho and chinook species.

The growth of population increased the demand for food, and as the easily accessible fishing grounds became depleted, the fishermen were forced to venture farther from their home bases and into the ocean. Improved fishing methods and methods of preservation along with the larger, more efficient fishing vessels made this possible. As the industry expanded over larger areas, costs rose, and both fishing and those industries based on fishing required larger amounts of capital. The result was centralization of production by large organizations which often controlled not only the fishing fleets but also the processing and marketing industries.

On each coast the nations reached agreements on fishing areas. The United

States and Canada reached agreements on the halibut and salmon from Alaska to Washington. Japan and Russia negotiated on the islands north of Japan. In 1952 the governments of Canada, Japan, and the United States agreed that "the line of meridian 175° W. Longitude ... be adopted for determining the areas in which the exploitation of salmon is abstained or the conservation measures for salmon continue to be enforced."[57] Agreements between the United States and Canada not only limit the annual catches, but also co-ordinate conservation and replenishing efforts such as fish hatcheries and scientific studies. The most publicized joint effort is in Hell's Gate in the Fraser Canyon, where fish ladders assist the salmon to reach their spawning grounds.

Such co-operative planning should ensure reliable stocks for an indefinite future for both Canada and the United States, but their efforts are threatened by the encroachments of other nations. Large Japanese and, especially, Russian fleets are appearing off the North American coasts from the Bering Sea to California. A fleet includes not only large numbers of fishing vessels but also "mother" ships which completely process the catch, enabling the flotilla to remain at sea for long periods. These intruders claim to be gathering "groundfish" or fish not used by Canadians and Americans. It is impossible to believe that their fishing methods are so selective that they are not catching the salmon and halibut which Canadians and Americans, at considerable cost, have replenished.

There are three possible solutions to these intrusions: to establish similar large-scale fleets and send them far into the ocean even to fishing in Asian waters; to expand our territorial zones and by patrols forcibly drive away foreign vessels; to establish international fishing agreements. The establishment of large fleets is against Canadian customs and would require large capital outlays. Such an expense has not been accepted by private enterprise as profitable. Government policy has been to encourage the rights of individual and independent fishermen and has not considered the use of government funds to establish large fishing projects. Instead, the government has strongly supported numerous Law of the Sea Conferences in the hope of establishing international regulations.

About fifty nations have established fisheries zones beyond twelve miles, in many cases as far as two hundred miles. Before 1977 Canada had been approaching a similar stance for some time. In 1964 it established a nine-mile fishing zone outside of its three-mile territorial limits, and six years later proclaimed a twelve-mile territorial zone, which was accepted by the United States in a reciprocal agreement (1970). In 1971 fishing zone "3" was designated as a straight line extending from Cape Scott, at the northern end of Vancouver Island, to the Queen Charlotte Islands. On 1 January 1977 it unilaterally proclaimed a twelve-mile territorial limit plus a 188-mile fishing zone, thus extending its control to two hundred miles. This added 700,000 square miles to Canadian territory, and when these limits were extended to the Canadian Arctic in March 1977 another 400,000 square miles were added.

The United States, which is also a major fishing nation, had opposed this distance, but with both Canada and Mexico adopting the 200-mile zone and with foreign vessels increasing off its coast, it reversed its attitude and proclaimed the zone two months after Canada. Both Canada and the United States have taken steps to support their positions. In March 1976, the Canadian cabinet increased operating expenses by $4 million to a total of $12 million for offshore patrols in the year 1976-77. Surveillance and enforcement involve ships and aircraft of the Fisheries and Marine Service, Department of Transport, and Department of National Defence. The last will supply four destroyers for Pacific coast duties.

However, the establishment of the new zones by both countries resulted in revived tensions between American and Canadian fishermen. Disputes arose about the direction of ocean boundaries from the Atlantic coast and also from the Strait of Juan de Fuca and Dixon Entrance. The Reciprocal Fisheries Agreement of 1973 was not renewed in 1977 and interim policies were adopted. Canadian–American fisheries disputes have been almost continuous since the United States became independent and a solution to this newest problem may demand patience and co-operation for many years.

In 1977, Foreign Fisheries Regulations made under the Fisheries Act set out operational restrictions on foreign fishing vessels, including quotas, mesh size limitations, and closed areas.[58] On the Pacific coast, Canada has determined the Total Allowable Catches (TAC) and the allocations of surplus to other countries. (On the Atlantic these figures were made by multilateral agreements through ICNAF.) Except for the United States, with which Canada has a Reciprocal Fishing Privileges Agreement, each foreign fishing vessel and each ship engaged in servicing the foreign fishing fleets is required to have a licence to operate in the new zone and must report its position and catches weekly.[59] All data is fed to a computer data management system, called FLASH, which is co-ordinated to give an updated survey of conditions and to permit a sophisticated capability for predictions of stock abundance.

Canada recognizes its inability to police and enforce these claims against stronger nations, and to prevent confrontations has conducted bilateral negotiations which have led to agreements in the Pacific region with Poland, Japan, Korea, and the U.S.S.R.

Russia, which in 1971 had made a renewable agreement with Canada by which Russian vessels were permitted into restricted zones for the purposes of servicing their vessels and for loading and unloading, was the first nation to make an agreement recognizing and complying with Canada's jurisdiction in the two hundred-mile zone. In November 1976, after the election of President Carter, Russia indicated its acceptance of United States rights and in December established its own two-hundred-mile zone. South Korea also accepted the United States zone and established its own.

The two-hundred-mile zones of other countries not only threaten the Japanese people's diet, but also add to the problems of unemployment and territorial rights. Distant-water fishing has been providing about four million tons of Japan's total annual catch of more than ten million tons. Seventy per cent of Japan's distant ocean catch falls within the new United States and Soviet zones and their two-hundred-mile limits will cause a drop estimated at between fifty per cent and eighty per cent of Japan's distant-water haul. From the Canadian and the United States zones, Japan takes mostly low-value fish, but from the Soviet waters of the Sea of Okhotsk and the Kamchatka Peninsula come the major catches of salmon, crab, and herring. In spite of opposition to the two-hundred-mile fishing zones of Canada, the United States, and Russia, the Japanese government was forced to retaliate to Russia's action for the protection of its own rights. In March 1977 the Japanese government approved a bill increasing Japan's territorial waters from three to twelve miles, while at the same time establishing its own two hundred-mile fishing zone.[60] Exempted from the twelve-mile limit are five strategically located international straits used by American warships. China and South Korea will not be excluded from the two-hundred-mile zone in the Sea of Japan, Yellow Sea, and the East China Sea. Both China and North Korea have protested the agreements reached by Japan and South Korea on the East China Sea, claiming that regulations for this common sea should be by agreement of the four nations. An interim agreement for 1977 only, nullifying the former Russian–Japanese fishing agreements, reduced the catch of Japanese fishermen in the Russian zone to about sixty-three per cent of previous years, and reduced the catch of Russian fishermen to about sixty-nine per cent of their former catch in Japanese zones. Meanwhile, for many years Japan has been developing the artificial breeding of salmon and other fisheries resources and the adoption of two-hundred-mile zones has resulted in an intensification of scientific research in this field, with the expectation that artificially bred salmon will result in a larger catch than that currently caught from the whole Pacific. This expectation has also increased the demands for the elimination of pollution in local waters.

When Prime Minister Trudeau visited Japan in 1976, he was told that the Japanese did not agree with the limitations and that further negotiations were necessary. From the discussion, agreement was reached to permit licensed Japanese fishing off both the Atlantic and Pacific coasts for a year while negotiations continue towards a bilateral agreement. Similarly, Canada and the United States agreed to continue their present practices and "to consult as necessary to ensure harmonious implementation" for a year until agreement is reached on controversial zones such as the Dixon Entrance and the extensions from the Strait of Juan de Fuca.

These various agreements will cover major fisheries off Canada's Pacific coast and more than eighty-eight per cent of the foreign catch within Canada's 200-mile zone.[61]

Canada does not intend to withdraw food from a hungry world, but if conservation is not practised there will not be enough food for everyone. Canada and the United States have stated that they intend to protect the needs of their own fishermen, and to establish conservation and management measures which will protect and rebuild fish stocks. Canadian fish should be caught by Canadian fishermen and processed by Canada, but the harvest would be distributed to other nations. Such a policy depends on the co-operation of other nations in controlling their fishing fleets and on the success of Canadian efforts to conserve and replenish the fishery resources. Canada believes that salmon should be caught with the exclusive management powers of the state of origin and further that there should be a ban on high seas fishing of anadromous species. Although there is no formal North Pacific organization such as the ICNAF (replaced in 1978 by NAFO) of the Atlantic, mechanisms do exist through which the same kinds of agreements can be achieved on the Pacific.

However, it must be acknowledged that some countries are strongly opposed to the two-hundred-mile zone. To discuss international agreements on problems relating to the sea, numerous Law of the Sea Conferences (UNCLOS) have been held since 1958. Because of many divergent interests, negotiations have been slow. Unanimous agreement on the two-hundred-mile zone has been impossible so that, although there has been an increase in the number of states supporting the zone, there is no international agreement. Zones must be established unilaterally and accepted by bilateral agreements. Another major problem on the agendas of the Law of the Sea Conferences has been to reach an agreement on the mining of the seabeds.[62]

With technological advances in recent years, the mining of the seabeds, where nodules are estimated to value $3 billion, has become a source of international disputes.[63] There are several aspects to this problem. What is the status of the two hundred-mile-limit? How should the proceeds from the international seabeds be divided? Those nations which do not have the necessary technical equipment and even those which are landlocked with no coastline believe that the benefits must be divided among all nations. This is a reflection of the developing nations' (the "have-nots") attempt to obtain a more equitable share of the world's resources, of which some nations such as Canada have an abundance.

Should nations have the right to unilaterally mine within their territorial limits or in the international ocean for their own profit? This question is of particular importance to the United States, which is the most advanced in undersea mining. Such a practice would lead to distress in both producer and consumer states. What protection is offered to present land-based mineral industries and their employees? Canada, once the world's largest producer of nickel, has been threatened in recent years by competition from other nations. Major production of undersea nickel could be disastrous to the industry.

At the Law of the Sea Conferences Canada is urging a solution which would protect land producers of nickel, copper, cobalt, and manganese, while allowing mining of these minerals from the international marine bottoms for the benefit of the international community.

Along with the problems of fisheries conservation and undersea mining is that of the growing pollution which is affecting ocean life and coastal communities. The most publicized pollution threat is that of oil, which is common to the entire Pacific Rim. Both Japan and the western United States are dependent on imported oil. Not only does the incidental discharge of wastes from ships reach a formidable total, but the construction of gigantic oil tankers up to 200,000 dwt presents new dangers.[64]

With the discovery of large Alaskan oil reserves which must be transported to the energy-starved United States, the problem of oil pollution has become a critical issue to the Pacific coast. Arguments for and against tanker transport have been contested before the courts and governments for many years without a decision. Alternate overland pipeline routes have been similarly supported and opposed without a clear resolution of the problems. In a world where oil stocks are declining while the demands for petroleum products are increasing, there is no doubt that the oil of Alaska must be brought south. Carried by pipeline across Alaska to Valdez, oil would be carried on supertankers to some southern point where it could be piped inland. The west coast route has a long history of maritime disasters, and there is no reason why these ships should be immune. In 1976 nineteen tankers throughout the world went aground or blew up, spilling more than a quarter of a million tons of oil. As each different terminal is proposed the dangers are evident: Kitimat is at the end of a long narrow inlet, and Port Angeles is on the stormy Strait of Juan de Fuca. In 1977, against the strong opposition of Washington State, the United States congress forbade the use of a terminal for supertankers in Puget Sound. The route into this narrow, intricate inlet would pass within eighteen miles of Canada, would threaten the rich salmon fisheries of the Fraser, and would be close to the most densely populated areas of Washington and British Columbia. Adding to the dangers is the failure to establish international standards. Tankers and vessels sailing under flags of convenience such as those of Liberia and Panama have a tragic history of unseaworthiness. The Pacific coast peoples from Alaska to California are united in their fear of the destruction which might be caused by the wrecking of one supertanker.

Eighty per cent of Russia's energy sources: coal, oil, and natural gas, and hydroelectric power, are located in Siberia, where there are believed to be some of the greatest of the world's deposits of oil and, especially, natural gas. However, as with mineral resources, the development of oil and natural gas fields calls for enormous amounts of capital. Foreign assistance is being sought for the exploitation of Siberia's resources on a co-operative basis, by which the foreign investors would provide technology and equipment against repayment in long-term deliveries of the product. Three such deals were signed with Japan in 1974 and 1975, involving Japanese credits totalling $1 billion for the development of eastern Siberian timber, coking coal deposits in southern Yakutia, and offshore oil and gas off Sakhalin. Talks on a much bigger tripartite deal with Japan and American companies for the development of natural gas reserves have not yet resulted in American agreement. Meanwhile, the U.S.S.R. is proceeding on a network of large diameter pipelines to link the oil and gas fields of Siberia to industrial centres and ports on the Pacific coast. From these centres, oil and gas could be shipped to Japan, the United States, Australia, and Canada. Along with the oil of Indonesia such a project would increase the number of trans-Pacific tankers.

The much publicized threat of oil spillage has overshadowed numerous other dangers of pollution which come from human carelessness and waste. Industrial wastes threaten the ecological balance of local, often isolated communities and are often ignored because of the small area affected far from centres of population. However, added together, especially when they are close to densely populated areas as in Japan or the Puget Sound–Georgia Strait waterways, they wipe out a vast quantity of sea life. Japan is becoming alarmed about the harm done to people from its increasing industrial pollution. Urban wastes have not only made sea life inedible but have also resulted in the closing of beaches and recreational areas. Floating debris from vessels and aircraft, especially with the advent of insoluble synthetics and plastics, has made beaches unsightly as well as being a nuisance and often a danger to fishermen and other boat operators. Increasing the problem of control is the fact that eighty per cent of ocean pollution is carried from the land by rivers and seaports. Thus control leads to possible federal–provincial/state clashes over jurisdiction and responsibility.

Formerly generally unnoticed, the dangers of uncontrolled dumping in ocean waters have been recognized by an intergovernmental conference of eighty nations in London, England, where the London Convention reached agreement on the necessity of regulating dumping. The conference accepted the fact that "the assimilative capacity of the ocean has finite limits; there is a saturation point to the ocean's ability to dilute, degrade, and dissipate waste is receiving waters."

The Canadian government recognizes the dangers of pollution in the Ocean Dumping Control Act, 1975, which permits fines up to one hundred thousand dollars for an offence. Prohibitive substances include mercury compounds, persistent plastics and other persistent synthetic materials, oils in all forms, high level radioactive waste and matter, substances used for biological and chemical warfare, containers, and scrap metal. Among the considerations to be taken into account for dumping are "possible effects on the amenities, possible effects on marine life, possible effects on other uses of the sea such as impairment of water quality or underwater corrosion of structure."[65]

Pollution threatens from the air as well as from the water. Factories belch toxic wastes which are carried into the ocean and over surrounding coastal districts. More potentially dangerous than these is the fallout from nuclear explosions. The French in the South Pacific, the Russians in the Arctic, and the Americans in Amchitka have selected these sites as the safest for the aftermath of their "clean" nuclear experiments. The damage to undersea life in all cases is unknown. China has experimented far inland. West coast people from British Columbia to Oregon know that by using the prevailing winds the Japanese were able to float fire bombs across the Pacific during the Pacific War. Four days after China explodes an atmospheric H-bomb, radiation increases are measured in Japan, three days later they are measured on the west coast of North America, and in a few more days they are measured on the Atlantic coast. As yet the measurements are low and of negligible concern to public health. Within two weeks the air mass will probably be back on its second trip around the world. The deadly effects which an Asiatic nuclear war would have on North America are obvious.

Conservation of our ocean resources, along with the threat of pollution, has been considered until recent times as a minor local problem, but as the dangers have become increasingly cumulative, provincial/state and federal governments have been forced to become involved. Today these problems are recognized as international, and only by international agreements can they be solved. Canada and the United States have illustrated that co-operation can save the west coast fisheries, but there is no incentive to such efforts if the resulting harvest is gathered by encroaching foreign fishermen. The nations of the North Pacific have united to save the sea otter and the fur seal. Thus conservation co-operation has been achieved to a limited extent, but these beginnings must be extended to cover all phases of ocean life. The Law of the Sea Conferences are making significant contributions towards international recognition of the problems common to all North Pacific nations.

THE PEOPLE

For over four centuries Europeans (and later Americans) with their mechanical knowledge and superior military equipment looked upon other peoples as inferior races, fit to be servants, labourers, or slaves. Westerners piously undertook to "carry the white man's burden," to spread Christianity among the "heathens," to, bring education and health services, and to introduce the "savages" to the advantages of democratic government while introducing the different aspects of European culture. This concept of inequality has been difficult to dissipate. Even the League of Nations, while admitting Japan to the council, could not accept the theory of racial equality.

In the last half of the twentieth century most formerly colonial people have gained independence, have established their own forms of government, and have begun the difficult task of reviving national dignity and cultures. The sensitivity created by centuries of subjection and non-recognition survived in their continuing mistrust of Europeans. On the other hand, actions by some white people have hindered assimilation into the international community: efforts to maintain white minority rule; segregation; interference in the internal affairs of Asiatic, African, and South American states; the restriction of immigration; the opposition to equality in citizenship of native peoples; and commercial and industrial practices which protected the developed nations.

None of the six nations of the North Pacific are developing nations, yet ignorance and mistrust continue to separate North American and Asiatic peoples.[66] The attitude ingrained during the long era of imperialism, strengthened in the western states and province by the long history of oriental exclusion, cannot be forgotten in one generation. The colour barrier remains. Canadians and Americans tend to qualify their recognition of Russian technological achievements or Japanese commercial and industrial success. The definitions of success may differ, but common to all people is the desire for security, peace, and happiness. Only better communication will lead both east and west to a better appreciation of each other and a recognition that all are members of the world community. Unfortunately, communication is not yet free.

The last century has seen an unprecedented movement of peoples from region to region and from continent to continent. Millions migrated from overcrowded Europe across the Atlantic to North America, with its vast unsettled spaces and wealth of opportunities. The people of both the United States and Canada are all immigrants or descendants of immigrants (even the so-called native peoples). There was also a movement of people across the Pacific Ocean. Overcrowded Asia had little to offer would-be settlers, and most North Americans who went there were visitors with specific duties to perform. In China, pressures of population forced the people to move north and south. To the Chinese and Japanese, North America offered unlimited opportunities. Chinese immigrants came to the American coast first as visitors, but remained as settlers. Faced with the prospects of unlimited immigration from the Asiatic millions, the white community successfully adopted restrictive measures. Nevertheless, thousands of Asiatics did arrive in North America. At first they settled along the west coast, but eventually they spread across the continent.

Canadian Orientals, from historical backgrounds, are reputed to be concentrated in British Columbia, but this is far from true. Chinese, Japanese, and East Indians are found in all the provinces and territories. In British Columbia ethnic Chinese are the ninth-ranking group, East Indians are fourteenth, and Japanese are fifteenth. According to the 1971 Census of Canada, less than two per cent of the province are of Chinese origin: 44,300 in a total population of 2,184,000. Whereas thirty-seven per cent of Canadian Chinese live in British Columbia, thirty-two per cent live in Ontario. Ontario has more Japanese (forty-five per cent) than British Columbia (thirty-four per cent). Since the establishment of independent governments in East Africa with their persecution of East Indians, many have come from there to eastern Canada, and the totals will have risen from 1971 when they showed forty-four per cent in Ontario and twenty-eight per cent in British Columbia. Since the Pacific War there has been a better understanding and acceptance of the oriental-ethnic peoples in Canada. Since 1949 they have had the franchise. Immigration regulations were modified in 1948, radically changed in 1967, and again relaxed in 1977 to allow citizenship to those with three years residence over the age of eighteen. There is no legal discrimination based on colour, nationality, or ethnic background. Numerous reasons account for this changing attitude. The worldwide acceptance of equality of all peoples demonstrated by the greatly enlarged membership of the United Nations is a powerful factor. Reaction to the persecution of the Canadian Japanese in 1942 along with recognition of the contributions which many made to the war effort has led to a better understanding of these people. Some so-called Chinese-Canadians are descendents of immigrants who arrived a century ago during the Fraser gold rush or of those who built the Canadian Pacific Railway. By their antecedents these people are more Canadian than many of the Europeans whose forefathers arrived much later. These ethnically oriental Canadians have moved out of the ghettos and are socially accepted. Most of them have made valuable contributions to Canada, and outstanding leaders can be identified in business, music, visual arts, and governments at all levels. They are no longer "hyphenated Canadians," but simply Canadians.

Unfortunately, complete toleration is not yet a fact, and oriental prejudices are still latent in some places. Rumours of Hong Kong investments and of the use of Japanese capital in industries meet with resentment. There have been incidents of unprovoked violence against East Indians in cities as far apart as Vancouver and Toronto.[67] Time will tell whether these examples of intolerance are isolated incidents, or whether anti-orientalism is still a dormant force liable to erupt at some crisis.

Three North Pacific nations, Japan, Canada, and the United States, support the belief that, in democracies, governments are theoretically quasi-managerial bodies' elected to execute the wishes of the majority of the citizens. In the confederated systems of Canada and the United States this responsibility of governing is complicated by the division of authority among the different levels of government, but foreign affairs are recognized as being under federal jurisdiction.

In Canada (and the United States) the federal government must subordinate the wide variety of regional interests and pressures to decisions which are most profitable to the country as a whole. While officially bilingual, Canada has the problem of balancing the English-speaking and French-speaking people in a country which is in truth multicultural. Ethnically, the British comprise 44.6 per cent of the population, the French 26.7 per cent, and the remaining "unofficial" peoples 26.7 per cent. Similarly, the divergent economic regions are often at variance. The western workers who depend on the extraction of raw materials consider Japanese trade to be of major importance, while the eastern workers watch the increasing importation of Japanese manufactured goods with alarm. The prairie farmers are enthusiastic over wheat sales to China and Russia, which carries over to the Pacific ports, but, as yet, eastern Canadian exports to China are negligible. The federal government must equate the threat to Quebec textile industries by Korean imports with the export of Saskatchewan potash. The Canadian government may pass an ocean anti-dumping act but it cannot control the river wastes, which are under provincial jurisdiction. The government in Ottawa must arrange to expand Canadian exports while at the same time protecting Canadian industries from destructive competition. It cannot be swayed from its overall policies by individual regional demands or by pressures from small vocal special interest groups.

Provincial governments are much more vulnerable to pressures, for their interests are narrower, and the concentrated demands of people with similar interests are more intense and closer to the seat of government. At the beginning of the twentieth century the British Columbia government, as well as most provincial federal members, strongly supported anti-oriental legislation. The federal government, concerned with the impact of actions on foreign governments as well as the welfare of the entire nation, disallowed the provincial legislation. Another factor in this decision was the fear of jeopardizing relations between Japan and Britain. When noisy demonstrators on the west coast protested the sale of scrap iron and copper to Japan in the late 1930's, the Canadian government, partially to protect Canadian industries and also to prevent reactions against Canadians in Japan, ignored them.

Through sophisticated media, governments of today may exert strong influence on public opinion. The strength of democracy is the acceptance and encouragement of opposition parties. On the North Pacific, Canada, the United States, and Japan have strong opposition parties, while in Communist China, Soviet Russia, and the Koreas they are discouraged. The opposition have been called "watchdogs," for they demand an accounting of the government's actions and reveal to the people the weaknesses or dangers of government proposals. The opposition exists as a constant reminder to the governing party that it offers an alternative which dissatisfied people, through regular elections, may select.

In times of war or crisis a policy of censorship is accepted as necessary, but in normal peaceful times people must be kept informed. When Hong Kong collapsed in 1941, the government hesitated to reveal details, and even when the findings of an investigating commission were issued they were suspect to many people. Today there are numerous studies and reports on various facets of Canadian life which have been completed and filed, unseen except for a few. In a successful democracy the people must be educated and informed. As governments increase in size, so does the bureaucratic system, and the citizens find it more and more difficult to gain information through the maze of departments. For some years Canadian information services were established in numerous centres where assistance could be obtained in obtaining information, but in 1976 these were closed. A substitute method for dissemination of information must be established. In recent times, strong pressures have been brought on the governments of both Canada and the United States to permit access to government documents. It is generally accepted that there must be exceptions, but these must be clearly and precisely described. With the knowledge of the facts it is the citizen's responsibility to insist on government actions acceptable to the majority. If we are to appreciate our position on the North Pacific, materials on all aspects of the region must be readily available.

The North Pacific is becoming one of the major power and economic centres of the world. Canadians must receive unbiased information of changing conditions. It is the duty of all Canadians, from the Atlantic to the Pacific, to recognize that they are citizens of a Pacific nation, that the future of Canada depends on their understanding of this region, and that they be familiar with government policies and actions to this region.

Since 1945 the North Pacific has challenged the North Atlantic's domination of international affairs, and in the foreseeable future it could become the leader. Around it are the three largest nations in territory, the most populated countries, three major trading nations, the leaders in technical knowledge, and the most powerful military forces ever to exist. There are vast natural resources still to be developed. Commercial and financial opportunities are expanding. Mutual agreements on the conservation and use of the ocean resources are increasing.

For centuries the European nations obstinately, but erroneously, believed that great wealth would come with their penetration of the Asiatic North Pacific. Joined by the United States, they forced open the door to China, only to have it closed against them by the Chinese in 1949. Since then the nations of the North Pacific have independently achieved world significance. China, with its need for food and technical assistance, has begun to open its own door again.

Today there is a recognition that expansion of trade and improved living conditions depend on mutual understanding and co-operation by all the

North Pacific nations. The region is becoming increasingly interdependent, and offers unlimited opportunities. If the earlier sectionalism of Pacific Asia and Pacific America are not to return, strenuous efforts must be made towards stronger trans-Pacific contacts. On the success of these contacts may depend prosperity and peace in the future.

Postscript

Canadians continue to give a low priority to North Pacific affairs. Seldom are events featured on the front pages of newspapers and a diligent search of the inside pages is necessary to discover current issues. Interest in foreign affairs is focussed on the crises of the Middle East, the wars and revolutions of numerous African states, the uncertainty of OPEC policies, the problems and dissensions within NATO, the threats of terrorist organizations, and the policies of the United States. The Canadian government, reflecting the attitude of the people, maintains a policy of neutrality with minimum involvement in international affairs. Canadians are less concerned with distant crises than they are with their own problems of numerous elections, inflation, the declining value of the dollar, the high cost of living, and unemployment.

Speculation is an inevitable outcome from the study of modern history. However, historians recognize that the future of any region can be influenced by extraneous circumstances or by unforeseen events. The patterns which have developed during the multipolar balance in the North Pacific over the last twenty years may forecast future events.

China, by its very size, has many internal problems which will require a period of peace to resolve. However, it will not permit any section to break away and any independence movements in the outlying provinces will be suppressed. In south-east Asia, China will probably co-operate with the independent states recently established, but it will not actively intervene in their affairs nor attempt to annex them, although at one time they were subject to the Chinese empire. On the other hand, China will continue to extend its influence in both the Asian and African states by economic and military aid.

Extensive industrialization is being encouraged in China. It may be expected to press the improvement of nuclear and intercontinental missiles and possibly could achieve a competitive position by the mid-1980's. China will slowly relax its isolationist policies as it becomes involved increasingly in world trade.

Chinese–Russian enmity will continue although every effort will be made to prevent conflict. China will attempt to counter the threatening encircling influence of Soviet Russia in southern Asia by propaganda. Any attempt by China or Russia to extend its influence into the other's territory will be met by instant reaction and protest before force is used.

Soviet Russia and the United States will continue a policy of co-existence, striving to prevent a serious confrontation. The inability of the two nations to renew the SALT agreement in 1977 illustrated their mutual fear and distrust. The United States is torn between its desire to withdraw from active foreign involvement and its fear of the aggressive expansionist policies of Soviet Russia with its increasing naval power and its growing influence in Asia and Africa. Although the United States is decreasing its military commitments in the Far East, and is granting self-government to its island possessions, it does not contemplate complete withdrawal. It cannot leave the future of the North Pacific to Japan, China, and Russia. While maintaining its military credibility, the United States will develop interests in other fields, returning to its earlier objectives of trade and increasing co-operation by educational, commercial, technical, and scientific exchanges.

In the face of rising nationalism and the withdrawal of the United States from Asia, Japan must face the problems of defence and must decide whether to re-establish military forces, which means a revision of the peace treaties and the constitution, and whether to adopt nuclear weapons. New alignments may be necessary. The problem of the four disputed islands north of Japan will continue to strain Russo–Japanese relations and Japan may therefore seek a closer relationship with China. The resurgence of an armed Japan in alliance with the United States presents a future problem to both China and Soviet Russia. In such an alliance Canada, with its United States defence ties, could be affected. Closer ties between Japan and China will increase Russian suspicions and opposition.

Canada will maintain its close ties with the United States, depending on it for protection, but recognizing the dangers of involvement implied by such dependence. Canada's main interest in the North Pacific will continue to be economic as it maintains its efforts to increase trans-Pacific trade, while its policies in the Law of the Sea conferences will be aggressive as it seeks to protect its fisheries, to balance the mining of the sea with its own interests, and to lessen damage caused by pollution. Fisheries problems between the United States and Canada have existed since the United States gained its independence. The extension of ocean boundaries has created new problems for the fishing areas on the east coast and in the west coast zones off the Strait of Juan de Fuca and Dixon Entrance. If past fishing disputes are to be accepted as examples, the negotiations over these new areas may be expected to drag on for several years as each side attempts to outmanoeuvre the other. Unsettled conditions or tentative agreements lead to frustrations which may in turn lead to critical confrontation. Meanwhile, Canada will press for international agreements by the North Pacific countries to define fishing policies.

The rise of Japan as an economic power necessitates further adjustments. Already, in the face of rising costs in Japan and the increasing opposition to its trading practices by other countries, Japan is modifying its industrial, commercial, and investment policies. United States opposition to increasing competition from Japanese industry and monetary policies has led Japan to reassess its export policies. New economic groupings may be expected in the future in which Japan would be a major partner. China and Soviet Russia would not be included, and all agreements with them would continue to be bilateral. Japan is looking towards increasing China trade and investments in Siberia. The United States, and more especially Canada, are dependent on China for large grain purchases. Canada hopes to extend its wheat sales to Russia on a more permanent basis. A broad regional economic union, similar to the OAS, might extend from Japan to Australia. Another possibility might include Japan, Canada, and the Republic of Korea. Taiwan would geographically fit into such an association, but both Japan and Canada would fear repercussions from China, where both are hoping to expand trade. Undoubtedly, the volume of Canadian trade to both the United States and Japan makes Canada vulnerable to the attitudes of both these countries.

In the foreseeable future, military or commercial pacts are unlikely except as bilateral arrangements between individual nations. This does not, however, preclude the possibilities of joint consultative agencies to discuss common problems. The powerful nations, while supplying aid and advice, have managed to localize the varied crises of the last decade. Pressures will continue on lesser states to limit their disputes in order to prevent active involvement by their powerful friends or allies with a resulting confrontation.

While continuing its support of the UN, NATO, and NORAD, Canada will continue to work for peace by working with these and other international agencies and consultative committees. A prosperous economy will continue to depend on foreign trade. Canada must continue its trading partnerships with the United States and Europe, but the greatest opportunities for expansion and diversification are in the North Pacific. Increasing contacts and the resolution of common problems ensure the future greatness of this region.

Chronology

1774 Perez reaches Queen Charlotte Islands
1776–83 American War of Independence
1776 Spanish settlement established at San Francisco
1778 Cook at Hawaii, Nootka, and Bering Sea
1779 Arteaga reaches Alaska
1784 Russian settlement established at Kodiak
1785–87 Hanna, first maritime fur trader on north-west coast
1785–88 La Pérouse expedition
1789 Nootka incident
1790 Nootka Convention
1791 Gray builds Fort Defiance
1791–93 Captain George Vancouver on north-west coast
1793 Alexander Mackenzie crosses North America
        Lord McCartney's unsuccessful mission to Peking
1788 Russian–American Company charter

1800–40

1803 Louisiana purchase
1803–6 Krustenstern voyage of circumnavigation
1804–6 Lewis and Clark expedition to mouth of Columbia
1811 Russians establish Fort Ross
        Astor establishes Fort Astoria
1814 Treaty of Ghent ends War of 1812–14
1818 Joint occupancy of Oregon
1819 American–Spanish agreement limits Spanish to 42° on west coast
1820 First American missionaries arrive in Hawaii
1821 Amalgamation of North West and Hudson's Bay Companies
1822 Mexico takes control of California
1823 Monroe Doctrine
1824 Russia–United States agreement sets 54°40′ as boundary
1825 Fort Vancouver built
1834 East India Company charter abolished
1836 First protestant missionaries arrive in Columbia River

1840–50

1839–42 First Opium War
1842 Treaty of Nanking
        Fort Victoria built
1844 Treaties of Wanghia and Whampoa

1846 Mexican War begins
      Oregon Treaty
1848 Treaty of Guadalupe Hidalgo
      Oregon Territory organized
1849 Colony of Vancouver Island established
      State of California constitution drawn up
      California gold rush

1850–70

1850–64 Taiping Rebellion
1850 Russia occupies Amur River to mouth
1853 Commodore Perry in Japan
      Washington Territory created
1854–56 Crimean War
1856 Arrow (Second Opium) War
1858 Treaty of Aigun
      Fraser River gold rush
      Colony of British Columbia founded
1859 Oregon becomes a state
1860 Vladivostok founded
      Treaties of Tientsin
1861 Telegraph line constructed across United States
1861–65 American Civil War
1866 Vancouver Island and British Columbia united
1867 Russia sells Alaska to the United States
      British North America Act
1868 Beginning of "Era of Enlightenment" in Japan
1869 First transcontinental railway completed in United States

1870–1914

1871 British Columbia becomes a province
1873 San Juan arbitration completed
1882 United States Exclusion Act
1885 Canadian Pacific Railway completed
      Dominion Franchise Act
      First Japanese immigrants to Hawaii
1889 Washington State admitted to United States
1894 Sino–Japanese War
1895 Treaty of Shimonoseki

1898 Spanish–American War
     United States annexes Hawaiian Islands
1899 Open Door Policy declared
1900 Boxer Rebellion
1902 Anglo–Japanese agreement
1903 Alaska boundary settled
1904 Russo–Japanese War
1905 Treaty of Portsmouth
     Trans-Siberian Railway completed
1907 "Gentleman's Agreement" on immigration
     Triple Entente (Britain, France, Russia)
1908 "Continuous passage" legislation passed
1910 Japan annexes Korea
1911 Convention on conservation of sea otter and fur seal
     Republic of China established
1914 *Komagata Maru* incident

1914–30

1914–18 First World War
1915 Japan presents Twenty-One Demands to China
1917 Lansing–Ishii Agreement
1918 Siberian invasion
1919 Paris Peace Conference
1921–22 Washington Conference
1923 Halibut Fisheries Convention
1924 United States Exclusion Act
1930 International Pacific Fisheries Commission

1930–53

1931 Japan invades Manchuria
1933 Japan withdraws from League of Nations
1934 Japan abrogates naval agreements
1934–35 Communist "Long March" in China
1936 Japan–Germany Anti-Comintern Pact
1937 Japan begins invasion of China
1939 Germany invades Poland; Second World War begins
1940 Ogdensburg Agreement
1941 (April) Soviet–Japan neutrality pact
     (June) German invasion of Russia

(December) Japanese air attack on Pearl Harbor
1942 Japanese evacuated from west coast of Canada and the United States
1945 (February) Yalta Conference
(June) United Nations charter adopted
(August) Atom bomb on Hiroshima
(September) Japanese surrender
1949 People's Republic of China established
NATO formed
Canadian franchise extended to Orientals
1950 United Kingdom recognizes People's Republic of China
1950–53 Korean War
1951 Japanese Peace Treaty

1953–

1953 United States–South Korea Mutual Security Treaty
1954 United States–Japan Mutual Assistance Agreement
1956 Japan admitted to U.N.
1960 United States–Japan Security Treaty
1964–72 Vietnam War
1971 People's Republic of China admitted to U.N.
1972 President Nixon visits Peking
Japan and People's Republic of China renew diplomatic relations
1977 Two-hundred-mile fishing zones adopted by Canada, United States, U.S.S.R., and Japan

Notes

NOTES TO CHAPTER ONE

1. Robert MacDonald, *The Owners of Eden* (Calgary: Ballantrae Foundation, 1974).
2. I. M. Muthanna maintains that immigrants from India crossed Beringia and that the Aztec and Inca civilizations were influenced by them. *People of India in North America, Part I* (Bangalore: Lotus Printers, 1975), pp. 4–12.
3. James J. Hester, "Early Man in the New World," ms. in Archeological Division, Provincial Archives, Victoria, 1974.
4. Douglas Leechman, *Native Tribes of Canada* (Toronto: W. J. Gage, n.d.).
5. Alfred Hulse Brooks, *Blazing Alaska's Trails* (Caldwell, Idaho: University of Alaska and Arctic Institute of North America, 1953), p. 115.
6. *The World and South-East Asia* (Sydney, Australia: Oswald Ziegler Enterprises Ltd., 1973), p. 10. James L. Henderson, editor, *Since 1945: Aspects of Contemporary World History* (London: Methuen, 1966), p. 138.
7. Charles G. Leland, *Fusang, or the Discovery of America by Buddhist Priests* (London: Trubner & Co., 1875), p. 6.
8. Herman R. Friis, *The Pacific Basin* (New York: American Geographic Society, 1967), p. 87.
9. T. W. Paterson, "Was Columbus a Latecomer by More than 3,000 Years?" Victoria, B.C.: *The Islander* (2 April 1967), p. 12.
10. Leland, *Fusang, or the Discovery of America by Buddhist Priests*, pp. 25–30. Charles Wolcott Brooks, *Japanese Wrecks Stranded... in the North Pacific Ocean* (Fairfield, Wash.: Ye Galleon Press, 1964), p. 21. Brooks believes Fusang was really Japan.
11. Brooks, *Blazing Alaska's Trails*, p. 7.
12. T. A. Rickard, "The Use of Iron and Copper by the Indians of British Columbia," *B.C.H.Q.*, Vol. III, No. 1 (January 1939), pp. 45–46. G. P. V. and Helen Akrigg, *British Columbia Chronicle* (Vancouver: Discovery Press, 1975), p. 287.
13. Brooks, *Blazing Alaska's Trails*, p. 21.
14. Beth Hill, "Japanese Glass Fishing Floats," *Westworld* (May–June 1976), pp. 30ff.

NOTES TO CHAPTER TWO

1. Goods in Venice increased 70 to 100 times the original cost to the Far East. T. A. Rickard, "Straits of Anian," *B.C.H.Q.*, Vol. V (1941), p. 161.
2. For early Christian Missions in Asia, see R. M. Panikkar, *Asia and Western Domination* (London: George Allen & Unwin, 1959), pp. 279ff.
3. Portugal also retained Brazil.
4. Richard Coke Wood and Leon George Bush, *The California Story* (San Francisco: Ferron Publishers, 1957), p. 20.
5. Spanish expansion and knowledge of the Pacific islands was increased by Spain's annexation of Portugal in 1580.
6. William Lytle Schurz, *The Manila Galleons* (New York: E. P. Dutton, 1939), p. 30.
7. *Ibid.*, p. 50. See also William Lytle Schurz, "Acapulco and the Manila Galleons," *South Western Historical Review*, Vol. XXII (1919), pp. 18ff.
8. Richard Hakluyt, *The Principal Navigations of the English Nation*, Vol. VIII (London: J. M. Dent, n.d.), pp. 233–35.
9. *Encyclopedia Britannica*, 11th edition.

10. Quoted from "Notes of Master Francis Fletcher," in Herbert E. Bolton, "Francis Drake's Plate of Brass," Special Publication No. 13 (San Francisco: California Historical Society, 1937), p. 33. See also R. P. Bishop, "Drake's Course in the North Pacific," *B.C.H.Q.*, Vol. III (July 1939).

11. The Dutch East India Company charter ended in 1799 during the French Revolutionary Wars, the French in 1769 following losses in the Seven Years' War, and the English in 1834.

12. P. C. Kuo, *A Critical Study of the First Anglo-Chinese War* (Taipei: Ch'eng Wen Publishing, 1935; rep. 1970), p. 4.

13. *Ibid.*, p. 6.

NOTES TO CHAPTER THREE

1. At first American traders were also individuals, but in later years large companies such as that of John Jacob Astor became powerful. There were no government monopolies granted.

2. Taras Hunczak, editor, *Russian Imperialism from Ivan the Great to the Revolution* (New Brunswick, N.J.: Rutgers University Press, 1974), pp. 72ff.

3. Some authorities believe that Deshnev did not round East Cape, but travelled overland from the Arctic to the Anadyr River. Alfred Hulse Brooks, *Blazing Alaska's Trails* (Fairbanks: University of Alaska, 1953), p. 25.

4. Yuri Semyonov, *Siberia: Its Conquest and Development* (London: Hollis & Carter, 1963), p. 88.

5. Beckles Willson, *The Great Company* (Toronto: Copp Clark, 1899), p. 245. The two might be said to have met in 1847 when the Hudson's Bay Company built Fort Selkirk (p. 85).

6. F. A. Golder, *Russian Expansion in the Pacific, 1641–1850* (New York: Paragon Book Reprint Corp., 1971), p. 331.

7. Hector Chevigny, *Russian Alaska* (New York: Viking, 1965), p. 38.

8. *Captain Cook's Voyages Around the World*, 3 vols. (Glasgow: J. Fowler, 1912), p. 375.

9. Semyonov, *Siberia*, p. 176.

10. *Cook's Voyages*, p. 375.

11. The H.B.C. charter was in perpetuity, the Russian–American Company's for twenty years, renewable.

12. Actually very few agricultural colonists were sent.

13. Stuart R. Tompkins and Max Moorhead, "Russia's Approach to America," *B.C.H.Q.*, Vol. XIII, Nos. 1, 2 (1949), pp. 232, 242.

14. John Francis Bannon, *The Spanish Borderlands Frontier, 1813–1821* (New York: Holt, Rinehart, Winston, 1970), p. 135.

15. Hubert Howe Bancroft, *History of California (1542–1800)* in *The Works of H. H. Bancroft*, Vol. XVIII (Santa Barbara: A. L. Bancroft, 1884), p. 3.

16. D. K. Fieldhouse, *The Colonial Empires* (London: Wiedenfeld & Nicolson, 1965), p. 17.

17. *Ibid.*, p. 26.

18. Herbert E. Bolton, *Fray Juan Crespi* (Berkeley and Los Angeles: University of California Press, 1927), p. 334. Point Santa Margarita is the north-west corner of the Queen Charlotte Islands, now called North Point.

19. *Cook's Voyages*: "Though some account of a voyage to the coast by Spaniards, in 1774 or 1775, had arrived in England before we sailed, the circumstances... prove that these ships had never been at Nootka" (p. 167); Bolton, *Fray Juan Crespi*, p. 351.

20. J. F. G. de la Pérouse, *A Voyage around the World* (London: G. G. & J. Robinson, 1799), p. 10.

21. *Ibid.*, p. 405.

22. *Ibid.*, p. 434.

23. *Ibid.*, p. 436.

24. *Captain Ledyard's Journal of Captain Cook's Last Voyage* (Corvallis: Oregon State University Press, 1963), p. 197.

25. *Cook's Voyages*, p. 145.

26. *Ledyard's Journal*, p. 70.

27. *Cook's Voyages*, p. 447.

28. Robert K. Buell and Charlotte N. Skladal, *Sea Otters and the China Trade* (New York: D. McKay, 1968), p. 42.

29. Captain George Dixon, *A Voyage around the World* (London: Geo. Goulding,

1789), pp. 300, 315. Portlock and Dixon were under a charter from the South Sea Company.

30. For accounts of early traders and explorers see F. W. Howay, "A List of Trading Vessels in the Maritime Fur Trade, 1785–1849," *Proceedings & Transactions of the Royal Society of Canada*, Vols. XXIV–XXVIII (1930–34) and Stuart R. Tompkins, "After Bering: Mapping the North Pacific," *B.C.H.Q.*, Vol. XIX, Nos. 1, 2 (1955).

31. John Meares, "Extract from Voyages Made in the Years 1788–89," *H.H.S. Reprints* (n.d.), p. 43.

32. T. A. Rickard, "The Sea Otter in History," *B.C.H.Q.*, Vol. XI (1947), p. 26.

33. Donald H. Mitchell, "The Investigation

of Fort Defiance," *B.C.S.* (Spring, 1970); Donald H. Mitchell and Robert J. Knox, "The Investigation of Fort Defiance," *B.C.S.* (Winter 1972–73).

34. Note that Heceta had reported the Columbia River in 1775.

35. Alexander Begg, *History of British Columbia* (Toronto: McGraw-Hill Ryerson, 1972), quotes Meares, p. 35.

36. The number of Chinese is uncertain, estimates varying from 29 to 70. See Derek Pethick, *First Approaches to the Northwest Coast* (Vancouver: J. J. Douglas, 1976), p. 207.

37. Marguerite Eyer Wilbur, editor, *Vancouver in California, 1792–94*, 2 vols. (Los Angeles: Glen Dawson, 1954), p. 124.

NOTES TO CHAPTER FOUR

1. John F. G. Stokes, "Hawaii's Discovery by the Spanish," *H.H.S. Papers* (20 March 1939), finds no historical facts to support the theory that Hawaii was discovered by the Spanish.

2 .Edward Joesling, *Hawaii: An Uncommon History* (New York: Norton & Co., 1972), p. 58.

3. *H.H.S. Annual Review* (1946), p. 17.

4. E. Towse, "Some Hawaiians Abroad," *H.H.S. Papers* (1904), p. 7.

5. Richard Henry Dana, *Two Years before the Mast* (London: William Tegg, 1856), p. 157.

6. E. E. Rich, editor, *The Letters of John McLoughlin from Fort Vancouver to the Governor....* third series (Toronto: The Champlain Society, 1941–44), p. 162.

7. Towse, "Some Hawaiians Abroad," p. 12.

8. Donald D. Johnson, "Powers in the Pacific," *H.H.S. Annual Report* (1957), p. 8.

9. C. L. Andrews, "Alaska under the Russians," *Washington Historical Quarterly*,

Vol. VII (1916), pp. 278ff.

10. From 1803 to 1849 there were thirty-six Russian voyages around the world. Krustenstern's was the first. Mairin Mitchell, *The Maritime History of Russia, 848–1948* (London: Sidgwick & Jackson, 1949), p. 18.

11. C. L. Andrews, "Alaska under the Russians," p. 229.

12. Mairin Mitchell, *Maritime History of Russia*, p. 229.

13. C. L. Andrews, "Alaska under the Russians," pp. 278ff.

14. Dana, *Two Years before the Mast*, p. 89.

15. Rich, *Letters of John McLoughlin*, p. 243.

16. Although Astor failed in this scheme he remained the dominant figure of the American fur trade until his retirement in 1833 at the age of seventy.

17. John S. Galbraith, *The Little Emperor* (Toronto: Macmillan, 1976), pp. 148, 153.

18. Robie L. Reid, "Early Days in Old Fort Langley," *B.C.H.Q.*, Vol. I (April 1937), p. 82.

NOTES TO CHAPTER FIVE

1. Ralph S. Kuykendall, "American Interests and American Influence in Hawaii, 1842," *H.H.S. Reports* (1931), p. 48.

2. Harold W. Bradley, "Thomas A. P. Catesby Jones," *H.H.S. Reports* (1931), p. 18.

3. John Van Arsdell, "B.C. Whaling: The

Indians," *Raincoast Chronicles First Five* (Madeira Park: Harbour Publishing, 1976), pp. 20–28.

4. David A. Henderson, *Men and Whales* (Los Angeles: Dawson's Book Shop, 1972), p. 15.

5. Charles Boardman Hawes, *Whaling* (London: Wm. Heinemann, 1924), p. 147.

6. Alexander Starbuck, *History of the American Whale Fisheries*, 2 vols. (New York: Argosy Antiquarians, 1964), p. 98. See also article by William Graves, "Whaling," *National Geographic Magazine*, Vol. CL, No. 6 (December 1976).

7. Starbuck, *History of the American Whale Fisheries*, p. 701.

8. Peter Trower, "B.C. Whaling: The White Men," *Raincoast Chronicles First Five.*

9. Herman Melville, *Typee* (London: Constable, 1922), pp. 33, 267.

10. Stephen Neil, *Colonization and Christian Missions* (New York: McGraw-Hill, 1966), p. 92.

11. Gwen R. P. Norman, "Evangelism in Yamanashiken," *Alaska and Japan* (Anchorage: Alaska Methodist University, 1972), p. 136.

12. John F. Fairbank, editor, *The Missionary Enterprise in China and America* (Cambridge: Harvard University Press, 1974), p. 128.

13. The Reverend William Scott, *Canadians in Korea* (Toronto: Board of World Missions, 1970), p. 14.

14. Fairbanks, *Missionary Enterprise in China and America*, p. 271.

15. Melville, *Typee*, p. 266.

16. Stuart Creighton Miller, "Ends and Means," in *The Missionary Enterprise in China and America*, p. 255.

17. *Ibid.*, p. 263.

18. K. M. Panikkar, *Asia and Western Domination* (London: Allen & Unwin, 1959), p. 292.

19. Kenneth Scott Latourette, quoted in Jessie G. Lutz, *Christian Missions in China* (Boston: D. C. Heath, 1965), p. 83.

20. Neil, *Colonization and Christian Missions*, p. 11.

21. Helen H. Robbins, *Our First Ambassador to China* (London: John Murray, 1908), p. 333.

22. *Ibid.*, p. 269.

23. *Ibid.*, p. 284.

24. *Ibid.*, p. 342.

25. *Ibid.*, p. 369.

26. Kenneth Bourne, *Britain and the Balance of Power in North America, 1815–1908* (London: Longmans Green, 1967), p. 75.

27. "Letters of Sir George Simpson," *American Historical Review*, Vol. XIV (October 1908), p. 79.

28. *Ibid.*, p. 80.

29. E. E. Rich, editor, *The Letters of John McLoughlin from Fort Vancouver to the Governor....* third series (Toronto: The Champlain Society, 1941–44), 31 October 1842, p. 75.

30. Glyndwr Williams, editor, *London Correspondence inward from Sir George Simpson*, 10 March 1842, Vol. XXIX (London: The Hudson's Bay Record Society, 1973), p. 145.

31. Norman A. Graebner, *Empire in the Pacific* (New York: Ronald Press, 1955), p. 35.

32. Frederick Merk, *The Monroe Doctrine and American Expansion, 1843–1849* (New York: Alfred A. Knopf, 1966), p. 167.

33. F. V. Longstaff and W. Kaye Lamb, "The Royal Navy on the Northwest Coast," *B.C.H.Q.*, Vol. IX (1945), p. 113.

34. British–American relations had been tense since American intervention in the rebellions of 1837. During the Webster-Ashburton talks on Maine there was some talk of the Americans accepting the British claims in exchange for California. See Bourne, *Britain and the Balance of Power in North America*, p. 123.

35. The British proposals arrived 6 June. On 9 May, Polk had declared a state of war with Mexico.

36. "Letters of Sir George Simpson," p. 89.

37. *Ibid.*, p. 89.

38. *Ibid.*, p. 122.

39. Captain J. C. Fremont, *Narrative of the Exploring Expedition to the Rocky Mountains in the Years 1842–44* (New York: D. Appleton & Co., 1849), p. 158.

40. Franklin D. Roosevelt, *Nothing to Fear*, 13 August 1938 (Freeport: Books for Libraries Press, 1970.)

NOTES TO CHAPTER SIX

1. Ken Adachi, *The Enemy That Never Was*, (Toronto: McClelland & Stewart, 1976), p. 3.
2. Charles Wolcott Brooks, *Japanese Wrecks Stranded... in the North Pacific Ocean* (Fairfield, Wash.: Ye Galleon Press, 1964), p. 7.
3. Richard O'Connor, *Pacific Destiny* (Toronto: Little, Brown, 1969), p. 127.
4. Harry Schwartz, *Tsars, Mandarins, and Commissars* (Philadelphia: Lippincott, 1964), pp. 50ff.
5. *Ibid.*, p. 51.
6. *The Times* (22 June 1854), p. 10.
7. *Ibid.*, (24 October 1854), p. 7.
8. *Ibid.*, (3 December 1854), p. 9; (9 April 1855), p. 7.
9. *Ibid.*, (25 October 1855), p. 4; (26 October 1855), p. 6; (30 October 1855), p. 8.
10. B. A. MacKelvie and Willard E. Ireland, "The Victoria Voltigeurs," *B.C.H.Q.*, Vol. XX (July/October, 1956), p. 233.
11. Donald C. Davidson, "The War Scare of 1854," *B.C.H.Q.*, Vol. V (October 1941), pp. 243ff.
12. C. P. Stacey, *Canada and the Age of Conflict*, Vol. I (Toronto: Macmillan of Canada, 1977), p. 41. It was the possibility in 1878 of another war over Turkey be-

tween Russia and Britain, with the fear of Russian naval attacks on the west coast, that caused Canada to begin the construction of defences at Esquimalt.
13. Henry Blumenthal, *France and the United States* (Chapel Hill: University of North Carolina Press, 1970), p. 131. Although the Americans believed this was a friendly gesture of support against British threats, it is more likely that the Russians, threatened by a war with Britain over Poland, wanted to free their navy from the Baltic and locate it in a position where it could attack British commerce. *New Cambridge Modern History*, Vol. X, p. 637.
14. On two of these today stand the University of British Columbia and Stanley Park. F. W. Howay, "Early Settlement on Burrard Inlet," *B.C.H.Q.*, Vol. I (April 1937), p. 101.
15. C. P. Stacey, "Britain's Withdrawal from North America," *Confederation* (Toronto: University of Toronto Press, 1967), pp. 14–22.
16. G. P. de T. Glazebrook, *A History of Canadian External Relations*, Vol. I (Toronto: McClelland & Stewart, 1966), p. 243.

NOTES TO CHAPTER SEVEN

1. John B. Daniell, "The Collins Overland Telegraph," *Northwest Digest*, Vol. XVI, No. 1 (January–February 1950), W. W. Bride, "Telegraph Line to Russia," *B.C. Digest* (August 1946).
2. In 1900 H. de Windt's Franco–American expedition visited Chuckchu Peninsula to study the possibility of a railway by means of a tunnel under Bering Strait which would eventually join Paris to New York. The idea was dropped in 1907 in favour of a shipping line. Yuri Semyonov, *Siberia: Its Conquest and Development* (London: Hollis & Carter, 1963), p. 364.
3. C. P. Stacey, "Britain's Withdrawal from North America," *Confederation* (Toronto: University of Toronto Press, 1967), pp. 14–22.
4. Esquimalt and Singapore had the only two

graving docks on the Pacific large enough to serve British naval vessels.
5. *C.A.R.* (1907), p. 120.
6. W. Kaye Lamb, "Pioneer Days of the Trans-Pacific Services," *B.C.H.Q.*, Vol. I (July 1937), p. 143.
7. K. M. Panikkar, *Asia and Western Dominance* (London: Allen & Unwin, 1961), p. 160.
8. Richard O'Connor, *Pacific Destiny* (Toronto: Little Brown, 1969), p. 149.
9. Hugh Borton, *Japan's Modern Destiny* (New York: Ronald Press, 1970), p. 275.
10. At the Congress of Berlin, 1878, Britain, Germany, Austria, France, and Italy forced Russia to surrender almost all of her gains from the Russo–Turkish War. Britain, which had not fought in the war, gained Cyprus.

11. Claude A. Buss, *The Far East* (New York: Macmillan, 1955), p. 163.
12. Michael Edwardes, *Asia and the European Age, 1848–1958* (London: Thames and Hudson, 1961), p. 143.
13. There is no indication that China will cancel this lease before 1997, but there is no guarantee otherwise. The shortening period undoubtedly accounts for much of the withdrawal of funds from Hong Kong, many of which are coming to Canada, especially to Vancouver. It is impossible to ascertain the amount of this flow of capital. By the Treaty of Nanking, 1842, Britain was granted Hong Kong in perpetuity.
14. George Woodcock, *The British in the Far East* (London: Wiedenfeld & Nicolson, 1969), p. 150.
15. William Woodruff, *Impact of Western Man* (New York: Macmillan, 1966), pp. 30, 128.
16. Mairin Mitchell, *The Maritime History of Russia, 848–1948* (London: Sidgwick & Jackson, 1949), p. 173.
17. A. T. Mahan, *The Influence of Sea Power upon History* (London: Sampson, Low, Marston, 1890), p. 42.
18. At the same time Spain sold the Caroline and Mariana Islands to Germany.
19. Sun Yat-sen, *The Three Principles of the People* (Shanghai: Commercial Press, 1929), pp. 281–83.
20. *Ibid.*, p. 15.
21. The Boxer Rebellion indemnity totalled U.S. $333,900,000, which was divided among thirteen nations. The largest amounts were: Russia 29%; Germany 20%; France 15.75%; Great Britain 11.25%; Japan 7.7%; and the United States 7.3%. Of its total $24,440,718 the United States returned $10,785,286 to China in 1924 and later set aside another $6,137,552 for educational services. Wen Hwan Ma, *American Policy towards China* (Shanghai: Kelly and Walsh, 1934), pp. 186–91; Paul Hibbert Clyde, *United States Policy towards China* (Durham, N.C.: Duke University Press, 1940), p. 218.
22. Kenneth Bourne, *Britain and the Balance of Power in North America, 1815–1908* (London: Longmans Green, 1967), pp. 276, 279.
23. Sun Yat-Sen, *Three Principles*, p. 5.
24. Panikkar, *Asia and Western Dominance*, p. 141.
25. A. Girdner and A. Loftis, *The Great Betrayal* (London: Macmillan, 1968), p. 34. "Some 25,000 Chinese arrived from Hong Kong in the single year 1850." R. C. Wood and L. G. Bush, *The California Story* (San Francisco: Ferron, 1957), p. 156, say that in 1850 there were about 46 Chinese in the United States and that in 1860 there were 4,000.
26. *The Times*, (18 October 1854), p. 8.
27. T. H. Watkins, *California: An Illustrated History* (Palo Alto: American West Publishing, 1973), pp. 88, 101.
28. Wood and Bush, *The California Story*, p. 156.
29. *Ibid.*, p. 156.
30. Mark Twain, *Letters from Hawaii*, 10 September 1866 (New York: Appleton, 1966).
31. Alfred H. Brooks, *Blazing Alaska's Trails* (Fairbanks: University of Alaska, 1953), p. 307.
32. Panikkar, *Asia and Western Dominance*, p. 151. During the Boxer Rebellion, U.S. exports of cotton goods to China fell from $9,823,000 in 1899 to $4,620,000 in 1901, resulting in the temporary closing of some United States cotton mills. Wen Hwan Ma, *American Policy towards China*, p. 168.
33. Ken Adachi, *The Enemy That Never Was* (Toronto: McClelland & Stewart, 1976), p. 96.
34. *C.A.R.* (1907), p. 384.
35. *Ibid.*, pp. 262, 284.
36. *Ibid.*, p. 296.
37. Girdner and Loftis, *The Great Betrayal*, p. 47.
38. *Ibid.*, p. 69.
39. In 1907 Hindus were driven from Seattle and Bellingham. *C.A.R.* (1907), p. 389.
40. In ten months to October 1907, 8,000 Japanese arrived at Canadian Pacific ports; 62 per cent came from Hawaii, which was not controlled by the Japanese government. R. MacGregor Dawson, *W. L. Mackenzie King*, Vol. I (Toronto: University of Toronto Press, 1958), p. 146.
41. American labour organizers, who were present, were partially responsible, but to what extent is uncertain. *C.A.R.* (1907), p. 95.
42. Dawson, *W. L. Mackenzie King*, p. 148.
43. *Ibid.*, p. 163.
44. Adachi, *Enemy That Never Was*, p. 95.
45. Brooks, *Blazing Alaska's Trails*, p. 350.

NOTES TO CHAPTER EIGHT

1. K. M. Panikkar, *Asia and Western Dominance* (London: Allen & Unwin, 1959, rev. 1961), pp. 213–14.
2. David Woodward, *The Russians at Sea* (London: William Kimber, 1965), p. 171.
3. Apparently Canadians were influenced by the belief that a foothold in Siberia might be of economic advantage in the future. C. P. Stacey, *Canada and the Age of Conflict*, Vol. I (Toronto: Macmillan of Canada, 1977), p. 278.
4. Of 196 Japanese immigrants who fought with the Canadian army in Europe, 53 were killed. Ken Adachi, *The Enemy That Never Was* (Toronto: McClelland & Stewart, 1976), p. 101.
5. Audrie Girdner and Anne Loftis, *The Great Betrayal* (London: Macmillan, 1969), p. 61.
6. The nine powers were United States, Great Britain, Japan, France, Italy, China, The Netherlands, Belgium, and Portugal.

7. Masamichi Royama, *Foreign Policy of Japan, 1914–1939* (Tokyo: Institute of Pacific Relations, 1941),. p. 33.
8. Sun Yat-sen, *The Three Principles of the People* (Shanghai: Commercial Press, 1929), p. 86.
9. Mairin Mitchell, *The Maritime History of Russia, 848–1948* (London: Sidgwick & Jackson, 1949), p. 261.
10. Claude A. Buss, *The Far East* (New York: Macmillan, 1955), p. 170.
11. J. W. Pickersgill, *The Mackenzie King Record*, Vol. I, *1939–1944* (Toronto: University of Toronto Press, 1960), p. 11.
12. In 1890 there were eight million Chinese in Manchuria, in 1920 there were over twenty-three million. Harry Schwartz, *Tsars, Mandarins, and Commissars* (Philadelphia: J. B. Lippincott, 1964), p. 83.
13. Ian Grey, *The First Fifty Years* (London: Hodder & Stoughton, 1967), pp. 261-65.

NOTES TO CHAPTER NINE

1. David Woodward, *The Russians at Sea* (London: William Kimber, 1965), p. 244.
2. Mairin Mitchell, *The Maritime History of Russia, 848–1948* (London: Sidgwick & Jackson, 1949), p. 109.
3. J. W. Pickersgill, *The Mackenzie King Record*, Vol. I (Toronto: University of Toronto Press, 1960), p. 206.
4. *Ibid.*, p. 151.
5. *Ibid.*, p. 297.
6. Graham F. Shrader, *The Phantom War in the Northwest* (Vancouver: U.B.C. Library Special Collection, 1969), pp. 213ff.
7. Ken Adachi, *The Enemy that Never Was* (Toronto: McClelland & Stewart, 1976), pp. 200ff.
8. Pickersgill, *Mackenzie King Record*, p. 354.
9. John B. Diefenbaker, *One Canada*, Vol. I (Toronto: Macmillan, 1975), p. 223.
10. Adachi, *Enemy That Never Was*, p. 296.
11. Audrie Girdner and Anne Loftis, *The Great Betrayal* (London: Macmillan, 1969), p. 275–76.
12. Adachi, *Enemy That Never Was*, p. 296. In August 1945 fifty-two Nisei trained for

intelligence work against Japan. C. P. Stacey, *Canada and the Age of Conflict*, Vol. I (Toronto: Macmillan of Canada, 1977), p. 213.
13. 3,964 were deported to Japan from Canada. *Vancouver Province* (31 July 1976), p. 5.
14. Adachi, *Enemy That Never Was*, p. 322.
15. A. Girdner and A. Loftis, *The Great Betrayal* (London: Macmillan, 1968), p. 456.
16. Statistics Canada, 1971, *Census of Canada: Population, Ethnic Groups*.
17. Franklin D. Roosevelt, *Nothing to Fear* (Freeport, N.Y.: Books for Libraries Press, 1946, rep. 1970), p. 412.
18. Pickersgill, *Mackenzie King Record*, pp. 516, 552 and R. H. Roy, "Canadians in the North Pacific 1943," *B.C.S.*, No. 14 (Summer, 1972).
19. Roy, "Canadians in the North Pacific," pp. 4ff.
20. Roosevelt, *Nothing to Fear*, p. 412.
21. H. Blair Neatby, *William Lyon Mackenzie King*, Vol. III, *1932–39* (Toronto: University of Toronto Press, 1976), p. 264.

22. Roy, "Canadians in the North Pacific," p. 5.
23. Mitchell, *Maritime History of Russia*, p. 208.
24. Donald Creighton, *The Forked Road* (Toronto: McClelland & Stewart, 1976), p. 73.
25. Richard O'Connor, *Pacific Destiny* (Toronto: Little, Brown, 1969), p. 234.
26. Members of the Council: China, Soviet Union, United States, and Commonwealth (including United Kingdom, Australia, and New Zealand but not Canada).
27. Harry S. Truman, *Memoirs*, Vol. II (New York: Doubleday, 1956), p. 62.
28. *Ibid.*, p. 71.
29. *Ibid.*, p. 62.
30. *Ibid.*, p. 90.
31. *Ibid.*, p. 352.
32. *Ibid.*, p. 398.
33. *World Almanac* (1975), p. 476; Lt. Col. Herbert Fairlie Wood, *Strange Battleground* (Ottawa: Minister of National Defence, 1966), p. 257.

NOTES TO CHAPTER TEN

1. In $ thousands: Exports 1962: 4,387; 1972: 24,444; Imports 1962: 2,910; 1972: 126,155. Statistics Canada, *Imports and Exports 1972*.
2. *Vancouver Province* (5 August 1976).
3. The *Vancouver Province* reported (*ibid.*): "According to authoritative diplomatic sources, Peking is now taking the stance that reunification can be accomplished only by military force." In the 15 November 1976 *Vancouver Sun*, Premier Chiang Ching-kuo is quoted as saying: "Except for battlefield contact in the shape of a bullet, we shall have nothing to do with mainland Chinese leadership."
4. Patwant Singh, *The Struggle for Power in Asia* (London: Hutchinson & Co., 1971), p. 31.
5. *Vancouver Sun* (3 September 1976).
6. First or second depends on numerous factors. For a comparison of forces see *Time* (3 May 1976), p. 36 and (17 May 1976), pp. 16–17. "By any numerical measures the Soviets lead the U.S. . . . but the U.S. is technically superior."
7. *Time* (16 January 1978), p. 12.
8. Harry S. Truman, *Memoirs*, Vol. II (New York: Doubleday, 1956), p. 414.
9. A. Doak Barnett, *A New U.S. Policy towards China* (Washington: The Brookings Institution, 1971), p. 16.
10. Katsushiro Narita, "Japan's Northern Territories," *Pacific Friend Magazine*, Tokyo, Vol. III, No. 9 (January 1976).
11. Japan became the fourth country to launch an earth satellite into orbit, in 1970, following the U.S.S.R., the U.S.A., and France.
12. *Japan in Transition*, Ministry of Foreign Affairs, Japan (1975).
13. *U.N. Statistical Yearbook*, 1975. By 1970 Japan dominated the trade of south-east Asia, but this trade is now growing less rapidly than Japan's trade with the industrialized nations—the United States, Canada, western Europe, and Australia. Japan prefers to make long-term contracts, especially for raw materials, with stable governments.
14. *The Pacific Rivals: A Japanese View of Japanese–American Relations by the Staff of the Asahi Shimbun* (New York: John Weatherhill, 1972), p. 285.
15. *Vancouver Sun* (18 May 1977).
16. Hedley Bull, editor. *Asia and the Western Pacific*, Australian Institute of International Affairs (Sydney: Thomas Nelson, 1975), p. 17.
17. Yasonobu Somura, "The Military Backdrop of the Law of the Sea," *Japan Echo*, Vol. IV, No. 3 (1977), p. 52. This is the only mention of Canada in this issue of *Japan Echo* which deals entirely with Japan and the sea, although the United States, the U.S.S.R., and western Europe have numerous references.
18. According to the Stockholm International Research Institute, $300,000 million were spent in the arms race in 1975. *The Soviet Union*, No. 1 (1977), p. 26.
19. Japan's interests in Asia include membership in the Asian Development Bank, Asian and Pacific Council (ASPAC), and the Japanese-sponsored South-East Asian Development committee. It is not a member of the social and economic Asso-

ciation of Southeast Asian Nations (ASEAN).

20. An article in the official Chinese newspaper, *People's Daily*, offered the intriguing suggestion of a union of Canada, Japan, and east and west Europe with China and other "Third World" countries to counter the domination of the United States and the Soviet Union. *Vancouver Sun* (1 November 1977).

21. "We have been the Number One peacekeeping country in the world." Secretary of State for External Affairs, the Honourable Don Jamieson, to the Empire Club, Toronto, 2 March 1978.

22. Donald Creighton, *The Forked Road* (Toronto: McClelland & Stewart, 1976), p. 66.

23. Department of External Affairs, *Statements and Speeches*, Nos. 76/20 and 76/21.

24. *Vancouver Sun* (1 February 1977), p. 1.

25. For debate on NORAD see *H.C.D.* (5 June 1975), pp. 6480ff.

26. *H.C.D.* (17 December 1975); *Vancouver Sun* (20 February 1975).

27. *H.C.D.* (9 May 1977), p. 5400; Barbara Johnson and Mark W. Zacher, *Canadian Foreign Policy and the Law of the Sea* (Vancouver: University of British Columbia Press, 1977), pp. 203, 211.

28. *H.C.D.* (4 April 1977), p. 4590.

29. *H.C.D.* (20 May 1976), p. 13701; *Weekend Magazine* (16 April 1977).

30. Department of External Affairs, *Statements and Speeches*, No. 76/77.

31. *H.C.D.* (14 May 1975), p. 5776.

32. A fourth bloc might be Russia–East Europe.

33. *H.C.D.* (11 June 1976), p. 14433.

34. Canada–Japan Trade Council, *The Export-Import Picture*, 1973.

35. Pierre E. Trudeau, *H.C.D.* (28 October 1976), p. 536.

36. *Vancouver Sun* (3 November 1977).

37. *H.C.D.* (3 July 1975), p. 7257.

38. *Vancouver Province* (14 February 1977).

39. *H.C.D.* (29 June 1976), p. 14936.

40. *H.C.D.* (26 June 1976), p. 10280.

41. A full discussion is in *H.C.D.* (30 January 1976), pp. 10489ff.

42. *Hawaii Tribune Herald* (18 October 1977).

43. The leading merchant naval nations are Liberia, Japan, and the United Kingdom. The U.S.S.R. ranks 7 and the U.S. 10. *Time* (3 May 1976), pp. 36–37.

44. *H.C.D.* (14 October 1976), p. 92.

45. *H.C.D.* (19 October 1976), p. 220.

46. *H.C.D.* (9 November 1976), p. 896.

47. *H.C.D.* (16 December 1976), p. 2069.

48. I. B. MacAskie, *The Beaver* (Spring 1975), pp. 9ff, and *Fisheries Canada*, Vol. XXIII, No. 4 (1971), pp. 3–9; Ian Smith, *Western Fish and Game* (November 1969), pp. 26ff.

49. Patrick Lane, "The Great Pacific Sealhunt," *Raincoast Chronicles First Five* (Madeira: Harbour Publishing, 1976), pp. 196–99.

50. F. W. Howay, W. N. Sage, H. F. Angus, *British Columbia and the United States* (Toronto: Ryerson Press, 1942), p. 320; C. P. Stacey, *Canada and the Age of Conflict*, Vol. I (Toronto: Macmillan of Canada, 1977), pp. 38–39.

51. Pacific Fur Seal Convention Act, 1957, c.31 s.1.

52. Whaling Convention Act, R.S. c.293, s.1, Can. Rev. Stat. c.W8 (1970). Only seven members now operate whaling fleets: Japan, the Soviet Union, Australia, Denmark, Brazil, Iceland, and Norway.

53. The Foundation claims that the quotas are meaningless, and the fact that they are never filled indicates that the number of whales continues to decrease. It adds that each year an increasing number of small whales is taken.

54. North Pacific Halibut Fisheries Convention Act, 1952–3, c. 43 s.1.

55. *British Columbia Manual 1930*, Provincial Bureau of Information, Victoria.

56. Pacific Salmon Fisheries Convention Act, 1957, c11 sl.

57. North Pacific Fisheries Convention Act, 1952–3, c44, sl.

58. Canadian allocations on the Pacific coast for 1977 (in metric tons):

	Rockfish	Black Cod	Hake
Japan	3,000	3,000	5,000
Poland			7,500
Rep. of Korea		250	
U.S.S.R.			7,500

Department of Fisheries, *Fisheries and Marine News*, February 1977.

59. *Reciprocal Fisheries Agreements*, signed 24 February 1977. Note article XII, "Recreation fishing vessels of each party in waters of the other shall continue." The temporary nature of these annual agree-

ments led to uncertainty and bickering between the rival salmon fishermen in the Strait of Juan de Fuca and Dixon Entrance.

60. The two-hundred-mile zone gives Japan economic control of a sea area twelve times larger than its land area. *Japan Echo*, Vol. IV, No. 3 (1977), p. 33.

61. *H.C.D.* (4 June 1976), p. 14164.

62. For a detailed study of the UN conferences on the Law of the Sea and Canada's participation, see Barbara Johnson and Mark W. Zacher, *Canada's Foreign Policy and the Law of the Sea* (Vancouver: University of British Columbia Press, 1977).

63. *Vancouver Province* (13 September 1976).

64. In 1950, there were no tankers exceeding 25,000 dwt. By 1975 there were as many as 500 exceeding 200,000 dwt. *Japan Echo*, Vol. IV, No. 3 (1977), p. 37.

65. Ocean Dumping Control Act, 1975. See also Environment Canada, Fisheries and Marine Service, *A Guide to the Ocean Dumping Control Act* (September 1975). For a list of Canadian standards for foreign vessels entering Canadian waters, see *H.C.D.* (25 July 1977), pp. 7957–58.

66. Canada does not extend bilateral aid to Korea in view of its strong economic performance. Department of Industry, Trade, and Commerce, *Bulletin*, 1977.

67. Typical articles are those of Doug Collins in the *Vancouver Sun* (26 June 1976) and Angela Ferrante in *Maclean's* (7 February 1977), p. 18.

Bibliography

ABBREVIATIONS

B.C.H.Q. British Columbia Historical Quarterly
B.C.S.   B.C. Studies
H.C.D.   House of Commons Debates (Hansard)
H.H.S.   Hawaiian Historical Society
C.A.R.   Canadian Annual Review

Adachi, Ken. *The Enemy That Never Was* (Toronto: McClelland and Stewart, 1976)
Akrigg, G. P. V. and Helen. *British Columbia Chronicles*, Vol. I. *Adventures by Land and Sea*,
    Vol. II. *Gold and Colonists* (Vancouver: Discovery Press, 1975-1977)
Alexander, W. D. "Early Trading in Hawaii," *H.H.S. Reports* 1904
—— "The Russians on Kauai," *H.H.S. Reports* 1894
—— "The Uncompleted Treaty of Annexation of 1854," *Papers of H.H.S.*, No. 9 (1897)
Allen, Edward Weber. *The Vanishing Frenchman* (Rutland, Vt.: Charles E. Tuttle Co., 1959)
Andrews, C. L. "Alaska under the Russians," *Washington Historical Quarterly*, VII, 1916
Ari, Tsuguo. *Alaska and Japan* (Anchorage: Alaska Methodist University Press, 1972)
Atkinson, W. D. "Early Voyages of the Pacific Ocean." *H.H.S. Reports* (1893)
Bancroft, H. H. *The Works of H. H. Bancroft*, Vol. XVIII, "History of California (1542-1800)"
    (Santa Barbara: Wallace Hebberd, 1886, rep. 1963)
Bannon, John Francis. *The Spanish Borderlands Frontier, 1513-1821* (New York: Holt, Rine-
    hart & Winston, 1970)
Barnett, A. Doak. *A New U.S. Policy toward China* (Washington, D.C.: The Brookings Institu-
    tion, 1971)
Battistini, Lawrence H. *The United States and Asia* (New York: Frederick A. Praeger, 1955)
Beaton, Kenneth J. *Serving with the Sons of Shuk* (Toronto: United Church of Canada, 1941)
Begg, Alexander. *History of British Columbia* (Toronto: McGraw-Hill Ryerson, 1972)
Bemis, Samuel Plagg. *John Quincy Adams* (New York: Alfred A. Knopf, 1949)
Berry, Don. *A Majority of Scoundrels* (*Informal History of the Rocky Mountain Fur Company*)
    (New York: Harper & Brothers, 1961)
Beyond the Reef. Records of Conferences of Churches and Missions in the Pacific, 22 April–
    4 May 1961
Bishop, R. P. "Drake's Course in the North Pacific," *B.C.H.Q.*, Vol. III, 3 (July 1939)
Blue, G. V. "A Hudson's Bay Company Contract for Hawaiian Labour," *Quarterly of the
    Oregon Historical Society*, Vol. XXV (1924)
Blumenthal, Henry. *France and the United States* (Chapel Hill: University of North Carolina
    Press, 1970)
Bolton, Herbert E. "Francis Drake's Plate of Brass," California Historical Society (March 1937)
—— *Fray Juan Crespi* (Berkeley: University of California Press, 1927)
Borton, Hugh. *Japan's Modern Century* (New York: Ronald Press, 1970)
Bourne, Kenneth. *Britain and the Balance of Power in North America, 1815-1908* (London:
    Longmans, Green, 1967)
Boxer, C. R. *The Portuguese Seaborne Empire, 1415-1825* (London: Hutchinsons, 1969)
Bradley, Harold W. "Thomas A. P. Catesby Jones." *H.H.S. Reports* (1931)
Bride, W. W. "Telegraph Line to Russia." *B.C. Digest* (August 1946)
Brooks, Alfred Hulse. *Blazing Alaska's Trails* (Fairbanks: University of Alaska, 1953)

Brooks, Charles Wolcott. *Japanese Wrecks Stranded . . . in the North Pacific Ocean* (Fairfield, Wash.: Ye Galleon Press, 1964)

Brookes, Jean Ingram. *International Rivalry in the Pacific Islands, 1800-1875* (Berkeley: University of California Press, 1941)

Buell, Robert Kingery and Charlotte Northcote Skladal. *Sea Otters and the China Trade* (New York: David McKay Co., 1968)

Bull, Hedley, editor. *Asia and the Western Pacific*. Australian Institute of International Affairs (Sydney: Thomas Nelson, 1975)

Buss, Claude A. *The Far East* (New York: Macmillan Co., 1955)

Cady, John F. *The Roots of French Imperialism in Eastern Asia* (Ithaca, N.Y.: Cornell University Press, 1954)

The Canadian Family Tree. Canadian Citizenship Branch, Department of the Secretary of State (Ottawa, 1967)

Canada-Japan Trade Council, Ottawa. *Canada-Japan* (annual)

——— *Canada-Japan: The Export-Import Picture*

——— *A Study of Canadian Manufacturers and Japan* (December 1972)

Cecil, Jane. *A Spanish Voyage to Vancouver Island and the North-West Coast of America*, translation of the narrative of schooners *Sutil* and *Mexicana*, 1792 (London: Argonaut Press, 1930)

Chatteron, E. Keble. *Whalers and Whaling* (London: T. Fisher Unwin, 1925, rep. 1974)

Chevigny, Hector. *Russian America* (New York: Viking Press, 1965)

Classen, H. George. *Thrust and Counterthrust* (Don Mills: Longmans of Canada, 1965)

Clyde, Paul Hibbert. *United States Policy towards China: Diplomatic and Public Documents* (Durham, N.C.: Duke University Press, 1940)

Clyde, Paul H. and F. Beers Burton. *The Far East: A History of Western Impact and the Eastern Response (1830-1970)* (Englewood Cliffs, N.J.: Prentice-Hall, 1948; rev. 1971)

Conroy, Hilary and T. Scott Mujakawa. *East across the Pacific*. American Bibliographical Center (Santa Barbara: CLIO Press, 1972)

Cook, Captain James. *Voyages Round the World*, 3 volumes (Glasgow: J. Fowler, 1810)

Creighton, Donald. *The Forked Road: Canada 1939-1957* (Toronto: McClelland and Stewart, 1976)

Crone, G. R. *The Discovery of the East* (London: Hamish Hamilton Ltd., 1972)

Dahlie, Jorgen. "The Japanese in B.C.: Lost Opportunity." *B.C.S.* (Winter 1970-71)

Dalzell, Kathleen E. *The Queen Charlotte Islands* (Terrace: C. M. Adam, 1968)

Dana, Richard Henry Jr. *Two Years before the Mast* (London: William Tegg, 1856)

Daniell, John B. "The Collins Overland Telegraph." *Northwest Digest*, Vol. XVI, No. 1 (January-February 1950)

Davidson, Donald C. "Relations of the Hudson's Bay Company with the Russian America Company on the North West Coast, 1839." *B.C.H.Q.* Vol. V (1941), p. 45

——— "The War Scare of 1854." *B.C.H.Q.* Vol. V (1941), p. 243.

Davidson, George. *The Tracks and Landfalls of Bering and Chirikoff* (San Francisco: Geological Society of the Pacific, 1901)

Davies, John Paton Jr. *Dragon by the Tail* (New York: W. W. Norton, 1972)

Daws, Gavan. *The Shoal of Time: A History of the Hawaiian Islands* (Honolulu: University Press of Hawaii, 1974; rep. 1977)

Dawson, R. MacGregor. *William Lyon Mackenzie King*. Vol. I (Toronto: University of Toronto Press, 1958)

Dawson, Will. *The War That Was Never Fought* (Princeton: Auerbach, 1971)

Day, A. Grove. *Explorers of the Pacific* (New York: Duell, Sloan and Pearce, 1966)

——— *Hawaii and Its People* (Toronto: Little, Brown & Co., 1955)

Dennett, Tyler. *Americans in Eastern Asia* (New York: Barnes and Noble, 1922, rep. 1963)

——— *Roosevelt and the Russo-Japanese War* (New York: Doubleday, Page, 1925)

Denton, L. L. *The Far West Coast* (Toronto: J. M. Dent & Sons, 1924)

Diefenbaker, John G. *One Canada: The Crusading Years 1895-1956* (Toronto: Macmillan, 1975)

Divine, Robert A. *Foreign Policy and U.S. Presidential Elections, 1952-1960* (New York: New Viewpoints, 1974)

Dixon, Captain George. *A Voyage around the World* (London: George Goulding, 1789)

Dryden, Cecil. *Dryden's History of Washington* (Portland, Ore.: Binford & Mort, 1968)

Edwards, Michael. *Asia in the European Age, 1498-1958* (London: Thames & Hudson, 1961)

Endacott, G. B. *A History of Hong Kong* (London: Oxford University Press, 1958, rev. 1973)

Endicott, Stephen Lyon. *Diplomacy and Enterprise (British Chinese Policy 1933-1937)* (Vancouver: University of B.C. Press, 1975)

Eugene, Perry M. "The Story of Frances Barkley." *Northern Messenger,* Montreal (23 January 1931)

Facts about Korea. Minister of Culture and Information (Seoul, Korea, 1971)

Fairbank, John K. *The Missionary Enterprise in China and America* (Cambridge, Mass.: Harvard University Press, 1974)

Far Eastern Economic Review. Canadian Supplement. Hong Kong (17 December 1973)

Ferguson, Ted. *A White Man's Country* (Toronto: Doubleday Canada, 1975)

Ferns, Henry and Bernard Ostry. *The Age of Mackenzie King.* (Toronto: James Lorimer & Co., 1976)

Fieldhouse, D. K. *Economics and Empire, 1830-1914* (Ithaca, N.Y.: Cornell University Press, 1973)

——— *The Colonial Empire* (London: Wiedenfeld and Nicolson, 1965)

Fitzgerald, C. P. *A Concise History of East Asia* (London: Heinemann, 1966)

Fitzgerald, C. P. and Myra Roper. *China: A World So Changed.* (London: Heinemann, 1972)

Fremont, Captain J. C. *Narrative of the Exploring Expedition to the Rocky Mountains in the years 1842-1844* (New York: D. Appleton & Co., 1849)

Friis, Herman R., editor. *The Pacific Basin.* American Geographical Society (New York, 1967)

Galbraith, John S. *The Little Emperor* (Toronto: Macmillan of Canada, 1976)

Girdner, Audrie and Anne Loftis. *The Great Betrayal (The Evacuation of the Japanese-Americans)* (London: Macmillan Co., 1969)

Glazebrook, G. P. de T. *A History of Canadian External Relations,* The Carleton Library (Toronto: McClelland and Stewart, 1966)

Goetzmann, William H. *Exploration and Empire* (New York: Alfred A. Knopf, 1966)

Golder, F. A. *Bering's Voyages,* 2 vols. American Geographical Society (New York, 1925)

——— *Russian Expansion in the Pacific, 1641-1850* [1914] (New York: Paragon Book Reprint Corp., rep. 1971)

Gosnell, R. E. *The Yearbook of British Columbia, 1911-1914* (Victoria: B.C. Legislative Assembly, 1914)

Gough, Barry M. *The Royal Navy and the Northwest Coast of North America 1810-1912: A Study in British Maritime Ascendancy* (Vancouver: University of British Columbia Press, 1971)

Government of British Columbia:

Department of Industrial Development, Trade and Commerce. *China, A Market Study* (n.d.)

——— *Growth Trends in the Japanese Economy*

——— *The Pacific Rim: An Evaluation of B.C.'s Trade Opportunities*

Department of the Provincial Secretary. *British Columbia Heritage Series* (1952)

Government of Canada:

Agriculture Canada. *Canadian Grain Exports* (1975/76)

Department of Manpower and Immigration. *Immigration Statistics* (1971)

——— *Quarterly Immigration Bulletin*

Department of the Minister of State. Bulletins

Department of the Secretary of State for External Affairs. *Annual Review* (1975)

——— *Pacific,* "Foreign Policy for Canadians Series" (1971)

——— *Joint Communiqué of the Seventh Meeting of the Canada-Japan Ministerial Council.* Pub. no. 49 (24 June 1975)

——— *Statements and Speeches*

House of Commons. *House of Commons Debates* (Hansard)

Department of the Environment and Fisheries. *A Guide to the Ocean Dumping Control Act*

——— *Fisheries and Marine News*

——— North Pacific Fisheries Convention Act, C.44 s.1 (1952-53)

—— North Pacific Halibut Fisheries Convention Act, C.43 s.1 (1952–53)
—— Ocean Dumping Control Act (1975)
—— Pacific Fur Seal Convention Act C.31 s.1 (1957)
—— Pacific Salmon Fisheries Convention Act C.11 s.1 (1957)
—— Reciprocal Fisheries Agreement (24 February 1977)
—— *The Seal Hunt* (n.d.)
—— Whaling Convention Act, R.S. C.293 s.1
Department of Industry, Trade and Commerce. *Canadian Commerce*, "Japan, Pacific Trade Partner" (September/October 1971)
—— *Canada's Trade with Pacific Countries* (June 1976)
—— *Markets for Canadian Exporters: The People's Republic of China* (1976)
—— *Markets for Canadian Exporters: Japan* (1977)
Statistics Canada. *Canada: The Annual Handbook*
—— *Canada Year Book* (annual)
—— *Canadian Statistical Review* (monthly)
—— *Exports by Countries* (1975)
—— *Imports by Countries* (1975)
—— *Census of Canada, Population: Ethnic Groups* (1971)
—— *Summary of Foreign Trade* (annual)
—— *The Wheat Review* (monthly)
Standing Senate Committee on Foreign Affairs. *Report on Canadian Relations with Countries of the Pacific Region* (March 1972)
Graebner, Norman A. *Empire in the Pacific* (New York: Ronald Press, 1955)
Graves, William. "Whaling." *National Geographic Magazine*, Washington, D.C., Vol. CL, No. 6 (December 1976)
Greer, Richard E., editor. "Hawaiian Historical Review: Selected Readings." *H.H.S. Reports* (n.d.)
Gregorovich, Andrew. *Canadian Ethnic Group Bibliography*. (Toronto: Department of Provincial Secretary and Citizenship of Ontario, 1972).
Grey, Ian. *The First Fifty Years: Soviet Russia 1917/67* (London: Hodder & Stoughton, 1967)
Guthrie, William. *A New System of Modern Geography* (London: C. Dilly, 1782)
Hacking, Norman R. and W. Kaye Lamb. *The Princess Story* (Vancouver: Mitchell Press, 1974)
Hakluyt, Richard. *The Principal Navigations of the English Nation*, Vol. VIII (London: J. M. Dent, n.d.)
Hallett, Mary E. "A Governor-General's View on Oriental Immigration to British Columbia, 1904–1911." *B.C.S.* No. 14 (Summer 1972)
Hawes, Charles Boardman. *Whaling* (London: William Heinemann, 1924)
Hawkins, Freda. *Canada and Immigration* (Montreal: McGill–Queen's University Press, 1972)
Healy, David. *U.S. Expansion: The Imperialist Urge in the 1890's* (Madison: University of Wisconsin Press, 1970)
Henderson, David A. *Men and Whales* (Los Angeles: Dawson's Book Shop, 1972)
Henderson, James L., editor. *Since 1945: Aspects of Contemporary World History* (London: Methuen, 1966)
Hester, James J. "Early Man in the New World." ms. in Archeological Division, Provincial Archives of British Columbia
Hibbert, Christopher. *The Dragon Wakes: China and the West 1793–1911* (London: Longman, 1970)
Hill, Beth. "Japanese Glass Fishing Floats." *Westworld* (May–June 1976)
Historical Statistics of the United States, Colonial Times to 1970 (U.S. Department of Commerce: Bureau of the Census, 1975)
Ho, Samuel P. S. and Ralph W. Huenemann. "Trade with China." *B.C.S.* (Spring 1972)
Hohenberg, John. *New Era in the Pacific* (New York: Simon and Schuster, 1972)
Hopkins, J. Castell, editor. *The Canadian Annual Review* 1916–18 (Toronto: Annual Review Publishing Co.)
Howay, F. W. "A List of Trading Vessels in the Maritime Fur Trade." *Proceedings and Transactions of the Royal Society of Canada*. Vols. XXIV–XXVIII (1930–34)
—— "Early Shipping in Burrard Inlet, 1863–1870." *B.C.H.Q.* Vol. I, No. 1 (January 1937)
—— "Last Days of the Atahualpa." *H.H.S. Papers* (1933)

Howay, F. W., W. N. Sage, and H. F. Angus, editors. *British Columbia and the United States* (Toronto: Ryerson, 1942)

Howay, F. W. and E. O. S. Scholefield. *British Columbia from the Earliest Times to the Present* (Montreal: S. J. Clarke Publishing, 1914)

Huculak, Mykhaylo. *When Russia Was in America* (Vancouver: Mitchell Press, 1971)

Hunczak, Taras, editor. *Russian Imperialism from Ivan the Great to the Revolution* (New Brunswick, N.J.: Rutgers University Press, 1974)

Hunter, T. Murray. "Coast Defences in B.C. 1939–41." *B.C.S.* (Winter 1975/76)

Iriye, Akira. *The Cold War in Asia* (Toronto: Prentice-Hall, 1974)

Japan in Transition (Tokyo: Ministry of Foreign Affairs, 1975)

Joesling, Edward. *Hawaii: An Uncommon History* (New York: W. W. Norton & Co., 1972)

Johnson, Barbara and Mark W. Zacher. *Canadian Foreign Policy and the Law of the Sea* (Vancouver: University of British Columbia Press, 1977)

Johnson, Donald D. "Powers in the Pacific." *H.H.S. Annual Report* (1957)

Jones, F. C., Hugh Borton, and B. R. Pearn. *The Far East, 1942–44* (London: Oxford University Press, 1955)

Jones, Maude. "Naturalization of Orientals in Hawaii Prior to 1900." *H.H.S. Papers* (1933)

Kahn, Herman. *The Emerging Japanese Superstate* (Englewood Cliffs, N.J.: Prentice-Hall, 1970)

Kalbach, Warren E. *The Impact of Immigration on the Canadian Population* (Ottawa: Census Division, Dominion Bureau of Statistics, 1970)

Kemble, John Haskell. "Coal from the Northwest Coast, 1848–1850." *B.C.H.Q.* Vol. II (1938)

Kenn, Charles. "A Visit to the California Gold Fields by Reverend Lowell Smith." *H.H.S. Papers* (1965)

Kenyon, Karl W. *The Sea Otter in the Eastern Pacific Ocean* (Washington: United States Fish and Wildlife Service, 1969)

Kim, Hong W. "Japanese–South Korean Relations in the Post-Vietnam Era." *Asian Survey*, Vol. XVI, No. 10 (October 1976)

Kuo, P. C. *A Critical Study of the First Anglo–Chinese War.* (Taipei: Ch'eng Wen Publishing Co., 1935, rep. 1970)

Kuykendall, Ralph S. "American Interests and American Influence in Hawaii in 1842." *H.H.S. Reports* (1931)

La Gumina, J. Salvatore and Frank J. Cavaioli. *The Ethnic Dimension in American Society.* Ch. 4 (Boston: Holbrook Press, 1974)

Lai, Cheun-Yan. "The Chinese Consolidated Benevolent Association of Victoria." *B.C.S.* (Autumn 1972)

Lai, Vivian. "The New Chinese Immigrants in Toronto," in *Immigrant Groups (Minority Canadians)*, Jean Leonard Elliott, editor (Scarborough, Ont.: Prentice-Hall, 1971)

Lamb, W. Kaye. "The Advent of the Beaver." *B.C.H.Q.* Vol. II (July 1938)

———— *Canada's Five Centuries* (Toronto: McGraw-Hill, 1971)

———— "Early Lumbering on Vancouver Island, 1844–1866." *B.C.H.Q.* Vol. II. Nos. 1, 2 (January, April 1938)

———— "Empress to the Orient." *B.C.H.Q.* Vol. IV. No. 2 (April 1940)

———— "The Mystery of Mrs. Barkley's Diary." *B.C.H.Q.* Vol. VI (1942)

———— "Pioneer Days of the Trans-Pacific Services." *B.C.H.Q.* Vol. I (July 1937)

Lane, Patrick. "The Great Pacific Sealhunt." *Raincoast Chronicles First Five* (Madeira Park: Harbour Publishing, 1976)

Latourette, Kenneth Scott. *A History of Christian Missions in China* (Taipei: Ch'eng-wen Publishing Co., 1970)

La Violette, Forbes E. *The Canadian Japanese and World War II.* (Toronto: University of Toronto Press, 1948)

Lawrence, Scott. "Buddhist Columbia." *Raincoast Chronicles First Five* (Madeira Park: Harbour Publishing, 1976)

Laycock, George. *Alaska, the Embattled Frontier* (Boston: Houghton Mifflin, 1971)

Captain Ledyard's Journal of Captain Cook's Last Voyage. James Kenneth Munford, editor. (Corvallis: Oregon State University Press, 1963)

Lee, David Tung Hai, editor. *A History of the Chinese in Canada.* Chapters 5, 7, 9, 14 translated by the Foreign Languages Division (Ottawa: Secretary of State, 1970)

Leechman, Douglas. *Native Tribes of Canada* (Toronto: W. S. Gage, 1956)

Leland, Charles G. *Fusang, or The Discovery of America by Chinese Buddhist Priests in the Fifth Century* (London: Trubner & Co., 1875)

London, Jack. *Revolution and Other Essays* (New York: Macmillan Co., 1912)

Longstaff, Major F. V. *Esquimalt Naval Base* (Victoria: Victoria Book and Stationery Company, 1941)

Longstaff, Major F. V. and W. Kaye Lamb. "The Royal Navy on the Northwest Coast." *B.C.H.Q.* Vol. IX (1945)

Lower, A. R. M. *Canada and the Far East* (New York: Institute of Pacific Relations, 1940)

Lower, J. Arthur. *Canada on the Pacific Rim* (Toronto: McGraw-Hill Ryerson, 1975)

——— "Construction of the Grand Trunk Pacific Railway in British Columbia." *B.C.H.Q.* Vol. IV (July 1940)

Lutz, Jessie G. *Christian Missions in China* (Boston: D. C. Heath & Co., 1965)

McCabe, James O. *The San Juan Boundary Question* (Toronto: University of Toronto Press, 1964)

MacDonald, Robert. *The Owners of Eden* (Calgary: Ballantrae Foundation, 1974)

Macintyre, Donald. *Sea Power in the Pacific: Sixteenth Century to the Present* (London: Arthur Baker, 1972)

McKelvie, B. A. and Willard E. Ireland. "The Victoria Voyageurs." *B.C.H.Q.* Vol. XX (July-October 1956)

MacLean, Alastair. *Captain Cook* (New York: Doubleday & Co., 1972)

McNaught, Kenneth W. and Ramsay Cook. *Canada and the United States* (Toronto: Clarke, Irwin & Co. Ltd., 1963, rev. 1968)

Ma, Wen Hwan. *American Policy towards China* (Shanghai: Kelly and Walsh, 1934)

Mahan, Alfred Thayer. *Armaments and Arbitration* (New York: Garden Publishing Co., 1912, rep. 1972)

——— *The Influence of Sea Power upon History* (London: Sampson, Low, Marston & Co., 1890)

Malozemoff, André. *Russian Far Eastern Policy, 1881-1904* (Berkeley: University of California Press, 1958)

Manning, Clarence A. *Russian Influence in Early America* (New York: Library Publishers, 1953)

Marshall, James Stirrat and Carrie. *Pacific Voyages: Selections from The Scot's Magazine, 1771-1808* (Portland, Ore.: Binfords & Mort, 1960)

May, Ernest P. and James C. Thomson, editors. *America-East Asian Relations: A Survey* (Cambridge, Mass.: Harvard University Press, 1972)

Meares, John. "Extracts from Voyages Made in the Years 1788-89." *H.H.S. Reprints* (n.d.)

Melville, Herman. *Typee* (London: Constable & Co., 1922)

Merk, Frederick. *The Monroe Doctrine and American Expansionism 1843-1849* (New York: Alfred A. Knopf, 1966)

Michael, F. H. and G. E. Taylor. *The Far East in the Modern World* (London: Methuen, 1956)

Miller, Stuart Creighton. "Ends and Means," in *The Missionary Enterprise in China and America* (Cambridge, Eng.: Cambridge University Press, 1974)

Millien, C. E. Woo and P. Yeh. *Winnipeg Chinese* (Ottawa: Department of the Secretary of State, 1971)

Ministry of Foreign Affairs, Tokyo. *The Japan of Today* (1970)

——— *Japan in Transition* (1972)

Mitchell, Donald H. "The Investigation of Fort Defiance." *B.C.S.* (Spring 1970)

Mitchell, Donald H. and Robert J. Knox. "The Investigation of Fort Defiance." *B.C.S.* (Winter 1972-73)

Mitchell, Mairin. *The Maritime History of Russia, 848-1948* (London: Sidgwick and Jackson, 1949)

Morton, James. *In the Sea of the Sterile Mountains* (Vancouver: J. J. Douglas, 1974)

Morton, W. Scott. *Japan, Its History and Culture* (New York: Thomas Y. Crowell, 1970)

Mueller, Peter G. and Douglas A. Ross. *China and Japan: Emerging Global Powers* (New York: Praeger Publishers, 1975)

Muthanna, I. M. *People of India in North America (First Part)* (Bangalore, South India: Lotus Printers, 1975)

Narita Hasushiro. "Japan's Northern Territories." *Pacific Friend*, Tokyo. Vol. III, No. 9 (January 1976)

Neatby, H. Blair. *William Lyon Mackenzie King* (Toronto: University of Toronto Press, Vol. II, 1963; Vol. III, 1976)

Nee, Victor G. and de Baty Brett. *Longtime Californ'* (New York: Pantheon Books, 1973)

Neil, Stephen. *Colonialism and Christian Missions* (New York: McGraw–Hill, 1966)

Nevins, Allan, editor. *Polk, The Diary of a President* (London: Longmans Green, 1929)

Nicholson, Major George. *Vancouver Island's West Coast, 1762–1962* (Victoria: Major George Nicholson, 1965)

Norman, Gwen T. P. "Evangelism in Yamanashiken," in *Alaska and Japan* (Anchorage: Alaska Methodist University, 1972)

Norris, John. *Strangers Entertained* (Victoria: B.C. Centennial Committee, 1971)

O'Connor, Richard. *Pacific Destiny* (Toronto: Little, Brown & Co., 1969)

Ogden, Adele. *The California Sea Otter Trade, 1784–1848* (Berkeley: University of California Press, 1941)

Ormsby, Margaret A. *British Columbia: A History* (Toronto: Macmillan, 1958)

Owen, Henry. *The Next Phase in Foreign Policy* (Washington: Brookings Institution, 1973)

The Pacific Rivals: A Japanese view of Japanese–American Relations by the Staff of the Asahi Shimbum (New York: John Weatherhill, 1972)

Patton, James. *Exodus of the Japanese* (Toronto: McClelland and Stewart, 1972)

Panikkar, K. M. *Asia and Western Dominance* (London: George Allen & Unwin, 1959, rev. 1961)

Paterson, T. W. "Was Columbus a Latecomer by More than 3,000 Years?" Victoria, *The Islander* (2 April 1967)

Pelissier, Roger. *The Awakening of China, 1793–1949* (London: Secker & Warburg, 1967)

Pérouse, J. F. G. de la. *A Voyage around the World* (London: G. G. & J. Robinson, 1799)

Pethick, Derek. *First Approaches to the Northwest Coast* (Vancouver: J. J. Douglas, 1976)

——— *James Douglas, Servant of Two Empires* (Vancouver: Mitchell Press, 1969)

Pickersgill, J. W. *The Mackenzie King Record, Vol. I, 1939–1944* (Toronto: University of Toronto Press, 1960)

Pomeroy, Earl. *The Pacific Slope* (New York: Alfred A. Knopf, 1965)

Priest, H. C. *Canada's Share in World Trade* (Toronto: Missionary Education Movement, 1920)

Ralston, Keith. "Patterns of Trade and Investment on the Pacific Coast, 1867–1892." *B.C.S.* No. 1 (1968–69)

Reid, Robie L. "Early Days in Old Fort Langley." *B.C.H.Q.* Vol. I (April 1937)

——— "Inside Story of the *Komagatu Maru.*" *B.C.H.Q.* Vol. V (1941)

Rich, E. E., editor. *The Letters of John McLoughlin from Fort Vancouver to the Governor.* 3 series (Toronto: The Champlain Society, 1941–44)

Richardson, David. *Pig War Islands* (Eastbound, Wash.: Orcas Publishing, 1971)

Richman, Irving Berdine. *California under Spain and Mexico, 1535–1847* (New York: Copper Square Publishing, 1965)

Rickard, T. A. "The Sea Otter in History." *B.C.H.Q.* Vol. XI (1947)

——— "The Strait of Anian." *B.C.H.Q.* Vol. VI (1941)

——— "The Use of Iron and Copper by the Indians of British Columbia. *B.C.H.Q.* Vol. III (January 1939)

Robbins, Helen H. *Our First Ambassador to China* (London: John Murray, 1908)

Robinson, the Rev. J. Cooper. *The Island Empire of the East* (Toronto: Missionary Society of Church of England in Canada, 1912)

Rodney, William. "Russian Revolutionaries and the Port of Vancouver, 1917." *B.C.S.* (Winter 1972–73)

Rolle, Andrew F. *California: A History* (New York: Thomas Y. Crowell, 1970)

Roosevelt, Franklin Delano. *Nothing to Fear: Selected Addresses, 1932–1945*, B. D. Zevin, editor (Freeport, N.Y.: Books for Libraries Press, 1946, rep. 1970)

Roy, Reginald H. "Canadians in the North Pacific, 1943." *B.C.S.* (Summer 1972)

——— "The Early Militia and Defence of British Columbia, 1871–1885." *B.C.H.Q.* Vol. XVII (1954)

Royama, Masamichi. *Foreign Policy of Japan, 1914–1939* (Tokyo: Japanese Council, Institute of Pacific Relations, 1941)

Sage, Walter N. "Spanish Explorers of the British Columbia Coast." *Canadian Historical Review*, Vol. XII, No. 4 (December 1931)

Sansom, G. B. *The Western World and Japan* (New York: Alfred A. Knopf, 1958)

Scammon, Charles M. *Marine Mammals of the North-Western Coast of North America, 1874* (New York: Dover Publications, 1968)

Schurman, D. M. "Esquimalt: Defence Problems, 1865–1867." *B.C.H.Q.* Vol. XIX (1955)

Schurz, William Lylle. "Acapulco and the Manila Galleons." *South Western Historical Review*, Vol. XXII (July 1918)

——— *The Manila Galleon* (New York: E. P. Dutton, 1939)

Schwartz, Harry. *Tsars, Mandarins and Commissars* (Philadelphia: J. B. Lippincott, 1964)

Scott, A. D. "National Economic Issues: Notes on a Western Viewpoint." *B.C.S.* (Spring, 1972)

Scott, the Rev. William. *Canadians in Korea* (Toronto: Board of World Missions, 1970)

Semyonov, Yuri, translation by R. Foster. *Siberia: Its Conquest and Development* (London: Hollis & Carter, 1963)

Shrader, Graham F. *The Phantom War in the Northwest*, pamphlet in Special Collections, University of British Columbia, 1969.

"Letters of Sir George Simpson." *American Historical Review*, Vol. XIV (October 1908)

Singh, Patwant. *The Struggle for Power in Asia* (London: Hutchinson & Co., 1971)

Smith, Dorothy Blakey. *James Douglas, Father of British Columbia* (Toronto: Oxford University Press, 1971)

Soviet Union Quarterly, Moscow, U.S.S.R. Minister of Foreign Trade

Speck, Gordon. *Northwest Explorations* (Portland: Binford & Mort, 1950)

Stacey, C. P. "Britain's Withdrawal from North America," in *Confederation* (Toronto: University of Toronto Press, 1967)

——— *Canada and the Age of Conflict*, Vol. I, 1867–1921 (Toronto: Macmillan of Canada, 1977)

Stackpole, Edouard A. *The Sea-Hunters* (Philadelphia: J. P. Lippincott, 1958)

Starbuck, Alexander. *History of the American Whale Fishery, 1878*, 2 vols. (New York: Argosy Antiquarian Ltd., 1964)

Stephan, John J. *Sakhalin: A History* (Oxford: Clarendon Press, 1971)

Stephen, H. Morse and Herbert E. Bolton, editors. *The Pacific Ocean in History*. Addresses presented at the Panama Pacific Historical Congress, California, 19–23 July 1915 (New York: Macmillan, 1917)

Stokes, John F. G. "Hawaii's Discovery by the Spaniards." *H.H.S. Papers* (1939)

Sun Yat-sen. *San Min Chu I (The Three Principles of the People)* (Shanghai: Commercial Press, 1929)

Thiessen, John Caldwell. *A Survey of World Missions* (Chicago: Inter-Varsity Press, 1955)

Thorgrimmson, Thor and E. C. Russell, *Canadian Naval Operations in Korean Waters, 1950–1955* (Ottawa: Department of National Defence, 1965)

Towse, Ed. "Some Hawaiians Abroad." *H.H.S. Papers* (1904)

Tompkins, Stuart R. "Mapping the North Pacific." *B.C.H.Q.* Vol. XIX (January, April 1955)

Tompkins, Stuart R. and Max L. Moorhead. "Russia's Approach to America." *B.C.H.Q.* Vol. XIII, Nos. 1, 2 (1949)

Trower, Peter. "B.C. Whaling, The White Men." *Raincoast Chronicles First Five* (Madeira Park: Harbour Publishing, 1976)

Truman, Harry S. *Memoirs*, Vol. II (New York: Doubleday & Co., 1956)

Tuchman, Barbara W. *The Proud Tower (1890–1914)* (New York: Macmillan, 1966)

Tucker, Gilbert Norman. "Canada's First Submarine." *B.C.H.Q.* Vol. VII (1943)

——— "The Career of HMCS *Rainbow*." *B.C.H.Q.* Vol. VII (1943)

Tupper, Harmon. *To the Great Ocean (The Trans-Siberian Railway)* (New York: Little, Brown & Co., 1965)

Twain, Mark. *Letters from Hawaii* (New York: Appleton Century, 1966)

Van Arsdell, John. "B.C. Whaling, The Indians." *Raincoast Chronicles First Five* (Madeira Park: Harbour Publishing, 1976)

Vancouver, Captain George. *A Voyage of Discovery to the North Pacific Ocean* (London: G. G. and J. Robinson, 1798)

Vancouver Historical Journals. Archives Society of Vancouver (1958)

Wagner, Henry R. *Spanish Explorations in the Strait of Juan de Fuca* (New York: A.M.S. Press, 1933, rep. 1971)
––––– *Spanish Voyages to the Northwest Coast of America in the Sixteenth Century* (San Francisco: California Historical Society, 1959)
Walbran, Captain John T. *British Columbia Coast Names, 1592–1906.* (Ottawa: Gov't Printing Bureau, 1909; reprint, Vancouver: J. J. Douglas, 1971)
Waley, Arthur. *The Opium War through Chinese Eyes* (London: George Allen & Unwin, 1973)
Warner, Marina. *The Dragon Empress* (London: Weidenfeld & Nicolson, 1972)
Whetten, Lawrence L. *Contemporary American Foreign Policy* (Toronto: D. C. Heath & Co., 1974)
White, Patrick C. T. "The Oregon Dispute and the Defence of Canada," in *Character and Circumstance*, John S. Moir, editor (Toronto: Macmillan of Canada, 1970)
Whitebrook, Robert Ballard. *Coastal Exploration of Washington* (Palo Alto, Cal.: Pacific Books, 1959)
Wilbur, Marguerite Eyer, editor. *Vancouver in California, 1792–94.* 2 vols. (Los Angeles: Glen Dawson, 1954)
Williams, William Appleman, editor. *From Colony to Empire* (New York: John Wiley & Sons, 1972)
––––– *The Roots of the Modern American Empire* (New York: Random House, 1969)
Willmott, W. E. "Approaches to the Study of the Chinese in British Columbia." *B.C.S.* (Spring 1970)
––––– "Some Aspects of Chinese Communities in British Columbia." *B.C.S.* No. 1 (1968–69)
Willson, Beckles. *The Great Company* (Toronto: Copp Clark, 1899)
Wood, Richard Coke, and Leon George Bush. *The California Story* (San Francisco: Ferron Publishers, 1957)
Woodcock, George. *The British in the Far East* (London: Wiedenfeld & Nicolson, 1969)
Woodruff, William. *Impact of Western Man* (New York: Macmillan, 1966)
Woodward, Arthur. "Sea Otter Hunting on the Pacific Coast." *Historical Society of Southern California Quarterly.* Vol. XX. No. 3 (September 1938)
Woodward, David. *The Russians at Sea* (London: William Kimber, 1965)
The World and South East Asia (Sydney, Australia: Oswald Ziegler Enterprises Ltd., 1973)
Wright, J. Leitch. *Anglo-Spanish Rivalry in North America* (Athens: University of Georgia Press, 1971)
Young, Charles, Helen R. Y. Reid, and W. A. Carrothers, *The Japanese Canadians* (Toronto: University of Toronto Press, 1939)

Index